PRAGMATISM, OBJECTIVITY,

In this book, Steven Levine explores the relation between objectivity and experience from a pragmatic point of view. Like many new pragmatists, he aims to rehabilitate objectivity in the wake of Richard Rorty's rejection of the concept. But he challenges the idea, put forward by pragmatists like Robert Brandom, that objectivity is best rehabilitated in communicative-theoretic terms – namely, in terms that can be cashed out by capacities that agents gain through linguistic communication. Levine proposes instead that objectivity is best understood in experiential-theoretic terms. He explains how, in order to meet the aims of the new pragmatists, we need to do more than see objectivity as a norm of rationality embedded in our social-linguistic practices; we also need to see it as emergent from our experiential interaction with the world. Innovative and carefully argued, this book redeems and reactualizes for contemporary philosophy a key insight developed by the classical pragmatists.

STEVEN LEVINE is Associate Professor in the Department of Philosophy at the University of Massachusetts Boston. He has published articles on the work of Sellars, Brandom, McDowell, and Davidson, as well as on a range of issues in classical and contemporary pragmatism.

PRAGMATISM, OBJECTIVITY, AND EXPERIENCE

STEVEN LEVINE
University of Massachusetts Boston

CAMBRIDGE
UNIVERSITY PRESS

University Printing House, Cambridge CB2 8BS, United Kingdom

One Liberty Plaza, 20th Floor, New York, NY 10006, USA

477 Williamstown Road, Port Melbourne, VIC 3207, Australia

314–321, 3rd Floor, Plot 3, Splendor Forum, Jasola District Centre, New Delhi - 110025, India

79 Anson Road, #06-04/06, Singapore 079906

Cambridge University Press is part of the University of Cambridge.

It furthers the University's mission by disseminating knowledge in the pursuit of education, learning and research at the highest international levels of excellence.

www.cambridge.org
Information on this title: www.cambridge.org/9781108435925
DOI: 10.1017/9781108525534

© Steven Levine 2019

This publication is in copyright. Subject to statutory exception and to the provisions of relevant collective licensing agreements, no reproduction of any part may take place without the written permission of Cambridge University Press.

First published 2019
First paperback edition 2021

A catalogue record for this publication is available from the British Library

Library of Congress Cataloging in Publication data
NAMES: Levine, Steven (Steven Matthew), author.
TITLE: Pragmatism, objectivity, and experience / Steven Levine, University of Massachusetts, Boston.
DESCRIPTION: 1 [edition]. | New York : Cambridge University Press, 2018. | Includes bibliographical references and index.
IDENTIFIERS: LCCN 2018035536 | ISBN 9781108422895 (hardback : alk. paper) | ISBN 9781108435925 (pbk. : alk. paper)
SUBJECTS: LCSH: Objectivity. | Experience. | Pragmatism. | Rorty, Richard. | Brandom, Robert.
CLASSIFICATION: LCC BD220 .L48 2018 | DDC 121/.4–dc23
LC record available at https://lccn.loc.gov/2018035536

ISBN 978-1-108-42289-5 Hardback
ISBN 978-1-108-43592-5 Paperback

Cambridge University Press has no responsibility for the persistence or accuracy of URLs for external or third-party internet websites referred to in this publication, and does not guarantee that any content on such websites is, or will remain, accurate or appropriate.

For
Shawn Spencer,
Judith Levine Porino, and William Levine (1935 – 2014)

Contents

Acknowledgments	*page* viii
Introduction	1
PART I	19
1 Rorty and the Rejection of Objectivity	21
2 Brandom, Pragmatism, and Experience	43
3 Communication, Perception, and Objectivity	82
PART II	121
4 An Experiential Account of Objectivity	123
5 Pragmatism, Experience, and Answerability	157
6 Meaning, Habit, and the Myth of the Given	192
Conclusion	235
References	243
Index	254

Acknowledgments

Some of the material included in this book is drawn from previously published work. I am grateful for permission to use this work. Chapter 1 is a slightly altered version of "Rehabilitating Objectivity: Rorty, Brandom, and the New Pragmatists," *Canadian Journal of Philosophy*, 40 (4), December 2010, while portions of Chapter 2 are drawn from "Norms and Habits: Brandom on the Sociality of Action," *European Journal of Philosophy*, 23 (2), June 2015.

In writing this book, I racked up many intellectual debts – so many, in fact, that I am no longer responsible for any of my mistakes.

First off, I would like to thank all of my colleagues, past and present, at the University of Massachusetts Boston. It is a wonderful environment in which to work and think, and this book would have been very different had I been elsewhere. I single out two colleagues, Jeremy Wanderer and Danielle Bromwich, for special thanks. Jeremy not only read several chapters of the book but also has given me countless ideas and suggestions throughout the years. I thank Danielle not because I learned much from her about pragmatism (though she wrote her MA Thesis on Peirce, so I should have) but because she is such a great friend, intellectually and otherwise.

I am deeply grateful to Roberto Frega, Alex Klein, and Carl Sachs, each of whom read parts of the book. Their comments have been invaluable. I would also like to thank the two anonymous reviewers for Cambridge University Press. Their comments led to quite far-reaching changes in the book, making it much better than it would have otherwise been.

For philosophical conversation, criticism, and encouragement, I would also like to thank Doug Anderson, Maria Baghramian, Aude Bandini, Matt Boyle, Lee Braver, Robin Celikates, Shannon Dea, Bill DeVries, Paul Giladi, Mathias Girel, Russell Goodman, Federica Gregoratto, David Hildebrand, Christopher Hookway, Hans Joas, John Kaag, Buffalo Bob King, Jonathan Knowles, Robert Kraut, Mark Lance, David Macarthur,

Stéphane Madelrieux, Cheryl Misak, Dick Moran, Christian Neuhäuser, Mark Okrent, Pete Olen, Jim O'Shea, Gregory Pappas, Robert Pippin, Henrik Rydenfelt, Arvi Särkelä, Bob Stern, Italo Testa, and Jörg Volbers.

My final intellectual debt is to my teachers Richard Bernstein, Alice Crary, and Jay Bernstein. Their impact on the content of this book is incalculable.

I also want to thank my editor Hilary Gaskin for seeing the value of this project and for skillfully shepherding it through to the end. I thank Sophie Taylor, Thomas Haynes, and Sriganesh Krishnamoorthy for all of their help with production, and Stefany Anne Golberg, Elizabeth Sharp-Levine, Elizabeth Kelly, and especially Shawn Spencer for countless hours of proofreading.

My greatest debts are of a more personal nature. My mother, Judy Levine, has been incredibly supportive of my intellectual efforts throughout the years. I cannot thank her enough. The same goes for my brother Paul Levine (keep on rocking), my fabulous sisters Elizabeth and Julia Sharp-Levine, and their mother, Pam Sharp. I would also like to thank my in-laws, Liz and Ed Spencer, my sister-in-law and brother-in-law, Shannon Spencer and Rich Wallace, as well as their children, Tucker and Jonah, for all of their support and encouragement.

However, it is the woman who has to put up with me on a daily basis, Shawn Spencer, who has my deepest gratitude. But hopefully, she already knows that.

Introduction

Communication and Experience

In this book, I enter into a debate that has been going on at least since the publication of Richard Rorty's *Consequences of Pragmatism*, over whether a linguistic brand of pragmatism can articulate the central insights of the pragmatic tradition better than a type of pragmatism that takes experience as its central concept. Rorty began this debate when he argued that the classical pragmatic concept of experience is hopelessly confused and ought to be replaced by an analysis of the linguistic capacities that inform inquiry and thought in general. He claimed that the concept is confused because it falls prey to what Wilfrid Sellars calls the Myth of the Given, and that it ought to be replaced because "'language' is a more suitable notion than 'experience' for saying the holistic and anti-foundationalist thing which James and Dewey wanted to say" (Rorty 1985, 40). The classical pragmatists, like Rorty, wished to overcome the modern philosophical tradition, one in which epistemology is seen as 'first philosophy'. But, Rorty argued, a view that puts experience at its center cannot enact this overcoming because the concept of experience, in being Given, is too loaded with epistemological freight from that very tradition to do the job. If their wish was to leave modern 'subject-centered' philosophy behind, the pragmatists ought to have "dropped the term 'experience'" (Rorty 1998e, 297) rather than rehabilitate it by issuing a radical empiricism. They ought to have dissolved the epistemological problematic not by trying to bridge the divide between mind and world, but by seeing knowledge as a linguistic social practice in which we are answerable to one another rather than to the world itself.[1]

---

[1] A large literature has developed around the debate between classical pragmatism and Rortyian neopragmatism. See Bernstein 1992, Kloppenberg 1996, Hildebrand 2003, the papers in Hildebrand 2014, Koopman 2009, and Malachowski 2014.

Pragmatic philosophers who work in the analytical tradition and who have come after Rorty's neo-pragmatism have generally agreed with him about the theoretical importance of experience. While there have been a few contemporary analytical pragmatists for whom the concept of experience has more than an antiquarian importance, the concept has not been the center around which the contemporary analytical appropriation of the pragmatic tradition turns. As Rorty puts it, these philosophers

> tend to talk about *sentences* a lot, but to say very little about ideas or experiences, as opposed to such sentential attitudes as beliefs and desires ... Following up Sellars's criticism of the myth of the given, they do not think *anything* is "given immediately in experience" ... In short, contemporary philosophers who profess sympathy with pragmatism show little sympathy with empiricism – they would rather forget empiricism rather than radicalize it. (Rorty 1998e, 291–292)

But while agreeing with Rorty about the concept of experience, most analytical pragmatists who have come after Rorty – those who Cheryl Misak dubbed the 'new pragmatists' – disagree with him about whether taking the 'linguistic turn' necessitates, as he thinks, rejecting the idea of objectivity – the idea that we are answerable to the world in addition to other subjects. For Rorty, notoriously, the goal of our epistemic practices is not truth, correspondence with reality, but intersubjective agreement. To think that our representations can stand "in immediate relation to a nonhuman reality" (Rorty 1991b, 21) is to accept the philosophical fantasy that we can transcend the finite and historically contingent conceptual and linguistic framework that structures our world view. To reject this fantasy is to turn "away from the very idea of human answerability to the world" (Rorty 1998d, 142–143) and accept that "there is nothing to the notion of objectivity save that of intersubjective agreement" (Rorty 1998a, 6–7). In Rorty's language, it is to replace the language of objectivity with that of solidarity. In contrast, for the new pragmatists – and here I have in mind Cheryl Misak, Hilary Putnam, Jeffrey Stout, Bjørn Ramberg, Michael Williams, Huw Price, Robert Brandom, and Donald Davidson – any satisfactory pragmatic position must engage the question of how thought is constrained by and answerable to the world, in addition to other subjects.[2] While the new pragmatists agree with Rorty's 'humanist' notion

---

[2] We could also mention Susan Haack and Isaac Levi here. Misak claims that there are other thinkers that could be thought of as new pragmatists even though they do not see themselves as part of the pragmatic tradition. She references Simon Blackburn, John McDowell, and Crispin Wright. For wide readings of the pragmatic tradition that include such figures, see Bernstein 1995, 2010, and

that the world by itself cannot dictate to us what we should think about it, they "are united in their efforts to articulate a position that tries to do justice to the objective dimension of *human* inquiry" (Misak 2007, 1).³

I agree with the sentiment expressed by the new pragmatists that Rorty's neo-pragmatism is flawed because it does not accommodate a pragmatically reconstructed notion of objectivity. This book aims to articulate a pragmatic position that includes such a notion. Where I diverge from the new pragmatists concerns the strategy one must use to rehabilitate this concept.⁴ Whereas most new pragmatists think that objectivity is best rehabilitated solely in *communicative-theoretic* terms – i.e., in terms that can be cashed out exclusively by capacities that agents gain through taking part in linguistic communication – I argue that rehabilitation can best be achieved through *experiential-theoretic* means.⁵ In other words, I take it that to achieve the aims of the new pragmatists, we need to do more than see objectivity as a norm of rationality embedded in our social-linguistic practices, in the so-called game of giving and asking for reasons; we also need to see it as emergent from our experiential interaction with the world. In this way, my argument is an attempt to redeem and reactualize for contemporary philosophy a key insight developed by the classical pragmatists, especially James and Dewey.⁶

In making this argument, I do not mean to suggest that linguistic communication has *no* importance for answering the question of objectivity. For, as we shall see in Chapters 3 and 6, linguistic communication is necessary to articulate an important stratum of the concept of objectivity, and it plays a key role *within* the pragmatist account of experience. What I argue instead is that any account that thinks that an

---

Brandom 2011a. It should be noted that there are other very important pragmatists who, while not strictly speaking analytical philosophers, took the linguistic turn – i.e., Jürgen Habermas and Richard J. Bernstein. Both take it that pragmatism's account of instrumental reason must be supplemented with accounts of communicative reason, imported via speech acts theory or Gadamerian hermeneutics. In recent years, both have come to stress more strongly the importance of experience in the classical pragmatist's sense. See Habermas 2003 and Bernstein 2010.

³ For an analysis of the relation of the new pragmatists to the pragmatic tradition as a whole, see Bernstein 2007.

⁴ I adopt the language of "rehabilitation" from McDowell 2000a.

⁵ I say "most new pragmatists" because not all of them eschew experience. Here I am thinking of Putnam and Misak. While not focused on the term 'experience', Putnam came to think that the account of the mind–world relation at work in the pragmatists (especially James) and other allied thinkers (Austin and McDowell) is central to overcoming the antinomies that beset modern philosophy. See Putnam 1990b, 1998, and 1999. Misak argues that pragmatists need both language and experience in their picture if they are to make sense of objectivity. See Misak 2014.

⁶ I do not mean to suggest that Peirce did not think experience to be important. He did. But he did not take it to be a central object of investigation as James and Dewey did.

analysis of linguistic communication is by itself sufficient to rehabilitate objectivity cannot succeed.

The Two Pragmatisms

My claim is that an account of experience akin to that of James and Dewey is necessary to make sense of objectivity. This goes against the standard interpretation of these authors, which argues that they are not wholeheartedly committed to this ideal. For instance, in her recent book *The American Pragmatists*, Misak develops the idea that pragmatic tradition includes two distinct kinds of pragmatism: one represented by Chauncey Wright, Peirce, C. I. Lewis, and Sellars; the other represented by James, Dewey, and Rorty.[7] Although she recognizes that there is substantial overlap between these kinds of pragmatism, the first "tries to retain a place for objectivity and for our aspiration to get things right while the other is not nearly so committed to that." She goes on to say:

> On the one side of the debate we have Richard Rorty and his classical predecessors (James and Dewey) holding that there is no truth at which we might aim – only agreement within a community or what works for an individual or what is found to solve a problem ... On the other side of the divide, we have those who think of pragmatism as rejecting an ahistorical, transcendental, or metaphysical theory of truth, but nonetheless being committed to doing justice to the objective dimension of human inquiry – to the fact that those engaged in deliberation and investigation take themselves to be aiming at getting things right, avoiding mistakes, and improving their beliefs and theories. On this more objective kind of pragmatism, which emanates from Wright and Peirce, the fact that our inquiries are historically situated does not entail that they lack objectivity. (Misak 2013, 3)

I do not deny that there are reasons for breaking up intellectual space in this way, especially if one focuses, as Misak does, on truth. I agree with Misak that James and Dewey (and, of course, Rorty) do not do justice to the fact that truth is a distinct norm of thought and inquiry that cannot be reduced to what works (in the way of our thinking), nor to warranted belief. Although I do not think that Misak does justice to the complexities of James's or Dewey's theories of truth, one can agree with her that James sometimes leaves the reader with a sense that he thinks that truth is what is satisfying for me or for you and that Dewey sometimes seems

---

[7] See Mounce 1997 for a similar 'two-pragmatist' reading of the pragmatic tradition.

to suggest that a true idea is one that is warranted due to its merely solving a local problem.[8]

But the objectivity question operates at two levels for the pragmatist –[9] at the epistemic level and at the level of content – and truth does not play the same role at each level.[10] At the epistemic level, the question of objectivity concerns the question of how our *inquiries* must be structured so as to issue in judgments that can be counted as *knowledge*. At this level, which is the one that is usually discussed with respect to the pragmatists, one is concerned with how inquiry, though value laden, fallible, and without foundations, can nonetheless get things right. It can, so the thought goes, because inquiry is a self-correcting enterprise, the authority of which is determined solely by evidence and open, unconstrained reason giving by a community of inquirers. At the level of content, in contrast, the question of objectivity concerns how potentially knowledge-bearing thoughts or judgments can have *objective content* – i.e., can be rationally constrained by and answerable to the mind-independent world. Here the question is how the world can stand as the *norm* for the correctness of thought and judgment about it.

Before going on, it is important to point out that for the classical pragmatists, the second question is not completely independent of the first because, on their view, thought or judgment is rationally answerable to the world by being part of an inquiry-like structure – namely, a feedback governed cycle of perception, thought, and action in which reflective problem solving informs our bodily habits and skills and in which these bodily habits and skills prepare us for intelligent future practice. This cycle is inquiry-like in the sense that the patterns of the disciplined forms of inquiry that come to be developed in the modern sciences are implicit in, and are a development of, this anthropologically basic way of coping with the world. But, nonetheless, an answer to the second question will have a different emphasis than an answer to the first, having to do not with the correct procedures for getting objective knowledge, but with

---

[8] For more nuanced accounts of their theories of truth see Burke 1994 and Putnam 1997.
[9] Like Rorty, I sometimes in this book talk about 'the pragmatist' or 'the pragmatists'. Sometimes I use these terms in a very general sense to refer to all of the classical pragmatists. But more often, I, unlike Rorty, use them to denote those who take experience to be the central concept of the pragmatic tradition.
[10] In positing these two levels, I follow Rouse 2015, chapter 5. Objectivity, of course, has many other meanings, but these are the two that are germane for the argument of this book. I give a brief pragmatic account of 'ontological objectivity' in Levine 2017.

the way that subjects and their cognitive abilities are situated within, and constrained by, the environment.

The debate about truth between the two kinds of pragmatism almost always concerns the epistemological level of objectivity. It is at this level that Misak's claim that one needs an account of truth to make sense of objectivity has purchase. To illustrate, let us take Dewey and Peirce as our avatars of the two kinds of pragmatism. For Dewey, thought and judgment are epistemically objective because they are a product of a self-correcting enterprise that involves communication and reason giving between inquirers who have the right *virtues* of inquiry. Dewey names three central virtues: 'whole-heartedness', 'open-mindedness', and 'intellectual responsibility'. Dewey takes it that inquiry cannot be a-perspectival – a procedure that maximally abstracts from an inquirer's subjective endowments, as realists about epistemic objectivity like Nagel and William hold, because inquiry requires that one *cares* about, is *devoted* to, and is *interested* in one's object.[11] Without these evaluative and affective states, inquiry would not get very far. But whole-heartedness is not equivalent to having a succession of affective states, for "it requires consistency, continuity, and community of purpose and effort" (LW 7, 256).[12] So these states must, to constitute the virtue of whole-heartedness, fund the correct *habits* of attention such that one can focus on the object of one's inquiry in an undistracted and single-minded way. To be open-minded, in contrast, is to have the "active desire to listen to more sides than one; to give heed to facts from whatever source they come; to give full attention to alternative possibilities; to recognize the possibility of error even in the beliefs that are dearest to us" (LW 8, 136). So open-mindedness is the virtue that opens us to being sensitive to evidence and other points of view and attentive to the fact that the correctness or incorrectness of our beliefs is determined by the evidence rather than our preestablished opinion. Lastly, to be intellectually responsible, one must "consider the consequences of a projected step ... to be willing to adopt these consequences when they follow reasonably from any position already taken. Intellectual responsibility secures integrity; that is to say, consistency and harmony in belief" (LW 8, 138). Here, one learns to submit one's thinking to the logical and material entailments of the beliefs one has taken on and to accept responsibility for these entailments.

[11] See Tiles 1988, chapter 5, for a comparison of Dewey and William's views.
[12] With the exception of the *Essays in Experimental Logic* (Dewey 2007) and his 1897 Lectures on Hegel (Dewey 2010), references to Dewey are to *The Collected Works of John Dewey 1882–1953* (Early Works, Middle Works, and Late Works). *The Early Works* are abbreviated EW, the *Middle Works* MW, and the *Late Works* LW.

Peirce does not disagree that virtues such as these are necessary for correct inquiry; but he thinks that these virtues, to be effective, need to be connected internally to the *hope* for a belief that *would* continue to meet the aims of inquiry in the face of continued inquiry and reason giving – which is what a true belief is for Peirce.[13] Dewey, in his later work, accepts this conditional account of truth. "The best definition of *truth* from the logical standpoint which is known to me is that of Peirce ... 'Truth is that concordance of an abstract statement with the ideal limit towards which endless investigation would tend to bring scientific belief'" (LW 12, 343n). But it is true that for Dewey this logical conception does very little work in his thought. Dewey worried that focusing on it would divert our attention away from the methods by which our various inquiries actually fix belief and tempt us into reinstating a realist view of truth. But I think he had another worry. In his moral philosophy, Dewey argued that happiness is not "directly an *end* of desire and effort, in the sense of an end-in-view purposively sought for, but is rather an end-product, a necessary accompaniment, of the character which is interested in objects that are enduring and intrinsically related to an outgoing and expansive nature" (LW 7, 198). To make happiness one's direct end is the surest way to not achieve it, for then one does not cultivate a *genuine* and *direct* interest in the kinds of objects that will, in fact, make one happy. I think he has the same thought about truth: instead of focusing on truth itself, we should – in light of our cultivated interests and habits – directly plunge into the objects of our concern. It is this that will produce truth, but as a by-product of, or accompaniment to, an inquiry that looks into objects in the right way.

Misak claims that the marks of epistemic objectivity are these: "We aim to get things right, we distinguish between thinking that one is right and being right, we criticize the beliefs, actions, and cognitive skills of others, we think that we can make discoveries and that we can improve our judgment" (Misak 2000, 77).[14] It is not clear to me that Dewey's view of truth as a by-product rather than an end-in-view makes him incapable of doing justice to these marks. Open-mindedness and intellectual

---

[13] Misak argues, I think correctly, that this definition of truth is preferable to Peirce's more famous account of truth as the belief that an infinitely expanding community of inquirers would endorse at the end of inquiry. It is preferable because it avoids several serious problems to which the latter is subject, for instance, that inquiry can stop before the end of inquiry and that it seems impossible for us in the present to specify the conditions that will obtain at the end of inquiry. See Misak 2000 and 2004. See Habermas 2000 for other difficulties with the end of inquiry view of truth.

[14] In this passage, Misak is arguing that moral discourse can be objective. But the marks she identifies are general features of objectivity in all domains.

responsibility together involve an appreciation of the distinction between being right and merely thinking that one is right, and of the need to criticize and appraise reasons. And the virtue of whole-heartedness involves devotion to the object of one's inquiry, which entails a belief that we can make discoveries and improve our thought. I think it is clear that Dewey *was* interested in our getting things right, although not in our fetishizing our conclusions as having gotten things right (for this certainly 'blocks the way of inquiry'). Our getting things right will be a by-product of correct inquiry rather than its direct aim. Nonetheless, I agree with Misak that Dewey gets something wrong here. For, in my view, to inquire into something correctly by having the right virtues of inquiry *just is* to be aiming at getting beliefs that we would have no reason to revise – i.e., true beliefs. Take the virtue of open-mindedness, in which we learn to be sensitive to the evidence and the possibility of our being out of alignment with it. This virtue would seem to depend on the fact that the inquirer is looking for beliefs that not only are in alignment with the evidence but ones that *would continue* to be such. If this is so, then truth is not merely a by-product of inquiry but is internally connected to it.

But while this book at certain points takes up the issue of epistemic objectivity, it is primarily about objectivity at the level of content. Here, the question is how potentially knowledge-bearing thoughts or judgments can have contents that are rationally answerable to the mind-independent world. Here, truth is not germane in the same way.

For traditional versions of the correspondence theory of truth, the account of truth *does* determine one's account of the objectivity of content. According to this theory, a thought or judgment is true if and only if it corresponds to the facts. Whether a thought or judgment corresponds to the facts is an objective affair that is settled independently of what you, I, or anyone thinks. Truth is evidence and inquiry transcendent. But if this is the case, then if one grasps what it is for a thought or judgment to be true, which is what for a truth-theoretic semantics determines its content, then one also grasps that *what* one's thought or judgment corresponds to is independent of what you, I, or anyone thinks. For the correspondence theory, the concept of objectivity comes, as it were, for free. But this is not so for those who reject the traditional correspondence theory and the truth-theoretic accounts of content that depend on it, as all pragmatists do. If one thinks that the content of the concepts that comprise thought or judgment are not conferred directly through word–world correspondence relations, but rather through their role in judgments that themselves have a functional role in a subject's goal-directed cognitive system, then the question of whether the content these concepts articulate correctly answer to the object this content is purportedly about becomes an open one. One needs a positive account of the objectivity of content over and above an account of truth.

Misak, predictably, argues that James and Dewey can't give a positive account of this concept of objectivity either:

> One kind of pragmatism thinks that our history and evolution makes us into the interpretive engines we are and, although we cannot completely pry apart interpretation from the truth of the matter, there nonetheless is a matter that we are interpreting. That is Peirce, and we shall see, C. I. Lewis. The other kind of pragmatism thinks that not even by abstraction can we say that there is something that stands apart from our interpretation of it. That is Dewey and, in a different sort of way, James and Schiller. (Misak 2013, 116)

For Misak, the question here is not one directly about truth, but about whether one can avoid idealism by developing an account of thought or judgment in which it is constrained by something that stands apart from it. For all of the pragmatists, this is a difficult question because they think that our access to the world is always mediated – by signs, concepts, habits, purposes, and interests. For this reason we can never, as Misak says, *completely* pry apart the matter interpreted from our interpretation of it.[15] To think that we can is to fall prey to what Sellars calls the Myth of the Categorical Given, the myth that the intrinsic nature of things is directly revealed to us simply through being Given, prior to our learning to use concepts, signs, etc.[16] In light of this, Misak's claim becomes the following: Peirce, Lewis, and Sellars can, without falling prey to the Myth of the Given, account for the fact that thought is constrained by and answerable to something that stands apart from it, while James, Dewey – and, of course, Rorty – cannot.

I aim, in the course of this book, to demonstrate that Misak's claim is wrong. In the first part of the book, I argue that certain new pragmatists that Misak thinks of as part of the Peircean line of pragmatism – i.e., Brandom and Davidson – cannot, in fact, account for objectivity.[17] They cannot because their views are predicated on the same move that underlies Rorty's position – namely, the rejection of experience. In the second part

---

[15] The language of interpretation is C. I. Lewis'. When the sensory given is taken in a certain way by conceptual judgment one 'interprets' the given.
[16] See Sellars 1981, 11.
[17] See Misak 2013, 248 and 253 for her readings of Brandom and Davidson as part of this pragmatist line.

of the book, in contrast, I argue that James and Dewey ought not to be grouped with Rorty because they, while not falling prey to the Myth of the Given, retain a robust place for the objectivity of content in their thought.

Two Concepts of Experience

One way to express the central thought of this book is this: for a pragmatist to have a satisfactory account of the objectivity of content, an account of how thought is rationally constrained by and answerable to the world, he or she must be a type of empiricist. In this, I agree with John McDowell, who had done more than anyone else in contemporary philosophy to emphasize this point. In *Mind and World*, McDowell articulates what he calls a 'minimal empiricism', a view in which experience serves as a 'tribunal for our thinking'. If empirical thinking is to be correct or incorrect depending on whether it answers to how things are in the world, and if our way of getting in touch with the world unavoidably involves experience, then our thinking – if it is to be in touch with the world – must in some way be answerable to experience. If thought is to be objective, of the way things genuinely are, it must be objective by way of a consideration of our experiential encounter with the world.

I agree with McDowell when he argues, on the basis of his minimal empiricism, that Rorty, Brandom, and Davidson can't make sense of the objectivity of thought because they eschew experience. Indeed, in the first part of this book, I cash out this thought in great detail. But my grounds for making this point are different than McDowell's. This is because I argue, in the second part of the book, that to articulate the connection between objectivity, thought, and experience correctly, we need to go beyond the account of experience found in McDowell's minimal empiricism to the more radical accounts of experience found in the pragmatic tradition.[18]

---

[18] In chapter 1 of his book *The Pragmatic Turn*, Richard Bernstein argues that the pragmatic tradition is best seen in light of the question about mind and world identified by McDowell rather than in terms of the theory of meaning articulated by Peirce in his 1878 *Illustrations of the Logic of Science* papers, and taken over and transformed by James in his pragmatism. Bernstein makes this interpretive move by reminding us of the importance of Peirce's 1868–1869 *Journal of Speculative Philosophy* Cognition Series papers (where Peirce's anti-Cartesian program is first laid out) and by showing us that Peirce's theory of perception can make sense of the fact that it involves both 'secondness' and 'thirdness' without falling prey to the Myth of the Given. See Bernstein 1964 for the origin of this interpretive strategy. My book follows Bernstein's interpretive reorientation, but it focuses on James and Dewey rather than Peirce. This entails that certain aspects of the theory of meaning downplayed by Bernstein must be included as part of a pragmatist answer to the problems surrounding the relation of mind and world identified by McDowell.

Introduction

According to McDowell's well-known account experience can be a tribunal for our empirical thought because it involves, prior to thought or judgment, an actualization of conceptual capacities. It's not that sensory consciousness is first brought about by the causal affection of the world and then *worked on* by conceptual capacities. It's rather that in experience "conceptual capacities are drawn on *in* receptivity" (McDowell 1996a, 9). The pragmatic account of experience also takes it that experience inextricably involves an actualization of spontaneity within receptivity, and that this actualization is necessary to understand how experience can be a tribunal. But it has a different conception of spontaneity than McDowell and, therefore, a different account of experience.

There are two analytically distinct notions of experience at play in the pragmatic tradition that are important for us – notions that, as Brandom points out, align with the German distinction between *Erlebnis* and *Erfahrung*. Both *Erlebnis* and *Erfahrung* have long histories and complex meanings, which go far beyond the pragmatic tradition.[19] And my use of these terms does not capture all of the meanings that the concept of experience has, even in the pragmatic tradition.[20] What I want to do here is to simply sketch, in a preliminary way, two idealized notions of experience so that we have a common basis upon which to proceed. As the book progresses, these notions will become significantly enriched and intertwined.[21]

Consider Jimi Hendrix's song "Are You Experienced?" What did he mean in asking this? One thing he asked was whether one has had, in one's conscious life, concrete states and episodes characteristic of an LSD trip. To have this experience is to consciously undergo certain kinds of states and episodes, to live through them. One has not had an LSD trip unless one has had those kinds of experiences. In this sense, experience is "what the Germans call an *Erlebniss* – anything that can be regarded as a concrete and integral moment in a conscious life" (James 1988a, 21). But Hendrix also meant something else by his question: has one, through having these concrete states and episodes, learned anything from them? Has one, through past experiences of LSD, become a wise and thoughtful person – "not necessarily stoned, but beautiful," as he puts it? Or take Brandom's

---

[19] See Jay 2005 and Carr 2014 for excellent histories of this concept.
[20] For example, I do not consider the meaning that experience has in James's *Varieties of Religious Experience* or in his late, more Bergsonian work.
[21] While James and Dewey used the terms *Erlebnis* and *Erfahrung* on occasion, I do not mean to suggest that these are the terms that they use to capture their concepts of experience. I have introduced these terms simply to help domesticate the complexity of the concept.

example: when we ask job applicants whether they have any experience, we are not asking whether they have lived through concrete moments in their conscious lives (and so are not zombies); we are asking whether they have acquired a certain kind of know-how through past training and habituation (see Brandom 2011a, 7). We are asking whether they have gone through a temporally extended *learning process* that involves both conscious and nonconscious states and episodes. In this sense, experience is akin to what the Germans, especially those in the Hegelian tradition, call *Erfahrung*.

Let me say a bit more about these concepts of experience. For Brandom and his teacher on this point, Rorty, "*experience*," in the sense of *Erlebnis*, is "the epistemologists' name for their subject matter, a name for the ensemble of Cartesian *cogitationes*, Lockean ideas" (Rorty 1979, 150). In other words, they understand an episode of *Erlebnis* to be "the occurrence of a self-intimating event of pure awareness" (Brandom 2011a, 6–7). But the assimilation of *Erlebnis* to self-intimating impressions and ideas has little to do with how this concept of experience works in James's *Principles of Psychology*, which is my main source for this conception of experience.[22]

James's account of experience is complex. On the one hand, he famously gives an account of thought in which it is undergone by an agent as part of his or her personal consciousness, as constantly changing, as streamlike or sensibly continuous with other thoughts, and of objects. Thoughts are given in experience as having these characteristics. On the other hand, experience for James, unlike for the classical empiricist, is active and not simply passive. We must characterize this active side carefully. James wrote this in the margins of his copy of the *Critique of Pure Reason*: "Of course Kant is on sound psychological ground that in distinguishing receptivity from activity, only he makes the latter furnish a part of the content, whereas it is limited to furnishing emphasis, to selecting from the content."[23] For Kant, the manifold of sense is understood as a manifold of discrete atomic impressions. Because impressions are discrete and separate, the faculty of judgment must bring to bear a concept to unify the manifold, must engender form onto sensory matter. The content of the experience is a product of this engendering and, therefore, of the combination of form and matter. For James, in contrast, form does not need to be

---

[22] For a presentation that lays out in great detail the affinities between the notions of experience found in the *Principles* and in Dilthey, the great exponent of *Erlebnis*, see Kloppenberg 1986.
[23] Quoted in Skrupskelis 1989, 174. In the original, Kant is abbreviated as 'K'.

imposed *onto* the sensory matter by the Understanding. This is because relations are given as already included in the sensory muchness. What is needed is not the imposition of form onto disorganized sensory matter, but the *selecting and emphasizing* of relations *already imbricated* in the matter by attention, discrimination, and potentially, by conceptualization. What is given to us originally is not a manifold of sensory atoms but a *vague sensory whole* that requires selective attention to make explicit certain of its features.

It is clear that what James means by experience in the sense of *Erlebnis* diverges quite considerably from what Rorty and Brandom mean by that term. Rorty and Brandom mean by experience an immediate episode in which the mere presence to the senses of the outward order has justificatory purport for the experiencing creature. James is clearly not working with this notion of experience. While James thinks that what is present to a creature's senses is given in the innocent sense that one has no control over what stimulates our sense organs (given how one is positioned), this is not what they *experience*. What one experiences depends both on what is present to the senses *and* on what one attends to, discriminates, and potentially conceptualizes – which itself depends on patterns and habits instituted by past acts of attention, discrimination, and conceptualization. For James, as we shall see, experience is always *funded*, meaning that the present operation of these capacities is shot through by prior operations of these capacities. His conception of *Erlebnis* contains an account of *Erfahrung*, an account of how experience as lived is mediated and enriched through time.

The second conception of experience, experience as *Erfahrung*, also sees experience as inextricably active and passive. But this conception, which is Dewey's, puts the point in an action-theoretical context, one that places experimentation at its center:

> Experience is primarily a process of undergoing: a process of standing something; of suffering and passion, of affection, in the literal sense of these words. The organism has to endure, to undergo, the consequences of its own actions ... Undergoing, however, is never mere passivity. The most patient patient is more than a receptor. He is also an agent – a reactor, one trying experiments, one concerned with undergoing in a way which may influence what is still to happen ... Experience, in other words, is a matter of *simultaneous* doings and sufferings. (MW 10, 8)

Experience in its most basic sense is, for Dewey, the temporally extended sensorimotor process through which an agent interacts with an environment through simultaneously acting on and being acted on by it. This process is more basic than knowing. If we discern the pattern of this interaction, we can grasp Dewey's conception of experience. At this juncture, there are two important things say about this pattern.

First, experience displays a pattern of *problem-solving* behavior. Because we act in a precarious and continually changing environment, sometimes the habitual connections between what we do and what we undergo no longer support fluid activity. In this case, the "situation" in which we act "becomes *tensional*" (Dewey 2007, 7) or indeterminate. Here, the meaning of the situation in which we pre-reflectively act is disrupted. When this happens, we must engage in a process of reflection and deliberation by utilizing meanings that are constituted communicatively in the space of reasons. Here, we, alone or with others, analyze the situation, develop hypotheses, and act on them to ascertain the consequences of their institution. Here we try "to make a backward and forward connection between what we do to things and what we enjoy or suffer from things in consequence." If this connection is ascertained by reflection, the "undergoing becomes instructive – discovery of the connection of things" (MW 9, 147). This discovery is "instrumental to gaining control in a troubled situation," and so is the basis for reestablishing fluid action. But it is more than that, for "it is also instrumental to the enrichment of the immediate significance of subsequent experiences" (Dewey 2007, 10).

With this, we come to the second and more fundamental characteristic of experience – namely, that it is a *developmental learning process*. Here is how Dewey puts it: "Experience as trying involves change, but change is meaningless transition unless it is consciously connected with the return wave of consequences that flow from it. When an activity is continued *into* the undergoing of consequences, when the change made by action is reflected back into a change made in us, the mere flux is loaded with significance. We learn something" (MW 9, 146). We learn something in experience because the connections discerned by the reflective processes that reestablish routine behavior *feedback* into our system of *habits* and *bodily skills*. This change in our habits is the 'change made in us' by what is learned. Habits, we could say, are the repository for the significances and meanings that are learned through experience. Experience understood as *Erfahrung* is the cycle by which our habits become meaningful and significant through incorporating what has been learned through past problem solving, and where this reflective problem-solving activity is made more intelligent and flexible through being funded by these enriched habits. When this cycle moves forward felicitously, there is what Dewey calls growth, which is his naturalistic term for what the classical tradition calls *Bildung*.

The Itinerary of This Book

Let me outline the trajectory of this book. In so doing, the importance of these two concepts of experience will become apparent. In Chapter 1, I examine the origin of the new pragmatic strategy to rehabilitate objectivity by tracing it back to Rorty's rejection of experience. I show how Rorty's rejection of objectivity is predicated on his prior rejection of experience and how Brandom's redemptive reading of Rorty fails because it overlooks this connection between experience and objectivity. While Brandom argues that Rorty eschews objectivity by generalizing the lessons of his fundamentally Sellarsian social-pragmatic account of subjective incorrigibility, I argue that the origin of his hostility is to be found in his eliminativist treatment of sense experience. The overall goal of this chapter is to motivate the two paths that can be followed to rehabilitate objectivity in the wake of Rorty's dismissal – the communicative and the experiential-theoretic paths.

In Chapter 2, I critique Brandom's rationalist pragmatism, which I take to be the most powerful product of the new pragmatism. Brandom's view is more complex than Rorty's because, while he follows Rorty in rejecting the concept of experience when it is understood episodically (*Erlebnis*), he accepts it when it is understood as a learning process (*Erfahrung*). I argue that, despite this difference, Brandom's view still fails to account for our answerability to the world. To have a satisfactory experiential-theoretic account of objectivity, one needs both concepts of experience, *Erfahrung* and *Erlebnis*, and Brandom's rejection of the latter undermines his rehabilitation of the former.

In Chapter 3, I examine Brandom's and Davidson's communicative-theoretic accounts of objectivity, accounts that make no mention of experience. Both argue that grasp of the concept of objectivity depends on intersubjective communication, for broadly Wittgensteinian reasons. In the absence of the criteria instituted by communicative reason giving, we would not be able to draw the distinction, with respect to a thought or judgment, between its seeming to be correct and its being correct, and so we would not be able to understand that what is correct always potentially transcends what we take to be correct. I argue that while communication can account for grasp of the distinction between something seeming to be correct and its being correct, it does not provide for a grasp of the fact that what is correct is settled by the way the world is. But without this, one does not understand that thought is answerable *to* the world for its correctness rather than the other way around.

To explain this more primitive grasp requires an account of the *spatial conditions* of perception. Here I follow Strawson and Evans, who argue that grasp of the concept of objectivity depends not on communication but on the ability to reason spatially by using what Evans calls a rudimentary theory of perception. In using spatial concepts to explain why a perceivable object is not in fact perceived, one gleans, within veridical perception, that it is because the object of perception is in the wrong spatial position. This is the basis of our understanding that things exist unperceived and that our access to things depends not only on us but also on how the independent world is spatially arranged. This is what fills out the missing piece of the content of the concept of objectivity.

But while I agree with Strawson and Evans that spatial consciousness is critical for grasp of objectivity, I disagree with them that the content of this concept is conferred through spatial reasoning. I argue that the concept of objectivity is an empirical concept and that grasp of it has *experiential conditions*. So, with respect to this concept, I endorse the basic idea that the pragmatists take over from the empiricist tradition – namely, that if the content of a concept cannot be traced back to experience, then the concept is spurious. If, however, we think of experience in a reductively empiricist way, this claim about the concept of objectivity will seem nonsensical. For if the concept of objectivity can be traced back to the impressions and ideas that comprise experience, then the content of this concept, which is meant to signify the mind-independent world to which our thought answers, will be filled out by states that reside in a subject's consciousness. But then what is objective will always be what is objective for an individual subject. An experiential account of objectivity seems to lead to a type of subjective idealism.

But this conclusion does not result if we follow the pragmatists and think of experience as either *Erlebnis* or *Erfahrung*. In the second part of the book, I argue that these two concepts of experience can be used to answer different sides of the overall question of objectivity. The first side concerns our *grasp* of the concept of objectivity. To have thought that is answerable to the mind-independent world, one must understand that what is the case is the case regardless of what one, or anyone, thinks. How is this grasp possible? The second side concerns the question of whether thought can, in fact, *be* objective. This question emerges because even if the conditions for a subject to grasp the concept of objectivity are fulfilled, their thought still might not be answerable to the world for its correctness.[24]

In Chapter 4, I argue that James's account of *Erlebnis* gives us the resources to answer the first side of the question of objectivity. Grasp of the concept of objectivity has two experiential conditions for James. First, it is based in our experience of the fact that objects persist through changes in our experience of them. Second, we grasp that persisting objects continue to exist even when unperceived because, in our experience of space as we move through it, we always 'know-together', or co-intend, presence and absence. Because we can reverse our attention at will, this knowing together applies not only to intuitively given spatial fields but also to our conception of space as an infinitely continuous unit. This, I argue, accounts for our most basic grasp of the concept of objectivity.

In Chapters 5 and 6, I use Dewey's notion of experience as *Erfahrung* to answer the second side of the question of objectivity: whether thought or judgment, regardless of what a subject grasps, can, in fact, be answerable to the world. In Chapter 5, I compare Dewey's experimental empiricism with McDowell's minimal empiricism, showing that both positions are motivated by the need to avoid a seesaw that they see taking place between empiricism and idealism/coherentism – between a view that accepts the Myth of the Given and one that cannot make sense of external constraint. Both think that we must understand experience as a tribunal in order to avoid this seesaw, but their views of experience differ considerably. While for McDowell experience involves the actualization of conceptual capacities within receptivity, Dewey thinks it involves the actualization of habits

---

[24] When discussing the pragmatists, interpreters do not usually ask about objectivity but about realism. (See Putnam 1987 and 1998, Hildebrand 2003, Kitcher 2012, and Godfrey-Smith 2013.) Realism involves two thoughts: one modest, one presumptuous (see Wright 1992, 1–2). The modest thought concerns the independence of reality – that the way matters stand with the world, and which beliefs are true of it, are questions settled independently of what we think. The presumptuous thought is that even though exactly which beliefs about the world are true is a question settled independently of thought, nevertheless our beliefs are able to capture in their net a substantial portion of the truth. So the question of realism with respect to the pragmatists is usually posed in this way: do they think that the existence and nature of the world is settled independently of thought, and do they think that we can come to know a substantial portion of the truth about the world? These two questions relate to my two questions about objectivity in the following way. My first question, which is about our grasp of the concept of objectivity, is distinct from either one of these questions. It is concerned with the conditions necessary for a subject to grasp that objects exist independently of their thought, not directly with their mind-independence or with their ability to know them. It is a kind of transcendental question. My second question about objectivity, in contrast, involves both questions of realism. On the one hand, if our thought is to be answerable to the mind-independent world, there must *be* a mind-independent world for it to answer to. On the other hand, if our thought is to *genuinely* answer to this world, it must be able to capture in its net substantial truths about it. I discuss the question of realism in Chapter 6 and the Conclusion.

or bodily skills. Because this is so, experience is intrinsically embodied and 'experimental', a temporal process in which we both act on and are acted upon by the environment in which we live.

In Chapter 6, I outline the concept of experience found in Dewey's later naturalistic empiricism. Dewey agrees with McDowell that experience is the product of a process of *Bildung*. But, for Dewey, this process both involves feedback relations between the communicative meanings that populate the space of reasons and the habits and bodily skills that make up our second nature *and* incorporates the environment insofar as habits are natural functions that cannot be individuated without making mention of both organism and environment. Based on this, I make two arguments. First, I argue that this naturalistic concept of experience can, unlike McDowell's, support a realist construal of answerability. Second, I argue that Dewey's concept of experience does not fall prey to the Myth of the Given, as Rorty claims. I end with this because the book aims to show that the pragmatists can give an experiential-theoretic account of objectivity without falling prey to the Myth of Given. In showing that Rorty's argument is groundless, I meet this last explanatory goal.

PART I

CHAPTER 1

Rorty and the Rejection of Objectivity

Introduction

As I mentioned in the introduction, in recent years a renascent form of pragmatism has developed that argues that a satisfactory pragmatic position must do justice to the objectivity of our thought and inquiry. This new pragmatism is directed primarily against Rorty's neo-pragmatic dismissal of objectivity. The new pragmatists agree with Rorty that semantic notions like truth and reference "are internal to our overall view of the world" (Rorty 1991a, 6). They agree with him that we cannot, in Putnam's terms, take "a God's-eye standpoint – one which has somehow broken out of our language and our beliefs and tested them against something known without their aid" (Rorty 1991a, 6). But they demur from his conclusion that this requires us to give up the notion that we can be answerable to the world in addition to each other. They demur because they think that internal to our view of the world that there are norms of correctness, of getting things right, that go beyond intersubjective justification or warrantedness. Since the commitments to both intersubjective justification and objective correctness are implicit in our discursive and inquiring practices, a pragmatic reconstruction of these practices – one that takes the point of view of the agent seriously – will show them both to be philosophically legitimate.[1]

Some new pragmatists – most notably Jeffrey Stout and Robert Brandom – argue that the aim of getting things objectively right is, in fact, consistent with Rorty's own best insights. If Rorty only took seriously the lessons of his pragmatic radicalization of the linguistic turn, the argument goes, either he would be a new pragmatist (Stout) or, in Brandom's story – the story with which I will be concerned in this chapter – he would

---

[1] See Chapter 3 for arguments to this effect by Brandom and Davidson. See Price 2003 and Stout 2007 for different versions of this strategy.

recognize that his position is at least consistent with a pragmatically reconstructed notion of objectivity. In this chapter, I argue that Brandom's attempted recruitments of Rorty for the new pragmatic cause fail because it misdiagnoses the basis of his hostility to the concept of objectivity.

Later in his career, the reason for Rorty's hostility toward objectivity became clear: the search for objectivity, as it has been construed in the philosophical tradition, is not consistent with human dignity and freedom. Rorty often put this thought in terms of his prophetic desire to help institute a second Enlightenment.[2] The great achievement of the first Enlightenment was the change that it effected in our moral view of ourselves. Instead of seeing ourselves as morally indebted to something outside of ourselves – i.e., God – we came to think that the 'source of normativity' was internal to our own moral being. The norms of moral action are not *given* but are something for which *we* need to take responsibility by deliberating together about what to do and what type of people we want to be. Rorty's envisaged second Enlightenment transfers this train of thought from the practical to the theoretical sphere. Just as we threw off our tutelage to an outside moral authority in the first Enlightenment, in the second we would additionally unburden ourselves of the need to bow down before the epistemic authority of objective reality, "the idea that there is something non-human out there with which human beings need to get in touch" (Rorty 2007, 105). For Rorty, objective reality cannot dictate to us how we should represent it because it is mute – i.e., it does not speak and offer reasons to us. This is something that only we do in the intersubjective space of giving and asking for reasons. In a second Enlightenment, we would realize this and accordingly shoot for solidarity rather than objectivity.

Where does the original source of this hostility to objectivity lie? In his paper, "An Arc of Thought: From Rorty's Eliminative Materialism to His Pragmatism," Brandom argues, I think correctly, that it stems from the constellation of ideas that informs Rorty's early eliminative materialism. However, I think Brandom stresses the wrong idea in this constellation. In his opinion, it is Rorty's views concerning the *incorrigibility* of the mental that led to his eschewal of the concept of objectivity, whereas I think that it is Rorty's views concerning the *eliminability* of sensory experience. What I try to show in this chapter is that it is Rorty's hostility to experience that underlies his later hostility to objectivity, and that any attempt to

---

[2] For more on this, see Rorty 1999b, McDowell 2000a, and Brandom 2011b.

pragmatically rehabilitate objectivity must address this if it is to be successful. Unless one does so, one will just be spinning Rorty's wheel.

It is important to stress what I said in the introduction, namely, that I agree with the new pragmatists that the pragmatic rehabilitation of objectivity is necessary and important. Where I disagree with them concerns the theoretical direction that such a project must take. The focus on Rorty is meant to sharpen this disagreement. While this might seem a roundabout way to get at our divergence, this focus is necessary because many of the new pragmatists arrive at their positions, in part, by working through the perceived deficiencies of Rorty's account of objectivity.[3] By criticizing Brandom's reading of Rorty, I aim to show that a pragmatic rehabilitation of objectivity requires a much more thoroughgoing revision of the Rortyian picture than he and the new pragmatists contemplate.

Incorrigibility and the Mark of the Mental

In Brandom's telling, Rorty's hostility to objectivity can be traced back to his thesis that incorrigibility is the mark of the mental. Before explaining how, for Brandom, this thesis leads to Rorty's later views of objectivity, I must first briefly explicate the thesis itself.

In his early paper, "Incorrigibility As the Mark of the Mental," Rorty makes the argument that what distinguishes the mental from all other realms of existence is the fact that certain events, thoughts, and sensations – and no other events – are subject to incorrigible first-person reports. The innovation here is defining the mental in epistemic rather than ontological terms. Instead of worrying about the ontological status of thoughts and sensations – about whether they are physical events that admit of topic-neutral explanations, etc. – Rorty urges us to focus instead on the linguistic criteria that we use to characterize and demarcate the mental. If we do so, we shall see that the only feature that thoughts and sensations have in common is that their avowal in sincere first-person reports cannot be rationally overridden by other agents. This incorrigibility is, for Rorty, the mark of the mental.

The Cartesian tradition, of course, also took incorrigibility to be the mark of the mental. But unlike the Cartesian, who accounts for incorrigibility by pointing to certain of the mind's ontological characteristics – i.e., transparency and immediate self-acquaintance – Rorty argues that

---

[3] See Brandom 2000c and 2011b, Misak 2000 and 2007, Ramberg 2000, Stout 2007, Price 2003, Putnam 1990a, and Williams 2000.

incorrigibility is a *socially and linguistically instituted phenomenon*. The raw materials for this argument come from Sellars' Myth of Jones given at the end of *Empiricism and the Philosophy of Mind*. Very briefly, the Myth of Jones attempts to show how a community of our ancestors – Sellars' famous Ryleans – who begin with an intersubjectively available language describing objects in space and time, could develop, through 'natural' additions to the language, the ability to make direct non-inferential reports about their own 'inner' episodes, whether thoughts or sense impressions. What Sellars wants to show is that this ability to make direct non-inferential reports about our inner episodes is not *Given*, as a Cartesian would have it, but *instituted* through the acquisition of non-innate conceptual abilities.

This institution occurs when the Ryleans introduce the concepts of thought and sensation into their language to explain certain anomalies for which their already available public concepts cannot account. In the case of thought, the Ryleans are puzzled by the fact that a line of rational behavior can go on without agents avowing their thoughts and intentions aloud while, in the case of sensation, they are puzzled by perceptual illusion – i.e., by the fact that they sometimes think that they are perceiving things that are not actually there. In response to these puzzles, the Rylean community (in the personification of the genius Jones) is pushed into making certain analogical extensions from concepts it already possesses. Predicates that apply to publicly available physical entities are now used as a model to form new concepts of theoretically posited inner episodes. In the case of thoughts, Jones simply takes the characteristics of public speech – intentional aboutness, truth-aptness, compositionality, etc. – and extends them to apply to a concept of certain inner episodes, thoughts. In the case of sense impressions, Jones analogically extends "the predicates of physical objects" by giving them a "new use in which they form sortal predicates pertaining to impressions, thus 'an (of a red rectangle) impression'" (Sellars 1968, 69). Of course, while each episode is modeled on a publicly available physical entity (verbal speech and the predicates of physical objects respectively), they have their own intrinsic features, being a 'thought about X' and a 'sensation of Y'.

When Jones initially teaches the Ryleans about these new concepts and the theory in which they are embedded, the episodes to which these concepts refer are inferentially posited theoretical episodes not available for immediate introspection. However, after a certain amount of training, the Ryleans learn to refer to these episodes directly by coming to use these concepts in direct non-inferential reports. Here (to use the example of sensations) the Ryleans come to "*directly* know (not merely infer by using the theory) on particular occasions that [they] are having sense-impressions of such and such kind" (Sellars 1991, 91).

Although Sellars provides the raw materials for Rorty's view, his account of the mental is ultimately found wanting. While his story is essential for explaining how mental terms enter the language, it fails to specify the mark of the mental correctly. The difficulty is that Sellars does not provide a single feature that characterizes both thoughts and sensations save the "one of being 'inner' states apt for the production of certain behavior" (Rorty 1970, 412). But the notion of something going on inside our bodies that accounts for our overt behavior does not give us a robust enough notion of the mental to contrast with the physical. To establish the mental as a 'new category of existence', what is needed is a publicly available linguistic practice that treats the authority of certain types of reports differently from that of others. "Only after the emergence of the convention, the linguistic practice, which dictates that first-person contemporaneous reports of such states are the last word on their existence and features do we have a notion of the mental as incompatible with the physical" (Rorty 1970, 414). Following Sellars' example, Rorty gives a mythical and naturalistic account of the origin of this convention. When explaining the behavior of agents who use the concepts of thought and sensation to make direct first-person reports, the Ryleans note certain features of their use that are helpful for this explanatory task.

> They found that, when the behavioral evidence for what Smith was thinking about conflicted with Smith's own report of what he was thinking about, a more adequate account of the sum of Smith's behavior could be obtained by relying on Smith's report than by relying on the behavioral evidence ... The growing conviction that the best explanation in terms of thoughts for Smith's behavior would always be found by taking Smith's word for what he was thinking found expression in the convention that what Smith said went. The same discovery occurred, *mutatis mutandis*, for sensations. (Rorty 1970, 416)

The upshot is that until a community took it that Smith's first-person reports were more reliable than the behavioral evidence for his thoughts, incorrigibility did not exist. In this sense, incorrigibility is arrived at from the 'outside-in' insofar as it is first posited as a facet of our explanations of one another. In showing that incorrigibility is not an intrinsic feature of our mental events but a socially and linguistically instituted status, Rorty can then argue that the mental itself is an *optional* category of existence. This is because it is possible that the social and linguistic practices that institute incorrigibility, and therefore the mental, can change such that there would no longer be states about which we are incorrigible. How could these practices change? Rorty canvasses the empirical possibility that through technological advances we could develop a new "practice of overriding reports about mental entities on the basis of knowledge of brain states" (Rorty 1970, 421). In other words, it is possible that we could develop third-person ways of detecting a person's mental states that are evidentially stronger than that person's own reports. Here our evidentiary practices would change in such a way that our "mental states would lose their incorrigible status and, thus, their status as *mental*" (Rorty 1970, 421).[4] If this change in status is truly possible, then, as Brandom puts it, "[t]he Cartesian mind is real, but it is a contingent, optional, product of our mutable social practices" (Brandom 2011b, 110).

Incorrigibility and Objectivity

We are now in a position to understand Brandom's story about the origin of Rorty's hostility to objectivity. Brandom sums up Rorty's position about the incorrigibility of the mental by pointing out that it is composed of two principle theses: (1) that incorrigibility is a *normative* phenomenon insofar as it concerns the incontestable authority of certain episodes and (2) that incorrigibility is underlain by the *social-pragmatic* thesis that the normative status of authority is instituted by social and linguistic practices. How do these ideas lead to Rorty's position on objectivity? Brandom points out that Rorty's 'post-ontological' philosophy of mind follows from his meta-philosophical view that, after the linguistic turn, ontology can only be done by examining the normatively governed linguistic practices by which we detail our view of reality. In this regard, Rorty remains, for all of his fulminations against Kant, a linguistic Kantian – just like his hero Sellars. Based upon this meta-philosophical view, Brandom thinks that a three-sorted ontology emerges:

> *Subjective* (Cartesian) things are those over which each individual knowing-and-acting subject has incontestable authority. *Social* things are those over which *communities* have incontestable authority . . . Finally, *objective* things are those over which *neither* individuals nor communities have incontestable authority, but which *themselves* exercise authority over claims that in

---

[4] Here we find the origin of the line of thought that will result in Rorty's story about the Antipodeans in chapter 2 of *Philosophy and the Mirror of Nature*.

the normative sense that speakers and thinkers are *responsible to* them count as being *about* those things. (Brandom 2011b, 110)

In this scheme, the category of the social is privileged because each ontological realm is instituted on social-pragmatic grounds – i.e., upon the grounds of what social-linguistic practices are taken as authoritative in each sphere. There is no further court of appeals concerning authority than what a community, through the game of giving and asking for reasons, takes or treats as authoritative. But just as a community can change its linguistic practices so as to eliminate incorrigibility and hence the mental, it can also, through a change in linguistic practice, eliminate the category of the objective. And with this we come to Brandom's thesis concerning the origin of Rorty's hostility to objectivity: this hostility emerged when Rorty came to treat the authority of the objective in the same eliminativist way that he treated the authority of the subjective.

Brandom thinks that two potential positions result from this treatment of the objective. The first position leads directly to the picture detailed by Rorty's second Enlightenment. Since our ontology falls out from the normative structure of authority operative in any given sphere, the category of objectivity is incoherent insofar as authority can only be accredited to normatively structured items. We can't grant "authority to something non-human, something that is merely *there,* to intrinsically normatively inert *things*" (Brandom 2011b, 111). While we can make sense of the idea of our entering into various theoretical consensuses concerning the nature of the 'objective world',

> the idea of something that cannot enter into a conversation with us, cannot give and ask for reasons, somehow *dictating* what we *ought* to say is not one we can in the end make sense of . . . Reality as the modern philosophical tradition has construed it . . . is the wrong *kind* of thing to exercise rational authority. That is what we do to *each other.* (Brandom 2011b, 111)

The second position that results from the social-pragmatic treatment of objectivity asks us to remember one of the key lessons of Rorty's thesis about incorrigibility – namely that the structure of authority that instituted the mental, while eliminable, is fully intelligible as it stands. Brandom puts the point this way:

> [Rorty's] claim was precisely *not* that the structure of individual *subjective* authority that instated mental events as incorrigible was *unintelligible*. On the contrary: we can understand exactly how we must take or treat each other in order to institute that structure and so the ontological category of things that exercises authority of that kind. The claim was rather that the

structure is *contingent* and *optional,* and that it is accordingly *possible,* and under conceivable circumstances even *advisable,* to *change* our practices so as to institute a *different* structure of authority. (Brandom 2011b, 112–113)

Brandom's strategy for rehabilitating objectivity takes the form of applying this lesson, forged in a consideration of subjectivity, to objectivity itself. Here we do not deny that objectivity makes *sense* but consider whether it is desirable to change our practices in such a way that this type of authority goes by the wayside. Rorty thinks that it *must* go by the wayside because reality is normatively inert. But as Brandom points out, Rorty's social pragmatism about normative statuses "does not entail that only the humans who institute those statuses can exhibit or possess them" (Brandom 2011b, 113). For since it is *we* who take or treat things as authoritative, we can put this authority 'where we like'. In other words, we can and should, from within our practices, "invest authority in non-human things: *take* ourselves in practice to be responsible to them in a way that *makes* us responsible to them" (Brandom 2008, 9). When this thought is put together with Brandom's thesis that semantic content is pragmatically rendered through the game of giving and asking for reasons, a hygienic notion of objective representational content emerges that is consistent with Rorty's normative social pragmatism.

> Rorty's two principle theses [that incorrigibility is a normative phenomenon and instituted in a social-pragmatic fashion] are compatible with acknowledging the existence of an objective representational structure of semantic authority. For, first, the referential, representational, denotational dimension of intentionality is understood as a *normative* structure. What we are talking or thinking *about*, what we *refer* to or *represent*, is that to which we grant a characteristic sort of *authority* over the *correctness* of our commitments ... And, second, we understand doing that, making ourselves responsible to non-human things, acknowledging their authority, as something *we* do – as conferring on them a distinctively *semantic* kind of normative status by our adopting of social practical-normative attitudes. The only question that remains is one of social engineering: what shape do our practices need to take in order to institute *this* kind of normative status? This is a Deweyian question that Rorty would have welcomed. (Brandom 2011b, 114–115)

For Brandom, the dimension of normative assessment that we institute by adopting certain practical attitudes is a non-optional 'quasi-transcendental' feature of our communicative practices insofar as agents sort and track these assessments (in their deontic scorekeeping) in light of an implicit distinction between the objective correctness of certain commitments and other lesser sorts of commitments. Brandom is not claiming that Rorty would endorse this strong view. His claim is more minimal – namely that the structure of authority that underlies objectivity is *consistent* with the notion that it is *we* who grant authority by making and taking reasons. If Rorty had recognized this, he could have endorsed the new pragmatic way of seeing things without endangering his central commitment to epistemological antiauthoritarianism.

The Rejection of Sense-Experience

Before we can understand why Brandom's argument that Rorty's views are consistent with a social-pragmatic conception of objectivity fails, we must provide our alternative genealogy of Rorty's eschewal of objectivity. As we mentioned in the introduction, it is not Rorty's social-pragmatic theory of subjective incorrigibility that is most responsible for his hostility to objectivity but, rather, his prior elimination of sensory experience.

We can see this by examining Rorty's early eliminativist paper, his 1965 "Mind-Body Identity, Privacy, and Categories." There, Rorty's goal is to "impugn the existence of sensations" (Rorty 1965, 182) by comparing them to entities (demons, witches, etc.) that were once thought to exist, but which, after improvements in our knowledge, are no longer discussed in polite company. As he says, "sensations may be to the future progress of psycho-physiology as demons are to modern science. Just as we now want to deny that there are demons, future science may want to deny that there are sensations" (Rorty 1965, 179). The main obstacle to making this argument is that "sensation statements have a reporting role as well as an explanatory function" (Rorty 1965, 179). In other words, the fact that science will be able to explain sensory phenomena in a more precise and comprehensive way than our folk psychology does nothing to undermine our intuition that sensory vocabulary plays a privileged role in our first-person reports. It is this that makes it seem that sensation statements and the phenomena that they report cannot be eliminated. But, Rorty says,

> the demon case makes clear that the discovery of a new way of explaining the phenomena previously explained by reference to a certain sort of entity, *combined with a new account of what is being reported by observation-statements about that sort of entity*, may give good reason for saying that there is no entity of that sort. The absurdity of saying "Nobody has ever felt a pain" is no greater than that of saying "Nobody has ever seen a demon," *if* we have a suitable answer to the question "What *was* I reporting when I said I felt a pain?" To this question the science of the future may reply "You

were reporting the occurrence of a certain brain-process, and it would make life simpler for us if you would, in the future, *say* "My C-fibers are firing" instead of saying "I'm in pain." (Rorty 1965, 179–180)[5]

This response is partially underlain by the Sellarsian argument, elaborated in the Myth of Jones discussed earlier, against the givenness of inner mental states. Just as the Ryleans integrated the concepts of thought and sensation into their conceptual repertoire and learned to use them in first-person non-inferential reports, we in the future will be able to integrate neurophysiological concepts into our first-person reports.[6] If we just focus on sensations, then instead of reporting that we are in pain, we will report that a certain C-fiber is firing. Here, terms like "'sensation', 'pain', 'mental image', and the like will drop out of our vocabulary ... at no greater cost than an inconvenient linguistic reform" (Rorty 1965, 185). But the elimination of sensation is also partially underlain, Rorty argues, by "an appreciation of the internal difficulties engendered in traditional empiricisms ... by the notion of a pre-linguistic item of awareness to which language must be adequate" (Rorty 1971, 231). In other words, if we grasp the difficulties that stem from the notion that there are pre-linguistic items to which language must be adequate and get past them, we will be able to see our way clear to a position in which reports about sensations may be replaced by reports about C-fibers.

The difficulties to which Rorty refers stem from the traditional empiricist commitment to the Myth of the Given. In its most familiar guise, the Myth of the Given is the myth that sense impressions can figure for a conscious subject as empirical *knowledge*, or as warrant for other episodes of empirical knowledge, simply through being Given, prior to concept formation, language learning, etc. But the traditional empiricist is also committed to a more basic thesis about *content*, namely, that sense impressions intrinsically have *intentional purport* without any conceptual stage setting or language learning. On this view, "sense is already a cognitive faculty, acts of which belong to the intentional order" (Sellars 1991, 44).

They are committed to this view of content because of their acceptance of an abstractionist theory of concept formation. It is important to

---

[5] Rorty recognizes the intuitive implausibility of this thesis. But he thinks this intuition is based upon the fact that dropping all sensation talk will be practically inconvenient. But philosophers must separate what is philosophically possible from what is convenient.
[6] Here I say "will be able" rather than "may be able" because I think Rorty's argument, like Sellars', is not based on an empirical prediction about future science but upon a rational reconstruction of our basic cognitive structure.

distinguish the theory of content that informs abstractionism and the abstractionist theory itself. Because, according to the abstractionist theory, there is nothing in the intellect that is not first in the senses; the formation of concepts requires an operation on antecedent sensory contents. On this view, a concept in the intellect – for example, the concept of red – is formed through a subject having multiple sense-experiences of red and abstracting out of such experiences a shared characteristic or quality – i.e., redness. The abstractionist theory of content emerges from a problem with this view. The problem is that the ability to notice and then abstract out of different experiences a shared quality like redness seems to require that one must already be able to *recognize* what it is these experiences share. If we are not to be led to the idea that this recognition depends on acquired concepts, which undermines the idea that the content of concepts has its origin in the sensory manifold, then we must say that subjects can notice *sorts* of things *prior* to their having a concept of that sort of thing. And subjects can do this because "the human mind has an innate ability to be aware of certain determinate sorts – *indeed, that we are aware of them simply by virtue of having sensations and images*" (Sellars 1997, 62). So without any conceptual stage setting or linguistic acquisition, the mere *having* of a sensation involves an awareness *of* certain determinate sorts or kinds, rather than being merely the causal antecedent to that awareness.[7] In sensing red, one is aware of red kinds; one is aware *that* something *is red*. This awareness is the prelinguistic awareness to which language must be adequate.

For the eliminative materialist, this view is obviously problematic because if sensations provide an agent with a 'knowing that something is the case' (e.g., that there is pain or a red triangle) prior to the acquisition of concepts or a language, then "there is a sort of pre-linguistic givenness about, e.g., pains [or sensations of red triangles, SL] which any language which is to be adequate must provide a means of expressing" (Rorty 1971, 228). This, in turn, supports the "intuition we will have the same experiences no matter what words we use" (Rorty 1971, 229). But with this intuition on the table, how can we 'impugn the existence of sensations'? For, on this account, the change in concepts that we use in our first-person reports (for example, from 'pain' to 'x C-fiber firing') is merely a *linguistic change* that does not affect the underlying experience. The words that

---

[7] As such, "the intellect can get its basic vocabulary from sense because this basic vocabulary already exists in the faculty of sense where it has been brought about by the action of external things" (Sellars 1991, 45–46).

report the experience are different, but their reference remains the same. But then the eliminativist claim about sensations, which seemed so radical, becomes the trivial thesis that we can change the vocabulary that we use to report our pre-existing experiences.[8]

The critique of the Myth of the Given is meant to ward off this criticism. For the "intuition that we will continue to have the same experiences no matter which words we use is in fact a remnant of ... the Myth of the Given" (Rorty 1971, 229). Rorty counters this myth by questioning the notion that there is a prelinguistic awareness to which language must be adequate:

> [T]he notion of a non-linguistic awareness is simply a version of the thing-in-itself – an unknowable whose only function is paradoxically enough, to be that which all knowledge is about. What *does* exist is the causal conditions of a non-inferential report being made. But there is no unique vocabulary for describing these causal conditions. There are as many vocabularies as there are ways of explaining human behavior. (Rorty 1971, 229)

There is no prelinguistic sensory awareness because sense impressions are causal intermediaries with the world that don't provide us with a consciousness of anything. As Sellars puts it, the "'of-ness' of sensation simply isn't the 'of-ness' of even the most rudimentary thought. Sense grasps no facts, not even such simple ones as something's being red and triangular" (Sellars 1975, 285). To be aware in the sense of having a conscious experience requires that one take up these causal conditions by using a concept in a perceptual judgment. Since Rorty follows Sellars in thinking that to possess a concept requires being able to use a word, for him conscious awareness is therefore bound up with the use of language. This is the Sellarsian doctrine of psychological nominalism – i.e., the doctrine that "*all* awareness of sorts, resemblances, facts, etc. ... is a linguistic affair. According to it, even the awareness of such sorts, resemblances, and facts as pertain to so-called immediate experience is presupposed by the process of acquiring the use of language" (Sellars 1997, 63).

Psychological nominalism is related to the traditional nominalist rejection of the rationalist idea that we have the innate ability to intuit universals, essences, or abstract entities – those that purportedly articulate a thing's intrinsic nature. Instead of rationally intuiting such abstract items as redness, our knowledge of red things is built up out of an acquaintance

---

[8] For this argument, see Bernstein 1971.

with red sense particulars, and our discernment of a common nature or essence of those particulars is a product of our acquired linguistic activity and the categorizations made possible by such activity. Because the discernment of the common natures of things depends on linguistic activity, there is, according to the psychological nominalist, no "awareness of logical space prior to, or independent of, the acquisition of language" (Sellars 1997, 66). In other words, there is no awareness of logically articulated facts, that something is thus and so, prior to this acquisition.

Sellars qualifies his psychological nominalism in two ways. First, the Myth of Jones demonstrates that there are inner thought-episodes (including perceptual episodes) that are not in any given instance linguistically articulated. Although thought-episodes *presuppose* the acquisition of a language insofar as they are semantically modeled on overt verbal episodes, they need not be linguistic in any particular instance. Rorty is usually not so careful as to make this qualification, often identifying thought and language. Second, perceptual episodes for Sellars have a sensory aspect even after the critique of the notion that they can by themselves play a cognitive role in our experience. While sensations are not the *object* of our perceptual experience, as act-object accounts of perception posit, we can say retrospectively, after their Rylean 'discovery' that they have qualitatively informed our perceptual experience all along.[9] For Sellars, this retrospective discovery of sensation is what makes the elimination of sense impressions in the scientific image such a pressing and difficult problem. Once again, Rorty is not so careful. In a move that Brandom will take over, Rorty couches Sellars' talk of sensation in terms of a creature's causal response dispositions to stimuli. On this account, sensory awareness is "awareness-as-discriminative behavior" (Rorty 1979, 182). Here a creature's sensing is construed in terms of what it *can do* and not in terms of what it *lives through* in experience. Sellars, of course, does use the language of discrimination, stimulus and response, for example, in his paper "Some Reflections on Language Games."[10] But he does not use it in *Empiricism and the Philosophy of Mind* or *Science and Metaphysics* to detail his theory of sense impressions. There, he consistently treats sense impressions as *states* or *episodes* and not as modes of behavior.

Because of his reductive interpretation of what Sellars' psychological nominalism entails, Rorty takes it that the critique of the Given results in the complete *epistemic neutralization* of sensation. By this we mean that the

---

[9] Sellars' account here is very complex. See chapter 5 of O'Shea 2007 and Levine 2016.
[10] This paper is included in Sellars 1991.

critique drains sense impressions of the immediate qualitative and phenomenal aspects that were taken to be their hallmark by the classical tradition. Sensations are epistemically inert causal conditions that, when 'coded' by a conceptual or linguistic system, leave no sensory remainder over and above the conceptual episode that eventuates. So when we respond to certain of our own inner causal states by deploying a concept (one that is originally part of the Ryleans' informal theory of thoughts and sense impressions) the character of our response is not determined *by the ontological nature of the states themselves* but by the vocabulary and the concepts that provide for the possibility of our giving a direct non-inferential report of these states. In this case, "what appears to us, or what we experience, or what we are aware of, is a function of the language we use. To say that 'X's appear to us as F' is merely to say that 'We customarily use 'F' in making non-inferential reports about X's'" (Rorty 1971, 228).

Since what we experience is a function of the language we use and the concepts we possess, when we exchange sensory concepts with neurophysiological ones, our very experience changes. The change in vocabulary is therefore not merely a linguistic change but a change in the very structure of our psychology. In ceasing to talk about sensations, we cease to have them.

The Rejection of Objectivity

The question that we must now address is how the argument for the elimination of sensation and sensory experience leads to Rorty's hostility to objectivity as a legitimate aim for our thought and inquiry. This connection comes out most clearly in Rorty's seminal *Philosophy and the Mirror of Nature* when he uses the Sellarsian argument against the perceptual Given to untangle "the basic confusion contained in the idea of a 'theory of knowledge'" – i.e., "Locke's confusion between justification and causal explanation" (Rorty 1979, 161). This is germane to Rorty's attack on the vocabulary of objectivity because he tries to demonstrate that the specifically modern conception of objectivity as the representation of how things are 'in themselves' is dependent upon the theory of knowledge having become, through the confusion of explanation and justification, first philosophy. Let us review this confusion and Rorty's response to it before coming back to how it is related to the elimination of sensory experience.

Rorty's exposition of the confusion of explanation and justification is embedded in a complex historical account of the emergence and eventual decline of epistemology. There are three basic stages in this emergence, Descartes' invention of the mind, Locke's confusion of explanation and justification, and Kant's confusion of predication with synthesis.[11] The move that sets the stage for Locke's confusion is familiar enough: Descartes invented the mind when he misinterpreted Rylean incorrigibility (the social practice of taking each other to be incorrigible) to be an ontological relation of immediate self-acquaintance. In defining the mind as the realm of immediate certainty, Descartes sets the stage for the assimilation of the items immediately known in this realm – i.e., thoughts and sensations. This assimilation was complete when Locke posited a single genus of representation, ideas, which included whatever is self-intimating for the mind. This, according to Rorty, is the key to the emergence of epistemology as an autonomous discipline because it makes it seem as if there is an object, our *representations* of the world, which can be reflexively accessed and examined prior to the world itself. Now epistemology has its own object, one that is prior to the objects of the special sciences.

Locke's view fails, according to Rorty, because he never fixes on a stable strategy to study this new sphere of the mental. On the one hand, he wants to give a quasi-Newtonian mechanistic explanation of the understanding, breaking it down into the smallest units possible (sense impressions), just as the corpuscular theory accounts for light in terms of the smallest particles possible. He wants this type of account not only to ape the most advanced forms of natural explanation but also to provide a plausible explanation of how the operations of the understanding are causally constrained by the sensory deliverances of the external world. On this score, naturalism and empiricism go hand in hand. However, Locke does not give up the notion that the products of the understanding are rational and so potentially knowledge bearing, for the whole goal of epistemology is to secure certain 'privileged representations' to ground the edifice of knowledge. To get around this problem, Locke construes representations in such a way that they can be the product of the causal impingements on our sensory apparatus while simultaneously standing in the rational relations characteristic of judgments and propositions in the space of reasons. So instead of separating the causal antecedents to knowledge (sensations) from the rationally articulated judgments and propositions in which

---

[11] Although Kant is essential to Rorty's story about the emergence of the theory of knowledge as a foundational discipline for the other areas of culture, the Lockeian stage of this emergence is most important for our purposes. This is because, for Rorty, Kant's basic mistake is to repeat the Lockeian confusion of explanation and justification. See Rorty 1979, 161.

knowledge is expressed (thoughts), Locke takes it that a "causal account of how one comes to have a belief should be an indication of the justification one had for that belief" (Rorty 1979, 141). In so doing, Locke confuses giving an explanation of our knowledge with giving a justification for it, and so commits himself to the Myth of the Given.

It is this confusion that gives weight to the notion, central to epistemology as first philosophy, that we can be in touch with the 'foundations of knowledge' – i.e., with "privileged representations" that "are automatically and intrinsically accurate" (Rorty 1979, 170). Rorty gives a very complex historical genealogy for this idea, finding its origin in the Platonic notion that knowledge should be modeled on a direct (noetic) perception of objects (e.g., mathematical truths) that don't allow themselves to be judged incorrectly. On this model, to be in touch with the foundations of knowledge is to be in touch with "truths which are certain because of their causes rather than because of the arguments given for them" (Rorty 1979, 157). In knowing these truths, we

> get beyond reasons to causes, beyond argument to compulsion from the object known, to a situation in which argument would be not just silly but impossible ... To reach that point is to reach the foundations of knowledge. For Plato, that point was reached by escaping from the senses and opening up the faculty of reason – the Eye of the Soul – to the World of Being ... With Locke, it was a matter of ... seeing "singular presentations to sense" and what should "grip" us – what we cannot and should not wish to escape from. (Rorty 1979, 159)

The Lockeian story about the foundations of knowledge, in which knowledge is based on the certainty that pertains to certain immediate presentations to sense, is made plausible by the Myth of the Given because the myth 'enchants' causality – i.e., smuggles into it epistemic properties – and so allows the notion of cause to *not* be the one that would be at work in a truly mechanistic account of cognition. For if that notion of cause *were* operative, Locke would owe us a story about how a mechanistically construed state could dictate to us what we *should* believe. Here we would need a story about how to move from 'is' to 'ought'. But because, for Locke, "knowing a proposition to be true is to be identified with being caused to do something by an object" (Rorty 1979, 157) – i.e., because causation *is* rational justification – this story is not even conceived of as being necessary.

To disentangle the Given and cut the Platonic cord requires, once again, the epistemic neutralization of sensation. Through our sensory contact with the world, we *do* directly confront the world causally, but the notion of causality at play here is not infected by the Given and hence one not epistemically relevant to propositionally structured knowledge. Unlike Locke, who only pretends to give a mechanistic explanation, Rorty accepts this burden and thinks of the causal impacts on our sensory apparatus as *merely* causal. As Brandom is fond of pointing out against those who read Rorty as a postmodern thinker for whom anything goes, Rorty thus thinks that our thought and perception are causally constrained.[12] But while "there is such a thing as brute physical resistance – the pressure of light waves on Galileo's eyeballs, or the stone on Dr. Johnson's boot," because Rorty separates explanation and justification, there is "no way of transferring this nonlinguistic brutality to *facts*, to the truth of sentences" (Rorty 1991c, 81). There is no way of doing this because there are no *rational* relations between language (as well as linguistically structured mental states) and the physical world at all. While the relationship between our thought and talk and the world is strictly causal, rational relations only pertain to items that are propositionally structured – i.e., items within the space of reasons.[13] As such, the space of reasons is autonomous insofar as items within it can only be rationally constrained by other items in this self-same space. But how then does the causal constraint provided by the world relate to the rational constraint generated inside the space of reasons? For Rorty, all we can say is that beliefs are caused to appear, and when they do, the self must accommodate them by changing their web or network of belief on pain of contradiction or tension (see Rorty 1991d, 93). We know through philosophical reflection that there is causal constraint, but we

---

[12] See Brandom 2000c, 160–161.

[13] At the end of his career, Rorty seemingly changed his mind about whether there are only causal relations between thought and belief and the world (See Rorty 2000a, Ramberg 2000, Stout 2007, Levine 2008 and in press b). For he comes to accept Davidson's idea that thought and world are two points of a three-pointed triangle and that the relations that thoughts have to the world are mediated by their relation to the other point of the triangle – namely, other subjects with which one communicates. So the relations between thought and belief and the world are not merely causal. But since he still rejects the idea that beliefs represent the world in a non-causal way, these relations we should say "are *neither causal nor representational*" (Rorty 2000a, 374). But there is less change in Rorty's view here than meets the eye. We can see this in a characterization of triangulation written at the same time as he supposedly changed his view:

> The point of this doctrine is that you cannot get along with just holistic inferential relations between beliefs and statements (as coherence theorists tried to do) nor with atomic relations of being-caused-by (as realists fixated on perception still try to do). You have to play back and forth between causation and inference in a way which does not permit any of the corners of a triangle to be independent of any of the others. (Rorty 2000b, 78)

So to say that the relations between belief and world are neither causal nor representational is not to say that these relations are somehow causal *and* inferential, natural *and* rational. It is just to say that we work *back and forth* between causation and inference such that a belief enters two distinct streams of relation. Here, the dualism between the causal and the normative remains in place.

can't, on pain of reinstating the Myth of the Given, answer the question of how this constraint rationally affects our view of the world.

It is this separation of the causal sphere from the rational sphere that underlies Rorty's infamous view of knowledge.[14] Since we cannot explain how constraint from the world is related to the justificatory process in the space of reasons, and only items in this space can justify other items in this space, in thinking about knowledge we must ignore the 'vertical' relation of mind to world and focus exclusively on the result of 'horizontal' conversational or justificatory processes. As Rorty puts it, "justification is not a matter of a special relation between ideas (or words) and objects, but of conversation, of social practice ... [W]e understand knowledge when we understand the social justification of belief, and thus have no need to view it as accuracy of representation" (Rorty 1979, 170). The move from objectivity to solidarity, or the move from being concerned with how our representations correspond to mind-independent facts to how our beliefs hold up in an ever-widening intersubjective process of justification, is therefore not a mere prejudice on Rorty's part but strictly follows from his underlying view about the relationship of reasons and causes.

It is here that we find the link between Rorty's attitude toward objectivity and the elimination of sensory experience. Simply put, they are linked because the argument for avoiding the confusion between justification and causation, which underlies his argument for overcoming objectivity in favor of solidarity, is based upon the same argument that Rorty previously used to eliminate sensory experience. This argument is his critique of the perceptual Given. In the sixties, Rorty tracked the consequence of this critique in the philosophy of mind, leading to his eliminative materialism, while in the seventies he sought out its consequences in epistemology, leading to his social-linguistic holism. The move from eliminative materialism to the rejection of objectivity was thus the carrying forward of this single Sellarsian line of thought.

In a passage from a later article on McDowell, but one that uses the language of *Philosophy and the Mirror of Nature*, Rorty demonstrates the interconnection of these moments:

> [A]dopting psychological nominalism, and thereby avoiding a confusion between justification and causation, entails claiming that only a belief can justify a belief. This means drawing a sharp line between experience as the cause of the occurrence of a justification, and the empiricist notion of

---

[14] I agree with McDowell when he argues that the dualism between reason and nature structures Rorty's thinking generally. See McDowell 1996a, 153.

experience as itself justificatory. It means reinterpreting "experience" as the ability to acquire beliefs noninferentially as a result of neurologically describable causal transactions with the world. (Rorty 1998d, 141)

In other words, untangling the central confusion of the epistemological tradition between justification and causal explanation requires reinterpreting experience in such a way that it is construed as a pre-personal causal transaction with the world rather than – as the empiricist tradition thinks – something that is justificatory for our thinking. This opens the way to Rorty's particular brand of antirealism.

Rorty argues that experience itself cannot dictate to us what we should think because our experiential transactions with the world can be taken up in different ways depending upon the system of concepts that circulate in one's community. When "something causal happens ... as many *facts* are brought into the world as there are languages for describing that causal transaction" (1991c, 81). So what facts there are depend on how the causal transactions are *taken* by the community, and this can't be determined by the causal transactions themselves. But then the *world itself*, which is only related to us via these transactions, cannot offer us *reasons* to think one thing rather than another. But if the world and its experiential deliverances cannot offer us reasons, then it cannot exercise authority over what vocabulary we should use to describe it.

Here we have the essence of Rorty's antirealism. It is not articulated by the thought that the existence of the world is causally dependent on minds or vocabularies. Because he thinks that experience is a causal transaction, Rorty can hold that "most things in the universe are causally independent of us" (Rorty 1998b, 86). But what he can't say is that these causally independent things have a genuine 'say' in determining the vocabularies we use to talk about them. Our freedom to use a vocabulary to describe and redescribe things is *not answerable* to the mundane world we are describing or redescribing; it is only answerable to the vocabulary that we develop with other subjects in the space of reasons.[15] And this, of course, is the ultimate lesson of Rorty's second Enlightenment.

Brandom's Interpretation

Now that we have our alternative story about the origin of Rorty's hostility to objectivity on the table, we can come back to why Brandom's argument

---

[15] For his rejection of the language of answerability, see Rorty 1998c and 1998d.

that Rorty's antiauthoritarianism is consistent with a pragmatically rendered notion of objectivity is flawed.

The first problem with Brandom's interpretation of Rorty is that it is, as I have tried to show, predicated upon a false genealogy. Brandom takes it that Rorty's rejection of objectivity is based on the social pragmatism that Rorty initially developed to eliminate subjective incorrigibility. Based upon this genealogy, Brandom can then argue that Rorty misinterprets the consequences of his own pragmatism insofar as a social pragmatism about objectivity, in contradistinction to Rorty's avowed understanding, allows for a community to engineer its linguistic practice in such a way that it can grant nonhuman things authority over their discursive practices. Here is the basis for Brandom's claim that it is within Rorty's power to accept a hygienic notion of objectivity, one that is not Given but *authorized* by a linguistic community. But if, as shown earlier, Rorty's elimination of the category of objectivity is not based on his social pragmatism but rather on his prior eliminativist thesis about sensory experience, then this argument does not pull through. Rorty rejects the vocabulary of objectivity because sensation, in being rendered a causal process through its elimination as an epistemic factor in our cognitive lives, cannot rationally mediate between the causal and conceptual orders. Because there is no mediation between these two orders, there is no way to account for how the world rationally constrains, via the deliverances of experience, our beliefs about it. But without an explanation of rational constraint, one cannot have a working notion of objectivity. Of course, for Rorty, this explanatory lacuna is a positive feature of his position insofar as he thinks it leads directly to his second Enlightenment.

Why does Brandom's interpretation of Rorty misidentify the origin of his hostility to objectivity? Brandom misses the real story because he is as invested in the strategy of eliminating sense-experience as Rorty. In his aptly titled paper, "No Experience Necessary: Empiricism, Non-Inferential Knowledge, and Secondary Qualities," Brandom states that we can make sense of perceptual knowledge "without postulating a layer of potentially evidentially significant (hence conceptually articulated) states in between purely causally occasioned and physiologically specifiable responses to environing stimuli and full-blown perceptual judgments" (Brandom 2002c, 2).[16] In other words, to explain the possibility of perceptual intentionality and knowledge, we don't need a layer of experience that,

---

[16] This paper has circulated in mimeo, but it is essentially the same as Brandom 2002b, which is published.

in being lived through, is rationally relevant to our beliefs and judgments about the world. All we need are full-blown perceptual judgments that are causally occasioned by environmental stimuli. To think otherwise is to fall into the Myth of the Given. Brandom's interpretation of Rorty is therefore redemptive: in showing that Rorty's social pragmatism can accommodate a hygienic notion of objectivity without utilizing the concept of experience, Brandom creates a genealogy for his thought that does not undermine his own central aim of rehabilitating objectivity in social-pragmatic terms. For if this rehabilitation could not be effected for Rorty, whose social-pragmatic transformation of Sellars sets the stage for Brandom's social-normative pragmatism, it would cast doubt on the cogency of his own project.

There is a second problem with Brandom's interpretation of Rorty. Even when taken on its own terms, it fails because it does not capture an essential feature of objectivity – namely that thought and perception that is objective is constrained by something that is *beyond our control*. If the category of objectivity is something we engineer, can we say that the world that is taken to be objective through the application of this category really is objective? To argue, as Rorty and Brandom do, that we are constrained by the world through its causal impact upon us does not address this question because the *category* of objectivity is a normative structure of authority that cannot, by their own admission, be accounted for or reduced to these causal impacts. So one can either (1) give an account of how the causal constraint provided by experience (understood in Rorty's reductionist way) leads to or grounds a type of rational or normative constraint in such a way that this constraint can become *part* of the content of the concept of objectivity or (2) provide a notion of objective constraint that is rendered solely at the normative or semantic level. Because of the way that they conceptualize the consequences of the critique of the Myth of the Given, both Rorty and Brandom think that the first course is impossible; accordingly Brandom, on Rorty's behalf, takes the second. But in accounting for the normative category of objectivity in just social-pragmatic terms, Brandom makes the category of objectivity *optional*, thereby leaving out the seemingly essential ingredient that what is objective is beyond our control. By staying within the terms of Rorty's social-linguistic pragmatism, Brandom cannot genuinely rehabilitate objectivity. In Chapter 4, I show how this conclusion applies to Brandom's stand-alone account of objectivity given in chapter 8 of *Making It Explicit*.

Of course, one might question whether the concept of objectivity has to capture the ingredient of constraint beyond our control. Indeed, Brandom might say that one of the consequences of pragmatism is that there simply is *no* such concept of objectivity, that it is a metaphysical illusion, and that his social-pragmatic account captures all that there is to the concept. How can we respond to this point? One of the aims of pragmatism, at least by my understanding, is to provide an elucidation of our concepts and a 'reconstruction' of our practices rather than a complete revision of them. This follows from pragmatism's suspicion of foundationalist positions that think that philosophical analysis can begin from a standpoint outside of our concepts and practices. For the pragmatist, philosophical analysis must begin in medias res – i.e., with all of the presuppositions that it in fact has – and commence in a process of problem solving that progressively elucidates the meaning of our concepts and reconstructs the shape of our practices. In moving so far from how the ordinary concept of objectivity operates in our thought and inquiry, by making the category of objectivity something that we control, Brandom completely revises the concept rather than elucidates it. Of course, this complete revision may be justified, but the burden is on Brandom to show that it is. I don't think Brandom has met this burden, especially when, as I will attempt to show in Part II of this work, we have a pragmatic account of objectivity that can, without falling prey to the Myth of the Given, accommodate the fact that thought and inquiry are objectively constrained by the world in a way that is beyond our control.

CHAPTER 2

Brandom, Pragmatism, and Experience

Introduction

In the last chapter, I argued that Rorty's rejection of sense-experience entails his later rejection of objectivity and that this entailment is underlain by certain dichotomies that structure his view. What I want to demonstrate in this chapter is that Brandom inherits these features of Rorty's thought and that this prevents him, despite his wishes, from making sense of our rational answerability to the world.

Brandom agrees with Rorty that pragmatism is not best thought of as a type of empiricism, much less a radical empiricism. Rather, he thinks that in its best guise, pragmatism ought to be rationalist in form. Brandom accordingly calls his pragmatism a 'rationalist pragmatism'. This view is filled out by two main components: (1) the social-linguistic pragmatism articulated in *Making It Explicit*, in which semantic content is conferred on our thought and talk through what subjects do in the social game of giving and asking for reasons and (2) the view, highlighted in *Between Saying and Doing*, in which subjects critically winnow their commitments through a feedback-governed test-operate-test-exit cycle (the TOTE cycle). So his rationalist pragmatism includes an account of content in which semantics answers to pragmatics and an account of empirical knowledge as a self-correcting enterprise. Brandom thinks of the latter process as a rationalist redescription of the pragmatist's concept of *Erfahrung*, experience understood as a developmental learning process. Brandom, therefore, does not reject the concept of experience *tout court*, as Rorty does, but only rejects the more limited concept of experience as an "episodic, self-intimating *Erlebnis*" (Brandom 2008a, 87). To make sense of content and knowledge, Brandom thinks, we do not need a notion of sense experience as a type of episode that subjects prejudgmentally live through. We do, however, need the notion of *Erfahrung* as a feedback-governed learning process by which we update and improve our commitments through time.[1]

In this chapter, I argue for two theses. First, I argue that Brandom's account of *Erfahrung* is structured by certain dichotomies that are a remnant the mind–body distinction. In light of this, he is unable to take on board the pragmatic idea that *Erfahrung* is a learning process that eventuates in habits and bodily skills. This, in turn, makes him unable to account for the guidedness and fluidity of the sensorimotor processes by which we cope with the world. Using Dewey's account of *Erfahrung* as a critical alternative, we can see that Brandom either gives an atomistic account of these processes – when, in fact, they are organic unities – or he gives an account that is intellectualistic. His account of experience is therefore not stable, veering back and forth between atomism and intellectualism. Second, I argue that conscious episodes of *Erlebnis* must be seen as part of this experiential learning process if we are to understand how it is rationally constrained by the world. To have a satisfactory theory of objectivity, one must utilize *both* concepts of experience, *Erfahrung* and *Erlebnis*, and Brandom's rejection of the latter undermines his attempted rehabilitation of the former.

Rationalist Pragmatism and Intellectualism

Let's begin by briefly characterizing the first component of Brandom's rationalist pragmatism. For Brandom, what is most salient about pragmatism, in all of its guises, is a claim about the 'priority of the practical', the view that explicit beliefs and representations depend on – and are somehow emergent from – a background of implicit practical abilities. What Brandom calls "*fundamental* pragmatism" understands "knowing *that* as a kind of knowing *how* ... That is, believing that *things* are thus and so is to be understood in terms of practical abilities to *do* something" (Brandom 2011a, 9). Here, pragmatism is seen as most opposed to an intellectualism in which our abilities to think and act are underwritten by an ability to explicitly grasp and apply rules or principles.[2]

---

[1] In Levine 2012, I did not pay sufficient attention to this point. I still do not think that Brandom's argument works, but his view is more in line with classical pragmatism than I took it to be in that earlier article.

[2] Opposing intellectualism is necessary to avoid what Brandom calls regulism – i.e., the notion that norms only guide our performances (theoretical and practical) as explicit rules that are self-consciously followed. Regulism is problematic because it generates a 'regress of rules', which can only be avoided, Brandom thinks, by holding that explicit rule following can only take place in a

On a typical construal, intellectualism is the chief vice of rationalism, and so one might think that fundamental pragmatism would be opposed to any form of rationalism. But this is not how Brandom sees things, claiming that his rationalist pragmatism "is not a form of intellectualism that stands opposed to fundamental pragmatism" (Brandom 2011a, 31). His rationalist pragmatism is not a form of intellectualism because, according to it, discursive intentionality (believing that something is the case) is a kind of practical intentionality – i.e., "the kind that includes practices of making claims and giving and asking for reasons" (Brandom 2011a, 31). In other words, in order to believe or know that something is the case, a subject must be able to *do* something – namely, to play the social game of giving and asking for reasons. And here we hook up with the central theoretical motivation driving *Making It Explicit*: namely, to replace the concept of representation as the central notion of semantics and epistemology with a concept that finds its natural home in our linguistic social practice – i.e., inference.[3]

Brandom replaces representation in three main steps. Let us go through them briefly. In a first step, Brandom articulates an inferential semantics in which the content of the concepts that articulate our assertions is conferred by the way in which such assertions are *used* in normatively governed patterns of material inference. For Brandom, to grasp the content of a concept requires having "practical mastery over the *inferences* it is involved in – to know, in the practical sense of being able to distinguish, what follows from the applicability of a concept and what it follows from," and to know what does *not* follow from the application of a concept and what it does not follow from. In other words, to grasp what it is to be committed to something being red is "treat 'That's red' as incompatible with 'That's green' ... as following from 'That's scarlet' and entailing 'That's colored'" (Brandom 1994, 89). So to grasp or understand the content expressed by this bit of vocabulary is to grasp what other commitments and entitlements its use in a proposition entails and precludes.

---

context where there is "a notion of primitive correctnesses of performance *implicit* in *practice* that precede and are presupposed by their *explicit* formulation in *rules* and *principles*" (Brandom 1994, 21). In other words, to explicitly follow a rule, an agent must already have a practical mastery, a know-how, which allows them to sort correct from incorrect performances (other's and their own) in practice.

[3] As we shall see in the next chapter, although Brandom replaces representation as the central concept of semantics and epistemology, he, unlike Rorty, is committed to rehabilitating this concept in social-pragmatic terms.

In a second step, Brandom argues that one's grasp of inferential compatibility and incompatibility relations depends on one's practical mastery of the 'norms implicit in linguistic practice' – i.e., of the *normative proprieties* or *deontic statuses* that specify what is correct or incorrect to do, what inferences one ought and ought not to make given those proprieties. Here an 'inferential semantics' is underwritten by a 'normative pragmatics' in which the ability to 'follow a rule' is achieved not by explicitly representing rules and principles but by having the *practical ability* to distinguish what does, and what does not, follow from one's beliefs, commitments, and entitlements. So what a subject must be able to *do* to believe or know that something is the case is to distinguish, in practice, between what is correct or incorrect to do, what inferences one ought or ought not to make given the norms or deontic statuses implicit in that linguistic practice.

Brandom's final step is to underwrite this normative pragmatics with a *phenomenalism* about norms. He argues that the normative or deontic proprieties or statuses in terms of which semantic contents are conferred on beliefs (and intentions), while practically ineliminable, are not theoretically primitive. These proprieties are not self-standing statuses that reside in a Fregean third realm but are, rather, instituted by the *practical attitudes* of those taking part in a language game, in what Brandom calls deontic scorekeeping. Norms get a grip because scorekeepers *take* or *treat* others as committed to and entitled to performances. As Brandom puts it,

> The natural world does not come with commitments and entitlements in it; they are products of human activity. In particular, they are creatures of the *attitudes* of taking, treating, or responding to someone in practice *as* committed or entitled (for instance, to various other performances). Mastering this sort of norm-instituting social practice is a kind of practical know-how – a matter of keeping deontic *score* by keeping track of one's own and other's commitments and entitlements to those commitments, and altering the score in systematic ways based on the performances each practitioner produces. The norms that govern the use of linguistic expressions are implicit in these deontic scorekeeping practices. (Brandom 1994, xiv)

We can now understand the contours of Brandom's view: his fundamental pragmatism is rationalist because what a subject must be able to do to believe that something is the case is take part in the practice of giving and asking for *discursively articulated reasons*. But this discursive demarcation of his pragmatism is not intellectualist because the discursive itself depends on *practical mastery* of the normative proprieties that govern inference, which themselves are instituted by how they are taken or treated by scorekeepers – by the *practical attitudes* of speakers and actors. So our discursive capacities depend on our participating in a social practice of making and taking normatively governed inferentially articulated reasons, and these depend on our ability to attribute and acknowledge commitments and entitlements.

I think it is safe to say that many pragmatists would still find this view to be overly intellectualist. For the norms implicit in practice are implicit in the *discursive* practice of *applying concepts and drawing inferences*, and the attitudes that institute these norms are *mental* attitudes toward conceptually contentful commitments and entitlements.[4] But this makes Brandom insensitive to a sense of practice that is at work in the classical pragmatists, and which is the basis of their critique of intellectualism – namely, the *habitual embodied practices* by which we pre-reflectively cope with our environment, both physical and social. For them, a subject's habitual sensorimotor engagement with the physical and social environment involves an embodied sense or understanding of a situation prior to the operations of discursive reason. This embodied understanding is governed by norms implicit in practice. So the pragmatist agrees with Brandom that we need a notion of norms operating implicitly in our practice. But while for Brandom norms are only implicit in our conceptual practices of making judgments and inferences, for the pragmatist norms are also implicit in our habitual embodied practices, both instrumental and social. For them, this type of bodily understanding is our basic way of 'being-in-the-world', and our discursive dealings with things emerge from this background.

---

[4] The question of whether *normative attitudes* are themselves conceptually constituted is, for Brandom, a difficult question. Normative attitudes can be undertaken without sematic self-consciousness – i.e., without the concept of an attitude. In this case, the attitude of taking or treating as correct or incorrect is a type of *doing* because one is not "*aware* of oneself *as* doing that" (Brandom 2005, 244). Here, one's practical attitudes are "only implicitly, and not explicitly propositional attitudes, that is, attitudes toward conceptual content" (Brandom 2005, 244). Taking or treating another subject as having commitments "*is* in fact ... attributing propositionally (hence conceptually) contentful commitments" (Brandom 2005, 243) to them not because one is aware of oneself as doing that but because the normative attitude is part of a scorekeeping practice that is structured in the right way. But, one wants to ask, how can one, in fact, attribute conceptually contentful commitments to another subject if one does not oneself grasp the contents attributed, even if only implicitly? If I have no sense of the content I am attributing, then what is the basis of the attribution? I agree with Laurier 2005a that Brandom never convincingly answers these questions.

The Two-Ply Account of Action and the Myth of the Practical Given

Brandom cannot take this richer sense of practice on board because of the way he conceptualizes the relationship between reason and the body. This can clearly be seen in his theory of action, which is modeled on his theory of perception.[5]

Following Sellars' account of action and perception as exits and entries into the space of reasons, Brandom aims to exploit "the structural analogies between discursive exit transitions in action and discursive entry transitions in perception to show how the rational will can be understood as no more philosophically mysterious than our capacity to notice red things" (Brandom 2000a, 79). To put it in Brandom's idiom, while perceptual belief is made possible by our having reliable dispositions to respond differentially to environmental states of affairs by acknowledging certain sorts of doxastic commitments, "[a]ction depends on reliable dispositions to respond differentially to the acknowledging of certain sorts of commitments (the adoption of deontic attitudes and consequent change of score) by bringing about various kinds of states of affairs" (Brandom 1994, 235). In other words, while in perception we non-inferentially respond to environmental stimuli by taking up a position in the space of reasons, in action we non-inferentially respond to our own taking up of a practical commitment or intention by bringing about a state of affairs through bodily action. "In action, alterations of deontic attitude, specifically acknowledgments of practical commitments, serve as stimuli eliciting nonlinguistic performances" (Brandom 1994, 235). Here we need reliable dispositions to respond differentially to stimuli not to acquire beliefs, as with perception, but to 'fulfill acknowledged commitments'.

Action for Brandom is therefore a two-stage process whereby a subject formulates a commitment to act through practical reasoning in the space of reasons and then 'makes true' that commitment by leaving that space through exercising a reliable response disposition. But if we follow Brandom in thinking that reliable response dispositions "are characterizable in a naturalistic, physicalistic vocabulary," and "are meant to capture the capacity we genuine knowers [and actors, SL] share with artifacts and merely sentient creatures" (Brandom 2002a, 350), then it is difficult to understanding how they can be sensitive to the reasons involved in the attitude of acknowledgment.

---

[5] Much of this section comes from Levine 2015a.

Roland Stout criticizes the view along these lines:

> Brandom's attempt to explain the process of acting according to reason as a two-stage process of acknowledging a rule and then responding to that acknowledgment can give us a distorted conception of the causal process that constitutes action. The distortion arises if in the two-stage model the rationality characteristic of agency is confined to the first stage – the production of attitudes ... [T]he first state involves sensitivity to rules (or reasons), but does not involve anything actually happening, and the second stage involves things actually being made to happen but involves no sensitivity to rules (or reasons). This fails to take seriously the idea of action as a process of rationally transforming the world – i.e., a process in which the changes characteristic of the action involve the rationality characteristic of agency. Instead the rationality characteristic of agency is manifested in the production of attitudes; the transformation of the world characteristic of action is not taken to be a manifestation of rationality in action, but rather a response to such a manifestation. (Stout 2010, 148)

The problem is that if bodily performances are reliable response dispositions that are merely caused by stimuli provided by acknowledged commitments, how can such responses be *rationally sensitive* to the content of the commitment that is to be made true? Perhaps a bodily action can be stimulated or launched by an acknowledged commitment, but how can the action that is launched be *guided* through time by the commitment if the action is not a manifestation of rationality but only a response to it?

Brandom answers this question by resisting Stout's suggestion "that a two-stage story must inevitably ... restrict rationality to one stage" (Brandom 2010a, 330). Response dispositions, Brandom claims, are themselves applications of concepts. As he puts it,

> the responsive capacity in question is itself a *rational* capacity. For in each case, the response must 'fit' the stimulus, and that 'fit' is a matter of the proper applicability of *concepts* ... [I]n action one must respond to a commitment to make-true some claimable by producing a situation in which it is true. The capacity to do that – in either direction – is a rational capacity. (Brandom 2010a, 329)

To ensure a fit between practical commitment and the state of affairs that makes the commitment true, we must consider our reliable differential response dispositions to be rationally sensitive to both the content of our normative attitudes and to what must be brought about in the world to make true that content.

But is Brandom entitled to a picture in which our response dispositions display this two-way form of rational sensitivity? I don't think so. To understand why, we must see that his two-ply theory of action is articulated in the way that it is to avoid the *practical Myth of the Given*. This is the myth that a theory of action can be grounded on "intrinsically motivating preferences or desires," which for Brandom are "the empiricist analogs, on the side of agency, to the preconceptual episodes of awareness to which epistemic authority is traced on the side of cognition" (Brandom 2000a, 31). When we understand Brandom's view of what is necessary in order to avoid the practical Myth of the Given, then we will be in a position to understand why he is not entitled to the thought that bodily response capacities are expressive of rational capacities.

In its more famous epistemological iteration, the Myth of the Given "is the idea that there could be a kind of state or episode, say perceptual experiences, such that the capacity to be in such a state or undergo such an episode both presupposes no mastery of concepts and also constitutes *knowing* something, or having *evidence* for a claim" (Brandom 2010b, 320). What is special about an episode of the given is that it has this authoritative status independently of all other items in our system of knowledge (insofar as it stands outside of the conceptually articulated space of reasons), yet it is also epistemically efficacious with respect to these items insofar as it can pass on its positive epistemic status to non-basic episodes. The notion that there are episodes that are *independent* yet epistemically *efficacious* is a myth because to be epistemically efficacious, these episodes must pass on epistemic warrant to items in the space of reasons, and to do this, they cannot be independent of this space. Because the efficacy and independence conditions cannot be met by a single episode, the notion that there *is* a single episode that meets both of these conditions is a myth.[6]

The Myth of the practical Given, in contrast, is the myth that there are intrinsically motivating states, preferences, or desires that are practically efficacious with respect to our bringing about a certain end or state of affairs, yet are independent of the system of conceptually articulated commitments and beliefs that could specify what it would be to successfully achieve that end and, therefore, guide us in the proper selection of means to that end. To be practically efficacious and independent at the same time, one must think that these given states "can have the properties both of itches and of the conceptually contentful desires that engage with conceptually contentful beliefs in practical reasoning" (Brandom 2011a, 74–75). But here one "runs together immediate inclination and conceptually articulated commitment

---

[6] This gloss is very quick. For a full account of the Myth of the Given parsed in terms of a tension between epistemic independence and epistemic efficacy, see DeVries and Triplett 2002.

in just the way Wilfrid Sellars criticizes, for beliefs rather than desires, under the rubric 'the Myth of the Given'" (Brandom 2011a, 51).

The problem with running these together is this: to meet the independence condition, one must think of desires as immediate inclinations on the model of non-cognitive itches, while to meet the practical efficacy condition, one must think of desires as conceptually contentful commitments. For the empiricist, because a desire is like an itch – i.e., a nonconceptual state that is foreign to the realm of reason – it is easily able to meet the independence condition. But once it meets this condition, it cannot be practically efficacious with respect to our bringing about a specified end. For when we have a desire, we are not motivated to act in just any old way but in the way that will make true the specific state of affairs desired. But if desire cannot specify what it would be to successfully bring about this state of affairs by incorporating a conceptually contentful claim about it, how can it motivate us to achieve *this* end and guide practical reasoning in its selection of means to that end? For this to be possible, desire must engage our system of conceptually articulated beliefs and so must not be independent of this system. If desire is truly independent, it cannot be practically efficacious with respect to achieving a specified end, and if it is efficacious for our successfully achieving that end, then it can't be independent of our conceptual system.

Brandom's general strategy for avoiding the Myth of the Given is to claim that instead of there being a single episode that meets both the efficacy and independence conditions, there are two such episodes, each meeting one of the conditions.

In the epistemological case, this strategy for avoiding the Given leads to a two-ply theory of perception in which agents have reliable dispositions to respond differentially to various kinds of stimuli by acknowledging a discursive commitment in the space of reasons. As Brandom puts it, "the ability to make non-inferential reports of, or to form perceptual judgments concerning, perceptible facts" is "the product of two distinguishable sorts of abilities: the capacity reliably to discriminate behaviorally between different sorts of stimuli, and the capacity to take up a position in the game of giving and asking for reasons" (Brandom, 2002a, 349). The ability to reliably discriminate between stimuli is something that full-fledged judgers share with nonrational creatures or even, as Brandom points out, non-sentient items that respond differentially to the environment (rusting chunks of iron). However, it is clear that this differential response is not yet the expression of the distinct responsiveness characteristic of those who can form perceptual judgments and possess perceptual knowledge. For this, the response that is reliably elicited must display understanding, must be a *conceptual* response that while not necessarily a *move* in the game of reasons – because it is non-inferentially elicited – is nonetheless a taking up of a position that has an inferential *status* in the selfsame game.[7]

This two-ply theory of perception thereby avoids the Myth of the Given because it does not posit, as the ground of our perceptual knowledge, sensory states or episodes that while nonconceptual, and so outside the space of reasons, are still epistemically authoritative with respect to items within that space. Rather, perceptual judgments, in being conceptually articulated, are inside the space of reasons (and so can pass on epistemic warrant to other states in this space), while the differential response dispositions that elicit these judgments are causal *pre-personal* responses to environmental stimuli. Here "we postulate the existence of something like sense impressions, whose properties systematically co-vary with the contents of the judgments they causally elicit from us. But these sense impressions are features of the physiology of perception. They are not something we are aware of, and they do not themselves have conceptual content. They merely occasion contentful judgments" (Brandom 1996, 253–254). So while perceptual knowledge has causal antecedents and is therefore constrained by the environment in that sense, these antecedents are not *themselves* episodes of awareness that have conceptual content. Brandom therefore avoids the Myth of the Given by *epistemically neutralizing* sense impressions, by substituting for them pre-personal causal response dispositions that play no role in the space of reasons. In placing "the interface between nonconceptual causal stimuli and conceptual response at the point where environing stimuli cause perceptual *judgments,*" his view thereby avoids "the Myth by seeing nothing nonjudgmental that could serve to *justify* perceptual judgments, rather than just to *cause* them" (Brandom 2002b, 93–94).

Brandom has a parallel strategy in the practical case. We saw earlier that if desire were truly independent of our conceptual system, it couldn't be

---

[7] For a response "to count as the application of a concept, for it to be properly characterized as a reporting or coming to believe that such-and-such is the case, is for it to be the making of a certain kind of move or the taking up of a certain kind of position in a game of giving and asking for reasons" (Brandom, 2002a, 351). But such responses are

> not the products of a process of inference, arising rather by the exercise of reliable capacities to non-inferentially respond differentially to various sorts of perceptible states of affairs by applying concepts. But *no* beliefs, judgments, reports, claims – in general, no application of concepts – are non-inferential in the sense that their content can be understood apart from their role in reasoning as potential premises and conclusions of inferences. (Brandom, 2002a, 352)

practically efficacious with respect to our making true a specific end or state of affairs, and if it were efficacious, by incorporating a claim about what it would be to successfully achieve a specific end it couldn't be independent of our conceptual system. Brandom's response to this dilemma is to drop all talk of desire, just as he dropped all talk of sense impressions, and ascribe to different states and episodes the functions of practical efficacy and independence. The independence condition is met – as it was in the case of perception – through the introduction of reliable differential response dispositions. The response dispositions that action involves are independent of our system of concepts because their exercise is a causal response to the stimuli provided by our practical attitudes, our acknowledgment of commitments in the space of reason. As such, bodily action itself is a nonconceptual response stimulated by a conceptually articulated commitment. This allows Brandom to avoid the practical Myth of the Given because the response dispositions by which we exit the space of reasons, while independent, are not practically efficacious – are not the items that specify the end to be made true nor motivate us to achieve that end. What specifies the state of affairs that is to be made true, and motivates us to bring it about, is the acknowledgment of a contentful practical commitment in deontic scorekeeping.

The point of this discussion has been to show that Brandom is not entitled to a view in which our bodily response capacities display a two-way rational sensitivity to our acknowledged commitments and to the states of affairs that make these commitments true. We can now see why: to avoid the practical Myth of the Given, Brandom must say that the reliable response dispositions that are exercised in bodily actions are independent of the realm of reason – i.e., only a causal response to the stimuli provided by the acknowledgment of a commitment. If such responses were not independent action would not be an exiting of the space of reasons and the two-ply account of action would collapse.[8]

The TOTE Cycle: Atomism or Intellectualism

The previous discussion was meant to show that Brandom's account of action couldn't make sense of the fact that bodily response dispositions display a two-way rational sensitivity, and this was meant to show that Brandom couldn't take on the pragmatist's richer sense of practice. But why is this a problem? It is a problem because without it, Brandom can't

---

[8] Brandom, therefore, has what Boyle calls an 'additive theory of rationality', where rationality does not permeate action and perception but is merely coupled with it. See Boyle 2016.

explain the fact that the activity by which humans cope with the world is not only *launched* by acknowledgment of a practical commitment but is also *guided* and *controlled* by it through time. In *Between Saying and Doing*, Brandom recognizes the problem:

> [I]t must be possible for actions to be controlled, and not just ballistic ('fire and forget'). That is, it must be possible for agents at least sometimes to adjust what they are doing on the basis of assessments of how successful current attempts are at reaching the desired goal.... [E]ven so simple an action as reaching for a doorknob must be specified as a Test-Operate-Test-Exit (TOTE) cycle, in which each incremental movement is observed, checked against its approach to the goal, and then followed by another movement calibrated by the results of the prior one, until the goal is reached. (Brandom 2008a, 63–64)

In *Between Saying and Doing*, this example is offered in the context of a consideration of a discursive practice in which standing practical commitments (to reach for doorknobs) mature into intentional doings when the circumstances are right. So the action envisaged here is an *intentional action*, involving the acknowledgment of a practical commitment to reach for the doorknob. But here we don't have the simple two-ply account of action enumerated earlier. Rather, intentional action is reconceived here to involve: (1) an acknowledgment of a practical commitment to make true this state of affairs and (2) a feedback-governed TOTE cycle in which we respond bodily to this acknowledgment, test the effects of this response, operate in response to that test, and then either exit – or if the goal has not been reached – test and operate again, and so on. Here we still have a two-ply theory of action, but instead of seeing bodily action as a simple one-step exit-transition, it is seen as involving a feedback-governed sensorimotor cycle in which "each cycle is mediated by its differential responses to the effects of its own performances" (Brandom 2008a, 182). This more complex picture can make sense of the fact that action is not just unleashed but guided and controlled by an acknowledged commitment because in involving response dispositions structured in this more complex way, it can *correct itself* in light of the state of affairs to be made true.

But, in fact, this updated two-ply account does not work any better than the older two-ply account. It can't because of the way that Brandom conceives of the composition of the TOTE cycle. Brandom takes it that the TOTE cycle is "algorithmically decomposable, that is, specifiable as the algorithmic elaboration of more basic differential response capacities" (Brandom 2008a, 190). To say that a practice P is algorithmically decomposable is to say that (1) all you need to take part in P is a set of primitive practices or abilities plus the algorithm by which these abilities are integrated; (2) that one could engage in each of these primitive abilities without having the capacity to engage in P. So, on this view, the TOTE cycle is composed a set of *atomic* abilities to respond differentially, responses whose exercise does not depend on the exercise of any others, plus the 'conditional branched-schedule algorithm' by which they are integrated.[9]

How is this algorithmic integration conceived of in the case of reaching for the doorknob? There are two potential readings, both of which are problematic. The first reading takes Brandom at face value when he says that in reaching for the doorknob, we *observe* our performance, *check* it against a standard of success, and based on that, produce another performance *calibrated* to reach the goal. Brandom seems to suggest here that the primitive abilities to reliably respond that comprise the TOTE cycle are integrated because each response is mediated by a *discursive* act of observation, calibration, and action, each of which involves a distinct doxastic or practical commitment. Here the act of reaching for the doorknob displays a type of "*discursive* intentionality, insofar as the differential responsiveness of the system to the results of its own performance is essentially mediated by states whose functional role in the feedback process can be understood only by taking them to be *propositionally* contentful" (Brandom 2008a, 183). This action is not just launched by a practical commitment but guided by it because as the action unfolds, the commitment involved in the action is continually *updated* in light of the states of affairs to be made true.

The virtue of this reading is that it can explain the guided and controlled nature of intentional action. But this reading makes Brandom's account intellectualist in an objectionable way. It is objectionable because if bodily action requires that each differential response is mediated by a distinct discursive act, then it is not able to explain a very basic feature of the phenomenology of action, namely, its *fluidity* – the fact that bodily movements are integrated and able to adjust flexibly to variations in circumstance without the intervention of distinct acts of reason. To think that distinct discursive acts are involved in each phase of the TOTE cycle would make the action of reaching for the doorknob 'clumsy and halting',

---

[9] For Brandom, there are two kinds of basic algorithm: a 'straight-schedule algorithm' and a 'conditional branched-schedule algorithm'. The former algorithm can simply follow a list of instructions, while the latter can "specify how it *alters* its differential response dispositions in response to the actual outcome of something it has done" (Brandom 2008a, 35).

as Dewey puts it. Sometimes, of course, the variability between performance and goal is so great that such discursive acts must be called upon to guide performance. But for basic kinds of actions like reaching for a doorknob, this is the exception, not the rule.

The second reading says that algorithmic integration happens when acknowledgment of a practical commitment to reach for the doorknob *causes* a cascade of response abilities structured in a way that conforms to a branch-schedule algorithm. While the *overall act* of reaching for the doorknob displays discursive intentionality because it is caused by an acknowledgment of a practical commitment, the cascade of response abilities caused by the commitment to make true this state of affairs only involves a type of *practical intentionality* that is meant to capture what is common in "what a predator does in stalking its prey and what a builder does in constructing a house" (Brandom 2008a, 178). On this reading, when Brandom says that reaching for the doorknob involves observing, checking, and calibrating, he is speaking metaphorically and not really referring to discrete discursive acts but to the fact that in the TOTE cycle, we not only respond differentially to the stimuli of an acknowledged commitment but also to the effects of that response, and the effects of that response, and so on.

But it is not clear how this avoids the original problem that we have been wrestling with – namely, how such responses can display the two-way rational sensitivity needed to account for the guided and controlled nature of intentional action without falling prey to the practical Myth of the Given. For, if the chain of responses is simply caused and hence independent of the acknowledgment that stimulates it, and every primitive ability to respond that comprises the chain is caused and so independent of every other, then it is unclear how one's response to can be rationally sensitive to the result of a prior response, and so self-correcting in light of the state of affairs to be made true.

Now Brandom would respond by saying that the cascade of atomic response abilities is goal seeking and self-correcting, not because these abilities are rationally sensitive themselves, but simply because they conform to a flexible branch-schedule algorithm. In this sense, response abilities are like those that comprise the activity of an automaton: "One of the striking things about automata that can execute conditional branch-schedule algorithms is that they are goal-seeking. The exit condition is not ... just ceasing to respond. It is sensible, and I think it is correct, to understand these systems as casting about, trying all sorts of things, until and unless a certain goal situation is brought about" (Brandom 2008b,

153). But this description does not even remotely describe what intentional action is like. Do we, in intentional action, *cast about* till we reach the goal of the action? It does not seem so. Rather, in intentional action, the goal that is specified by the content of the acknowledged practical commitment *inhabits, informs, and guides* the very doings that brings it about. Brandom still has no account of how this is possible, and so no account of how action is guided and controlled by a practical commitment rather than just launched by one.

Brandom, in my view, is stuck between the Scylla of intellectualism and the Charybdis of atomism. One side can't make sense of the fluidity of action, the other action's guided and controlled nature. What I want to claim now is that a pragmatist account of action, which involves their richer sense of bodily practice, can explain both of these features.

Pragmatism and Habits

On the pragmatist view, intentional action is not the coupling of a rational and a completely nonrational capacity, as the two-ply account has it, but rather the coupling of two rational capacities, one discursive, the other having a different sort of rational intelligibility. Intentional action is the coupling of an *active* rational capacity – the capacity to make and take reasons – with a *passive* rational capacity to act on standing *habits* or *bodily skills*. For the pragmatist, habits are acquired "skills of sensory and motor organs" (MW 14, 15) that, outside of direct conscious control, order the sensorimotor elements that subtend action. In actions that they do not dominate – i.e., intentional actions – habits are still "operative in some subdued subordinate form" (MW 14, 31). But while habits are passive in the sense that they are exercised outside of one's conscious control, they nonetheless are "projective, dynamic in quality, ready for overt manifestation" (MW 14, 31).

But while passive, habits have rational intelligibility. There are four reasons why this is so: they are reasons, are normatively accountable, involve a type of embodied sense or know-how, and can be changed through being intervened on. It is clear that habits that have been purposively acquired and inculcated through training can stand as reasons, for these habits were inculcated to serve the purpose of the practice of which they are a part. If a pianist develops a habit through training, it would be wrong to say that the pianist lacks a reason to exercise the habit just because their doing so is outside of their conscious control. They do have a reason to exercise the habit – namely, to successfully play a piece of music. If a historian is apt to see certain kinds of social formations as the result of social movements rather than functional social mechanisms, it's because they have acquired over time a habit of seeing the historical data in a certain way. They have a reason, of course defeasible, to see things this way. While this habit is not expressive of a current exercise of one's rational capacities, it has been brought about by *past exercises* of these capacities and takes part in the justificatory and reason-giving structure of those exercises.

But, of course, many if not most of our habits are not purposively inculcated through training. Take, for instance, a deep-seated culturally formed habit like our standing at certain distances from others in small spaces (like elevators).[10] But even this kind of habit is purposive – we have the habit of standing at a certain distance from others for the purpose of feeling at ease. Therefore, here, too, we have a reason to stand at that distance from others. Even though this reason is not at the moment *one's own*, the rationale behind this habit *can*, we shall see next, become one's own.

Because habits as purposive can be reasons, a sense of correctness and incorrectness can get a grip with respect to them. The particular sense of correctness and incorrectness at play here is centered on what, following Merleau-Ponty, we could call a "norm of optimality" – a norm that pertains to whether our sensorimotor responses are organized in a sufficiently optimal way to engage uninterruptedly in the action at hand.[11] The specification of whether our bodily habits and skills are sufficiently optimal is not determined by reason and its reflective monitoring but by the *situation itself* – i.e., by whether the action made possible by such habits and skills continues in an unimpeded fashion or not. To be optimal, habits must be sensitive not only to the sensorimotor coordinations demanded of our *bodies* but also to *what* our bodies are doing, to the demands of the action in which they are involved. So while the norm of optimality pertains to the coordination of our sensorimotor system, it also pertains to the *practical logic* of the action and practice in which one is engaged – whether playing the piano, carving a statue, standing in an elevator, negotiating a contract, or attending a dinner party. In all of these cases, the success of our habits and bodily skills is determined by whether they conform to the demands of these practices. To be successful, the materiality of our natural

---

[10] For more on this, see Dreyfus 2013 and Levine 2015b.
[11] See Merleau-Ponty 2013, especially part 2, chapter 3, and Dreyfus 2000. In Chapters 5 and 6, I argue that Dewey's naturalistic anthropology includes an account of natural normativity that is in essence the same as the norm of optimality.

bodies must incorporate, and be molded by, certain of our subjective purposes, those embedded in the logic of the practices that comprise our form of life.

According to the pragmatist, this incorporation infuses habits not with conceptual content but with a type of *embodied sense* or *know-how*, a sense of how one can meet the demands of the logic of the practice in which one is engaged.[12] As Bourdieu puts it, habits involve a "practical sense, or if you prefer, what sports players call a feel for the game, as the practical mastery of the logic or of the immanent necessity of the game – a mastery acquired through experience of the game" (Bourdieu 1990, 61). As it is for Brandom, subjects know how to go on in a practice without following an explicit rule. But in the pragmatists' view, this know-how does not just apply to our knowing how to apply concepts and draw inferences but also to how our bodies can successfully gear into, and so successfully complete, our worldly projects.

An account of intentional action that includes habits and bodily skills can make sense of its guided and controlled nature, as well as its fluidity, because, in having rational intelligibility, habits are *manifestations* of our rationality and not merely *responses* to an independent exercise of it. As such, action is expressive of a practical commitment and not merely caused by one. Take the action of reaching for the doorknob. An acknowledgment of a practical commitment to make this state of affairs true activates standing bodily habits and skills of reaching. These habits and skills involve an embodied sense of how to reach for the doorknob. Because this understanding is mostly offloaded from consciousness to bodily habits, in performing this action, consciousness does not need to coordinate the minor elements of the action. As such, it can concern itself with more 'universal things' like thinking about what to have for dinner (as one reaches for the doorknob). Because the coordination of these minor elements is mostly automatic, action can be fluid and in the flow rather than clumsy and halting – as it would be if it continually needed the guidance of discrete discursive acts. But while the coordination of the action is mostly outside of conscious control, it nonetheless remains sensitive to and so is guided by the acknowledgment of a practical commitment. This is because the habits and bodily skills involved in this action remain, throughout the performance, accountable to the norms of optimality entailed by the purpose of the action – the state of affairs that is

---

[12] Although he is wary of the cognitive connotation of the term '*know*-how', Dewey uses it and contrasts it with 'knowledge-that' at WM 14, 124–125.

to be made true. When these norms are violated, it signals to the actor that a divergence between performance and goal has developed and that a correction is necessary to reestablish equilibrium. This leads to a correction that remains in the flow or to a correction that requires a more extensive type of reflection that breaks the flow.

But if habits and bodily skills are, unlike Brandom's reliable response dispositions, manifestations of rationality and not just responses to an antecedent exercise of it, then does not the resulting view of action fall prey to the practical Myth of the Given? For this picture gives up the idea, central to Brandom's way of avoiding the Given, that bodily responses are independent of the practical attitudes that cause them. As we know, the sine qua non of the Myth of the Given is the notion that there are efficacious states (epistemological or practical) that simply in being Given operate either as forms of knowledge (sense impressions) or as practically efficacious (desires), without the benefit of prior learning, concept formation, etc. If we stick to the practical case, we can avoid this conception by recognizing that habits are efficacious states that, unlike desires, are acquired, relatively plastic, and changeable through intervention.

While habits are intrinsically propulsive and hence motivating if the right circumstances develop, they are acquired and subject to change over time. Habits are not, therefore, Given states of ourselves like desires but are the result of a learning process, the result of training or of a reflective intervention on our own habits.[13] Habits are subject to these processes because, while they operate prior to reflection, they *can* be reflected on and changed, at least to a degree. But how? While habits are forward looking, our reckoning with the undesirable consequences of their exercise is backward looking. An undesirable consequence could be that one has a tendency to respond irritably when one's spouse is driving too slowly or that one's left hand has the tendency to rhythmically follow the right hand too closely when playing the piano, etc. These undesirable consequences, whether noted by oneself or another, are what provoke reflection and deliberation about the habit. Unlike mere reflex behaviors or sub-personal bodily processes, which can only be the object of a witnessing of our own bodies from sideways-on, these habits – whether non-purposively inculcated (irritation at slow driving) or purposively inculcated (playing the piano) – can come with the scope of one's reflective self-knowledge. This reflection *begins* by taking one's body and its habitual activity as an object that is witnessed from the sideways-on. But *through a reflective process* that

[13] See Pollard 2006.

is temporal and effortful, these bodily habits can be transformed into being part of one's 'bodily-subjectivity' – i.e., can be experienced as part of something that *one oneself does*. While this process might seem mysterious, we can easily imagine a pianist saying: 'Before, I did not realize that my left hand did that, but now I not only realize it but can experience it in the flow of my playing'. Because the habit now falls within the scope of the pianist's reflective self-consciousness and is part of his or her bodily subjectivity, he or she is able to begin a process to control and change the habit.

As we all know from experience, this process is difficult and will often fail. But while some habits are more resistant to change than others, the fact that we can change them through training or reflective intervention shows that they are to some degree reason responsive, and so not completely outside the space of reasons. The Myth of the Given is therefore nullified not by taking recourse to a rationalism that posits a break between conceptually articulated reasons and bodily responses, but by extending the realm of reasons all the way out to bodily habits and skills.

The TOTE Cycle and the Reflex Arc: Dewey's Critique

There is no space for the pragmatist's notion of habit in Brandom's picture because his two-ply account of action and perception, whether the older or newer version, is structured by this break. For on his normative functionalist view, mind is understood as the normatively governed moves made in the space of reasons, while the body is understood as a causal concatenation of natural response abilities, whether to stimuli in perception or to acknowledged commitments in action. Here we have a dichotomy between mind and body, which Brandom reinterprets as the dichotomy of reasons and causes. While in action and perception normatively governed thoughts and utterances and causally governed response dispositions (to stimuli and practical acknowledgments) are somehow *coupled* casually, there is an ontological gulf between them that cannot be bridged.[14]

---

[14] In *Between Saying and Doing*, Brandom is sometimes committed to a position that reduces this dichotomy away. Brandom there argues that the "specifically *semantic* intentionality displayed in language-use, engaging in *discursive* practices, deploying an autonomous *vocabulary*, should be understood both as a development of and as a special case of the sort of basic *practical* intentionality exhibited already by ... feedback-governed transactions" (Brandon 2008a, 179). Since the feedback-governed TOTE cycle is itself understood in terms of atomic response abilities, this program, if successful, would give a 'bottoms up' explanation of discursive intentionality in

The classical pragmatists, especially Dewey, think that this dichotomy is ripe for critical dismantling. Dewey does so by providing a critique of the atomist picture of sensation, thought, and motor response that he thinks results from the underlying separation of bodily stimuli and response, on the one side, and thought on the other.[15] He does so by arguing that the distinction between these states are "not distinctions of existence, but teleological distinctions, that is, distinctions of function, or part played, with reference to reaching or maintaining an end" (EW 5, 104). In other words, while we can draw functional distinctions between sensory stimuli, thought, and bodily responses insofar as they help us interpret an agent's goal-directed action, we ought not think that these distinctions, or the underlying distinction between body and thought, cut nature at its joints.

This is the central point of Dewey's famous paper "The Reflex Arc Concept in Psychology," which articulates a type of teleological functionalism. There, Dewey discusses James's famous example of a child seeing a candle flame, touching it, and feeling pain (see James 1981, 36–37). Here we have a basic TOTE cycle in which the child learns from his exploratory sensorimotor activity. This TOTE cycle is understood by the reflex arc theorist to be comprised of atomic parts. It is, in Brandom's terms, algorithmically decomposable: "The sensory stimulus is one thing, the central activity, standing for the idea, is another thing, and the motor discharge, standing for the act proper, is a third" (EW 5, 97). Dewey rejects this account because "it assumes sensory stimulus and motor response are distinct psychical existences, while in reality they are always inside a co-ordination and have their significance purely from the part played in maintaining or reconstituting the co-ordination" (EW 5, 99). In other words, he rejects the idea that the TOTE cycle, whether brought about by an acknowledged commitment or not, can be seen as comprised of atomic response abilities, abilities to respond differentially to stimuli or to move one's body, as Brandom and the reflex arc theorist think. Instead

---

terms of these primitive abilities. In this case the categorical distinction between contents conferred in the space of reasons and reliable response dispositions would vanish since the former would, at the ultimate explanatory level, be just a version of the latter. The more moderate picture I consider in this chapter integrates the TOTE cycle into an updated two-ply account of action and perception. This picture has the advantage of making what Brandom says in BSD consistent with the rest of his work, where the two-ply account of action and perception is maintained.

[15] The view that thinks of sensory stimuli, thought, and motor response as separate existences is not a case of "plain science" but is rather "a survival of the metaphysical dualism, first formulated by Plato, according to which the sensation is an ambiguous dweller on the border land of soul and body, the idea (or central process) is purely psychical, and the act (or movement) purely physical" (EW 5, 104).

of thinking of a sensorimotor circuit as a "patchwork of disjointed parts, a mechanical conjunction of unallied processes," we ought to think of it as "organic unity" (EW 5, 97). It is the whole circuit that is the primary explanatory structure, and "the distinction between what has been called stimulus and response is made only by analytic reflection" (LW 12, 36). Dewey's argument for this is that the very possibility of discerning stimulus and response as isolated moments depends on an interpretation of the overall act of which these moments are a part, and this depends on discerning the overall act's goal or end.

Dewey's first argument for this conclusion is meant to undermine the idea that stimulus and response are atomic states whose significance and nature depend on nothing besides themselves. Take a stimulus, hearing a loud sound. The experiential character of this stimulus depends not just on what is Given but also on what is *taken*, which itself depends on the ongoing activity of the stimulated creature. As Dewey puts the point:

> That which is, or operates as, a stimulus turns out to be a function, in the mathematical sense, of behavior in its serial character. Something, not yet stimulus, breaks in on an activity already going on and *becomes* a stimulus in virtue of the relations it sustains to what is going on in this continuing activity... Even in the case of abrupt changes, such as a clap of thunder when one is engrossed in reading, the *particular* force of that noise, its property as stimulus, is determined by what the organism is already doing in interaction with a particular environment. One and the same environmental change becomes, under different conditions of ongoing or serial behavior, a thousand different actual stimuli – a consideration which is fatal to the supposition that we can analyze behavior into a succession of independent stimuli and response. (LW 5, 223)

But the significance that a stimulus has depends not just on the *horizontal* relations it has to our ongoing activities; it also depends on the *vertical* relations that it has to bodily capacities that are exercised *contemporaneously* with the stimulus. Consider the stimulus of the light that the child responds to by reaching. This act does not actually begin with a bare sensation of light

> but with a sensorimotor co-ordination, the optical-ocular, and that in a certain sense it is the movement which is primary, and the sensation which is secondary, the movement of body, head and eye muscles determining the quality of what is experienced. In other words, the real beginning is with the act of seeing; it is looking, and not a sensation of light. (EW 5, 97)

If we were able to take a cross section of this experience, we would find it to have *depth*; it is an act of seeing that is both sensory and motor, and the nature of their coordination depends on the total state of the creature at that moment. But, of course, this point not only applies to the present moment but also to the moment prior to the act of seeing. So what comes before the present act and prepares the ground for how we shall take it is not an isolated sensation but a whole act or sensorimotor coordination.

The upshot is that talk of 'stimulus' or 'response' as isolated states is misleading, since the significance and nature of any given state is bound up with its place in a larger organic unity or context. But if this is the case, then how do we so much as arrive at the concepts of 'stimulus' and 'response'? Dewey takes it that these concepts are arrived at through isolating a moment of a sensorimotor coordination and abstracting it from its horizontal and vertical dependencies. He argues that the organic sensorimotor circuit is explanatory prior to stimulus and response because this abstractive procedure, undertaken from the third-person point of view, is dependent on an interpretation of the end of the act with which the organism is engaged. To specify what in an act is 'stimulus' and what is 'response', an interpreter must take up a teleological stance to the total act of which these moments are a part. They must for two reasons.

The first reason is that because "it is only the assumed common reference to an inclusive end which marks each member off as stimulus and response, that apart from such reference we have only antecedent and consequent" (EW 5, 105).[16] In other words, we mark off the seeing of the light as the stimulus to the reaching, rather than as an event that is simply antecedent to the reaching, because the end of the act gives us basis to interpret one thing as *bringing about* the other. Instead of looking at stimulus and response as a succession of uncoordinated events, we are able, by positing an end, to look at them as *leading to that* end. The second reason is that it is only with reference to the end of the act that we can discern that the seeing of the light is a stimulus to the response of reaching rather than its being a response to a prior stimulus, perhaps turning one's head toward the light. So an end gives us a reference point not only to determine that a series of occurrences are connected insofar as they lead up to that end, but also to determine the specific role each occurrence plays. This determination of role, however, is merely pragmatic, relative to our interpretive interests. For the act of seeing can be both stimulus and

---

[16] Dewey does not think that he needs to take a stand on whether teleology is real or not. For whether "teleology is ... real or unreal, my point holds equally well. It is when we regard the sequence of acts *as if* they were adapted to reach some end that it occurs to us to speak of one as stimulus and the other as response" (EW 5, 105n).

response. The distinction between it being stimulus or response is one "of flexible function only, not of fixed existence; that one and the same occurrence plays either or both parts, according to the shift of interest" (EW 5, 102). It is for this reason that we can say that stimulus and response are not distinctions of existence but teleological distinctions that are pragmatically rendered to advance interpretation.

But if a sensorimotor circuit or TOTE cycle is not comprised of distinct response abilities, as Brandom and the reflex arc theorist think, how is its organic unity to be understood?[17] Take the sequence of seeing the candle and reaching for it. These two acts are unified within a 'larger co-ordination' because if

> the sight did not inhibit as well as excite the reaching, the latter would be purely indeterminate, it would be for anything or nothing, not for the particular object seen. The reaching, in turn, must both stimulate and control the seeing. The eye must be kept upon the candle if the arm is to do its work; let it wander and the arm takes up another task. (EW 5, 98)

In other words, the act of seeing does not just stimulate or launch a motor act, it continues to 'inhabit' it, for otherwise the action would be 'indeterminate', would not be guided and controlled in light of a specified end. And the act of reaching controls the seeing in the sense that it gives seeing a *telos* (it must focus on the candle, not look elsewhere). If the coordination between these acts is fluid and in the flow, it is not consciously represented but mostly off-loaded to bodily habits. The child does not need to derive the steps of this sequence of acts; rather, they only need to represent the goal that they wish to make true, which brings about mostly automatic bodily habits.

But unity is not accounted for just by the presence of habits but also by the fact that such habits are part of a feedback-governed process in which earlier experience is mediated by later experience, and later experience consummates and develops earlier experience. To illustrate, consider the next stage of the TOTE cycle, in which the child reaches for the candle and gets burned. In this case,

> the so-called response is not merely *to* the stimulus; it is *into* it. The burn is the original seeing, the original optical-ocular experience enlarged and transformed in its value. It is no longer mere seeing; it is seeing-of-a-light-that-means-pain-when-contact-occurs. The ordinary reflex arc theory proceeds upon the more or less tacit assumption that the outcome of the response is a totally new experience; that is to say the substitution of a burn

---

[17] See Rödl 2008 for an alternative Kantian account of unity arrived at through a critique of Brandom.

sensation for a light sensation through the intervention of motion ... [w]e do not have the replacing of one sort of experience by another, but the development (or as it seems convenient to term it) the mediation of an experience. The seeing, in a word, remains to control the reaching, and is, in turn, interpreted by the burning. (EW 5, 98–99)

To say that an experience is 'mediated' is to say that an earlier phase of an experience is interpreted by a later phase of the experience in light of its outcome or result. Because the seeing continues to inhabit and control the reaching, it can be interpreted by the result of the reaching, in this case by the burning. So, for instance, by being burned, the child has a better sense of *what it was that they experienced when they saw the light*. They now understand that the original seeing of the light was, in fact, a 'seeing-of-a-light-that-means-pain-when-contact-occurs'. The child is now *conscious* that this is (at least one) meaning of light, and this meaning feeds back into their system of habits and bodily skills, preparing them to cope with light in the future. Because of this backward-facing interpretation, their understanding of what they experienced is enriched, and this enriched experience prepares them in a forward-facing way for present and future experience. Here, the child has gone through a developmental learning process, which for Dewey *is* experience.

Erfahrung and Rational Constraint

Brandom well recognizes that, for the classical pragmatists, experience is a developmental learning process:

> Dewey's term for that process, in all its varieties, is "experience" ... Experience in this sense is not the ignition of some Cartesian internal light ... It is something *done* rather than something that merely *happens* – a process, engaging in a practice, an exercise of abilities, rather than a episode. It is experience not in the sense of *Erlebnis* (or *Empfindung*) but of Hegel's *Erfahrung* ... For the pragmatists, experience is not an input to the learning process. It just *is* learning: the process of perception and performance, followed by perception and assessment of the results of the performance, and then further performance, exhibiting the iterative, adaptive, conditional-branching structure of a test-operate-test-exit loop. The result of experience is not best thought of as the possession of items of *knowledge*, but as a kind of practical *understanding*, a kind of adaptive attunement to the environment, the development of habits apt for successful coping with contingencies. (Brandom 2011a, 6–7)

When understood as *Erfahrung*, experience is "one of Brandom's words" (Wanderer 2008, 191). But his understanding of it is different than the pragmatist's. As we have seen, and as Brandom himself notes in this passage, for the pragmatists, this cycle eventuates in a set of bodily habits and skills. For Brandom, in contrast, the TOTE cycle eventuates in a new set of *commitments* apt to inform successful future thought and action. Here, Brandom integrates the pragmatists' notion of experience as *Erfahrung* into his rationalist pragmatism, taking it to be a "naturalized version of the rational process of critically winnowing and actively extrapolating commitments, according to the material incompatibility and consequence relations they stand in to one another" (Brandom 2011a, 8).

For Brandom, the process of critically winnowing commitments through the TOTE cycle is not an autonomous discursive practice, one that could be engaged in without engaging in any other. For one can only update commitments and entitlements if one can utilize such deontic statuses by playing the intersubjective game of giving and asking for reasons. But the converse also holds. For

> one understands what a bit of vocabulary means only insofar as one knows what difference undertaking a commitment by its use would make to what else the one using it is committed or entitled to – that is, insofar as one knows how to update the set of commitments and entitlements in the light of adding one that would be expressed using that vocabulary (keeping deontic score). (Brandom 2008a, 79)

This ability to update one's commitments and entitlements entails a distinct norm of belief formation – i.e., the responsibility to update one's commitments by subjecting them to rational criticism:

> An essential part of what one is *doing* in committing oneself (doxastically or practically) to some claimable content is taking responsibility for *integrating* it into a whole constellation of such commitments, by following out the inferential consequences it has in the context of its fellows, and subjecting it to rational criticism by confronting it with an concomitant commitment that turns out to be materially incompatible with it. Engaging in that fundamental sort of discursive activity is what Kant called "synthesizing the transcendental unity of apperception." (Brandom 2008a, 186–187)

The question I want to ask now is this: how is this process of synthesizing the transcendental unity of apperception rationally constrained by the world? It is constrained, Brandom argues, because the discursive practices at play in the TOTE cycle are world involving – they *incorporate* objects, events, and worldly states of affairs:

> The way the world is, constrains proprieties of inferential, doxastic, and practical commitment in a straightforward way from *within* those

practices ... The possibility of incompatible commitments arising from the cycle of perception, inference, action, and perception, reflects the way the normative structure of perception and action incorporates elements of the causal order. As a result, empirical and practical constraints get built into what commitments (including inferential commitments) one can sustain entitlement to. (Brandom 1994, 332–333)

Brandom illustrates this with the example of dipping litmus paper into an acid. If one perceives a liquid to taste sour, it is permissible to infer that it is an acid. One can infer further – based on the content of one's concept of an acid – that if one dips litmus paper into the liquid it will turn blue. If it turns red instead, however, one's expectations will have been thwarted, and a material incompatibility will have been introduced into one's system of commitments. For someone to

> repair that incompatibility (to update her commitments), she is obliged either to relinquish the claim the liquid tastes sour, or to relinquish the claim that [the litmus paper] is red, or to revise her concept of an acid so that it no longer mediates the inference that caused the problem ... Entitling oneself to any of these moves involves further commitments it may not be easy to entitle oneself to, and none of them may ultimately be successful. But in any case, something has been learned. (Brandom 2008a, 185)[18]

We know that this learning process is constrained by the world because non-inferentially elicited perceptions input into one's system of commitments something *unexpected*. Based on the sourness of the liquid, one expects the litmus paper to turn blue, but one, in fact, perceives red. One is *surprised* by what one perceives, and this shows that one does not control what one perceives. So what engenders "*friction* between the world and the deployment of vocabulary in a practical cycle" is the fact that the "inferential links between observational concepts" (Brandom 2008a, 185) elicited non-inferentially are disrupted. In the case we are considering, what is disrupted is the inferential link between sour liquids and litmus paper turning blue when dipped into such liquids. "For what has been revealed is that, contrary to the material inference curled up in that concept, it is *not necessary* that sour liquids turn phenolphthalein blue. It is *possible* that a liquid both be sour and turn phenolphthalein red" (Brandom 2008a, 186). The use of modal vocabulary here signals that what has been revealed through doxastic updating is not merely 'subjective', merely about what a subject takes to be compatible or not with respect to their commitments, but 'objective', about

---

[18] I have changed Brandom's example slightly. I talk about litmus paper while he talks about phenolphthalein solution.

"the objective world they talk about and act in: its *laws*, what connections are *necessary*, what is really *possible*" (Brandom 2008a, 186).

Notice that we can't specify this learning process without making "reference to changes in the world that are both produced by the system's responses and responded to within each loop of the TOTE cycle" (Brandom 2008a, 178). This points us in two directions. On the one hand, the changes in the world that provoke discursive updating are partly produced by, and so mediated by, one's own prior responses, and so by the standing system of doxastic and practical commitments that resulted in such responses. On the other hand, in the TOTE cycle, one perceives and responds to these produced changes, the results of which feedback into one's system of commitments. So these results mediate our commitments about changes in the world that themselves have already been mediated by prior responses. The TOTE cycle, therefore, involves a double form of mediation, one by which our concepts come to be more and more adequate to the way things are

> Where enough discursive updating TOTE cycles of this sort have been engaged in to produce a relatively stable and successful discursive practice, objective facts about what actually follows from and what is incompatible with what will have been incorporated in the material inferences and incompatibilities that articulate the concepts expressed by the vocabulary deployed according to the practical norms implicit in that practice. This essentially holistic process involves getting onto how things objectively are not just by making true claims, but also by acknowledging the right concepts. (Brandom 2008a, 186)

Erlebnis and the "Rational Constraint 'Constraint'"

While Brandom integrates the notion of experience as a developmental *Erfahrung* into his theoretical picture, he also famously sides with Rorty "in rejecting the notion of experience ... 'Experience' is not one of my words – literally, it does not occur *in Making It Explicit*" (Brandom 2011a, 197).[19] Is Brandom contradicting himself? No, because, as we mentioned in the introduction, Brandom is working with two separable concepts of experience: experience as a developmental *Erfahrung* and experience as an episodic *Erlebnis*. What Brandom rejects here is the concept of *Erlebnis*,

---

[19] Here Brandom is parroting Rorty, who says that the "term 'experience' does not occur in the admirably complete index to Brandom's 700 page book; it is simply not one of his words" (Rorty 1998c, 122).

the concept of an episode that is lived through first-personally by a conscious subject prior to judgment that can nonetheless stand as a reason for judgment.

Brandom's primary reason for rejecting this concept is simply that it is not needed to articulate a hygienic theory of perception, one that avoids the Myth of the Given. For, as we saw earlier, according to his two-ply theory of perception, there is no need to posit a "layer of potentially evidentially significant ... states" and episodes to stand "in between purely causally occasioned and physiologically specifiable responses to environing stimuli and full-blown perceptual judgments" (Brandom 2002c, 2).[20] In perception, we rather reliably respond to environmental stimuli by directly issuing perceptual judgments.[21] Brandom recognizes that rejecting this layer of prejudgmental yet evidentially significant experience places an explanatory burden upon him, for an account of perception in which perceptual judgments are just *causally occasioned* by environmental stimuli seemingly has trouble making sense of the fact that such judgments have an empirical content that is *rationally constrained* by the way things are. It has trouble making sense of what Brandom calls the "rational constraint 'constraint'." Here is how Brandom puts it: "[T]o underwrite an intelligible notion of empirical conceptual content, the constraint on our thought exercised by the world in perception must be *normative*: it must settle how it would be *correct* to apply the concepts in question, how they *ought* to be applied. The concept of conceptual or intentional content, like the concept of meaning, is a normative concept" (Brandom 1996, 246). If the commitments non-inferentially elicited by environmental stimuli are to have a content that can *guide* doxastic updating rather than merely occasion it they must meet the "rational constraint 'constraint'."

In his paper "Perception and Rational Constraint," which is a critique of John McDowell's account of perception, Brandom tries to show that his two-ply account of perception can meet this constraint without need of the concept of experience (*Erlebnis*). Brandom agrees with McDowell that the rational constraint necessary for empirical content can't be accounted for

---

[20] Brandom also rejects the concept of *Erlebnis* because he thinks such episodes are 'self-intimating'. But to say that an episode is lived through first-personally does not entail that it is self-intimating in the Cartesian sense.

[21] It should be said that this is Brandom's way of avoiding the Myth of the Given; it is not, by his own admission, the only way, for he admits that positing a layer of potentially evidentially significant yet prejudgment experiential states and episodes does not *by itself* gives rise to the myth. One could hold, as McDowell does, that this experiential layer is informed by the activation of conceptual capacities that are not themselves Given but acquired.

by a picture of perception that accepts the Myth of the Given, or by a coherentism that thinks that rational relations only pertain between thoughts and other thoughts, or by a picture of perception that thinks of it solely as a causal interaction with the environment. But Brandom does not think that ruling out these views leads to a picture where thought can only be rationally constrained by experience. He avoids this conclusion by calling upon epistemological reliabilism, which for him is a social externalism.

The basic thesis of externalism – of whatever kind – is that "one can *be* justified without being *able* to justify. That is one can have the standing of being *entitled* to a commitment without having to *inherit* that entitlement from *other* commitments inferentially related to it as reasons" (Brandom 1995, 904). The basic thesis of a reliabilist version of externalism is that the justification condition for knowledge can be replaced by a reliability condition: "to count as knowledge, true perceptual beliefs must be the outcome of *reliable* belief forming processes, that is, processes that are ... *likely* to lead to true beliefs. Perceptual beliefs so formed are ones the perceiver should count as *entitled* to" (Brandom 1996, 249). While one can take oneself to be reliable, and so turn reliability back into a reason for one's commitment, this need not be the case for the perceiver to be entitled to their perceptual beliefs. All that is necessary is that they be reliable.

But Brandom's reliabilism is a *social* externalism rather than an externalism *simpliciter* because reliability is not, he thinks, a concept that can stand independently of scorekeepers *taking* others to be reliable. The ascription of reliability, Brandom thinks, only makes sense relative to an assessor's choice of reference class (see Brandom 2000a, 113). So to take Goldman's barn façades as our example, a non-inferential knower might be reliable in identifying barns when the reference class is barns in general, or barns in the state of Iowa, but they would not be reliable when identifying barns in barn façade county. So assessments of reliability are not made by 'nature itself', but by an assessor of reliability.

> Assessing reliability is one way of assessing a believer's entitlement to beliefs she finds herself with perceptually. This is as normative a matter as can be – a matter of what one *should* think, and not just what one *does* think ... And it is evidently not an assessment that somehow takes place outside the space of reasons. On the contrary, taking someone to be a reliable reporter is just endorsing an *inference* of a characteristic pattern: taking it that the fact that the *reporter* is noninferentially disposed (in the right sort of circumstances) to acquire a belief with a given content provides a good

reason for acquiring a belief with that content *oneself* (a reason the *attributor* of reliability could cite in *justifying* his own belief, if the one whose belief it is could not). (Brandom 1996, 251)

An assessment of reliability is therefore a *socially articulated inference from* the attribution of a non-inferentially acquired commitment *to* the undertaking and endorsement of that commitment by the attributor. In other words, a scorekeeper judges that the perceptual judgments of a candidate knower, elicited by reliable response dispositions, *are* reliable relative to an ascribed reference class or context, and bases the commitments they endorse on this assessment of reliability.

Brandom argues that this social reliabilist account of knowledge can do justice to the "rational constraint 'constraint'." In a long passage, he explains why:

> If a suitable story is told about the constitutive inferential engagement of these non-inferentially elicited judgments with other judgments, then their essential liability to rational criticism – and hence states as denizens of the space of reasons and products of spontaneity – is secured ... If a suitable story is told about how they are rationally criticizable by those who key their correctness to their correspondence to the facts reported, and their entitlement to the reliability of the noninferential process that elicits them – a matter of the assessors' rational willingness themselves to endorse respectively the claim in question and the inference form the reporter's making of it to that endorsement themselves – then rational constraint by and answerability of perceptual judgment to how things actually are is secured. (Brandom 1996, 254)

Brandom's point is that if one sees knowledge as a standing in a *socially articulated* space of reasons, then rational constraint does not need to come from one's *experience* of the world, as McDowell thinks, but can come from the rational assessment of one's perceptual judgments by *other* scorekeepers. Reliability inferences are rational and not causal and, as such, admit of rational evaluation and criticism. And these rational inferences are precisely *about* whether a candidate knower's non-inferentially elicited judgments are answerable to the facts – to the way things are in the world. So they are about how, in perception, the facts perceived exert a rational influence on a subject's thinking. But this rational influence is not assessed by the candidate knower himself but by another agent who is looking to form a reliability inference so as to ground their own undertaking and endorsement of a commitment.

If we are interested in how a candidate knower's observation report is rationally constrained by the world, we therefore don't need to point to *their* conscious perceptual experience; instead we can point to the causal covariance between unexperienced sense impressions and elicited perceptual judgments. While, for Brandom, a candidate knower *understands* the content of the elicited judgment they make, grasps its inferential significance, they gain no inkling *from their conscious lived experience* why it is *rational* for them to make that judgment. The rationality of the judgment comes on the scene in a second-person fashion (Brandom 1996, 257). Because of this, *experience* (*Erlebnis*) plays no role in accounting for the rational credentials of a non-inferential perceptual response to the world, for one's being *entitled* to it. But can experience be eschewed so easily?

Following McDowell, I think that Brandom's attempt to meet the "rational constraint 'constraint'" without utilizing a concept of experience (*Erlebnis*) is incoherent. Let's see how.

As we just saw, for Brandom the rational constraint provided by the facts does not come into view *for* the subject who experiences those facts. While a subject understands the content of their elicited perceptual judgment they do not know from their experience why it is rational for them to make that judgment. If we think of a perceptual judgment as expressed by a linguistically articulated observation report, as Brandom does, then the point is that one makes a report about certain facts but does not have experiential insight into why these facts call for this report. One just makes the report. McDowell argues that this makes one's reaction to these facts "a blind reaction to she knows not what" (McDowell 1996b, 294). For McDowell, in contrast, the experiential availability of the facts reported in an observation report and their being rationally constraining on the report "are not two distinct characters it has" (McDowell 1996b, 294). Rather, what a report *reports* are facts that are rationally constraining on the report. This is why it is not 'blind'.

We can understand what McDowell is driving at by examining the observation report of a scorekeeper who makes reliability inferences, and therefore takes a candidate knower's perceptual responses to be rational. Upon what basis are these inferences made? Once we ask this question it becomes immediately apparent that a difficulty arises. For how, McDowell asks, can Brandom

> be entitled to the idea that an *interpreter* ... is in touch with the relevant aspects of reality (the environmental circumstances supposedly reported on, and, now in addition, the responses that Brandom wants to be entitled to see as reports). It can only be *qua* responder – *qua* capable, herself, of responses that are intelligible as reports – that a person who is supposed to be an interpreter comes into *our* view (if she does, which I am bringing into

doubt) as able to observe the relevant aspects of reality: able to adopt, as a result of suitable impacts from the environment, mental postures with the appropriate empirical content. (McDowell 1996b, 295)

For an interpreter to assess a candidate knower's entitlement to the beliefs she perceptually finds herself with, the interpreter must be able to make reports about environmental circumstances and whether the candidate knower's responses to that environment are reliable. Do the facts that are reported here come into view as rationally constraining *for* the interpreter or not? If they *do* come into view for the interpreter, licensing them to think that another subject's responses are reliable, then we have found a subject whose first-personal *experience* of the facts is essential to the warrantedness of their belief and judgment – i.e., their judgment of reliability. But if an interpreter's judgments can be based on their conscious experience, then there is no principled reason why the candidate knower's non-inferential perceptual judgments can't be based on *their* conscious experience.

If, on the other hand, the facts are *not* available for the interpreter, do not come into view for them, then why should their reliability inference about another subject be seen as rationally responsive to the facts? What are they basing their judgment on? Well, perhaps their inference concerning the reliability of a candidate knower is based on *their* non-inferential response to the relation of environmental circumstances to the candidate knower, which is itself taken as reliable by *another* interpreter who is keeping score on them. This again would be what introduces rational constraint into *their* non-inferential response, making it more than mere causal covariance. But as McDowell asks: "How could multiplying what are, considered by themselves, blind responses, to include blind responses to how the blind responses of one's fellows are related to the circumstances to which they are blind responses, somehow bring it about that the responses are after all not blind" (McDowell 1998a, 408). As McDowell rightly says, the notion that one could account for the rational purport of observation reports in this way 'smacks of magic'.

The culprit in all of this is Brandom's eschewal of experience (*Erlebnis*). In not being able to utilize the resources of conscious experience to underwrite the rational credentials of a perceptual belief or judgment, Brandom is forced to credit another subject and their attributions with introducing such credentials into one's judgment. But then the question of what introduces rational credential into their attributions arises, and one is off on a vicious regress. The only way to avoid the regress is to accept that a subject's first-personal conscious experience can enter the epistemic process at certain points to rationally warrant a belief or judgment based upon such experience.[22] But if that is the case, then Brandom's account of rational constraint without experience (*Erlebnis*) fails.

Double-Checking

What I want to show now is that Brandom's inability to account for rational constraint without experience (*Erlebnis*) undermines his account of the constraint generated by experience understood as a developmental *Erfahrung*. If successful, this argument would show that his rationalist rehabilitation of experience as a developmental *Erfahrung* fails, and that one needs, to make sense of experience so understood, to integrate into it the notion of experience as an episodic *Erlebnis*.

As we know, *Erfahrung* is a learning process in which a subject, through the TOTE cycle, synthesizes materially incompatible commitments. What introduces constraint or friction into the process concerns the fact that non-inferentially elicited perceptual judgments produce surprising material incompatibilities. What I want to focus on here is this question: *when*, in light of these surprising material incompatibilities, does one have the task-responsibility to update one's commitments? The answer can't simply be when one acquires a seemingly new commitment – through testimony or the TOTE cycle – which seems materially incompatible with one's standing commitments. For, according to Brandom's default and challenge structure of entitlement, most of our prior commitments have *default entitlement*, and that a challenge to our existing commitments by a new commitment will be legitimate, and the material incompatibility created justified, only if the "challenge ... itself has, either by default or by demonstration, the status of an entitled performance" (Brandom 1994, 178). So while we have the task-responsibility to subject our commitments to rational criticism, we also have the task-responsibility to justify, in any given case, that very criticism. If this were not so, if criticism and challenge did not need entitlement, then the demand for justification could never be brought to an end, and the infinite regress brought about by foundationalist accounts of justification could not be avoided. But, Brandom argues,

> One of the lessons we have learned from thinking about hyperbolic Cartesian doubt is that doubts too sometimes need to be justified in order to have

---

[22] For why this does not land us back in the Myth of the Given, see note 21.

the standing to impugn entitlement to doxastic commitments. Which commitments stand in need of vindication (count as defective in the absence of a demonstration of entitlement to them) is itself a matter of social practice – a matter of the practical attitudes adopted toward them by the practitioners ... Claims such as 'there have been black dogs' and 'I have 10 fingers' are ones which interlocutors are treated as prima facie entitled. They are not immune to doubt in the form of questions about entitlement, but such questions themselves stand in need of some sort of warrant or justification ... [N]othing recognizable as a game of giving and asking for reasons results if justifications are not permitted to come to an end. (Brandom 1994, 177)

Here Brandom is thinking about challenges in an interpersonal context: I challenge your belief, and if the challenge is justified and has the status of an entitled performance, you have a task-responsibility to respond by giving reasons. Playing the game of giving and asking for reasons is an interpersonal process of synthesizing the transcendental unity of apperception. But we can also think about challenges in an intrapersonal context of fixing belief through the TOTE cycle. Here we can have a range of cases. If I have a belief that is contradicted by the having of a non-inferentially elicited perceptual judgment (formed in standard conditions), then the challenge of the new commitment to my prior commitments has a type of default entitlement, and I have immediate reason to begin the process of updating my commitments. If I think I left my wallet on the table but see it on the nightstand, then I have immediate reason to update my beliefs about where my wallet is. But take a second case, one where I perceive a green elf. The challenge that this poses to my prior commitment that green elves don't exist – given the default entitlement of everything else I am committed to – would not seem to have the status of an entitled performance (although it would seem to legitimately challenge other commitments – i.e., that conditions are standard, that I am sober, etc.). Because one has reason to not take this challenge to have the status of an entitled performance, one does not have reason to begin the process of updating one's beliefs about existence of green elves.

Brandom's acid example falls between these two cases. If one has a body of belief about acids that have default entitlement a single observation report contrary to one's expectations will not automatically lead one to begin the process of doxastic updating. It would, in fact, be irrational to update entrenched standing commitments before gaining entitlement to the challenge that brings about material incompatibility. The case, however, is not the like the green elf case, where one can simply dismiss the challenge posed by the observation, given everything else one knows. Rather, the observation report that underwrites the challenge takes on the status of a *hypothesis* that needs confirmation before the challenge gains entitlement. Confirmation in this case happens through *double-checking*. One double-checks one's results to gain entitlement to the challenge and the concomitant need, in the face of material incompatibility, to begin doxastic updating. Double-checking can be done in two ways: interpersonally through testimony and the TOTE cycle, or intrapersonally through the TOTE cycle. In the former case, I might consult an authority on acids who tells me that litmus paper in fact turns red in acid when such and such conditions are in place. When I double-check my results, I find that such and such conditions are in place, legitimating the apparent challenge to my prior commitments. In light of this, I must update my concept of an acid to take account of this new knowledge. When I double-check solely through the TOTE cycle, I gain entitlement to the challenge by checking *more carefully* than before whether the conditions were standard, whether the liquid really was sour, whether the litmus paper really turned red, etc. If by going through this cycle I get the same results, I gain entitlement to the commitment that brings about doxastic updating, whereas if get different results, I do not.

The question is this: can one explain the process of double-checking without utilizing the concept of experience (*Erlebnis*)?[23] As we saw, Brandom is able to account for perceptual knowledge without *Erlebnis* by claiming that entitlement is a status that is *attributed* to one's perceptual judgment by other scorekeepers. It is not a status that comes about through the reason-giving power of something being present to one in first-person experience. We can easily see how this works in the case of testimony. But it seems off-key when describing the entitlement we gain to a commitment when we double-check through the TOTE cycle. It seems off-key because the point of double-checking through the TOTE cycle is to verify one's past perceptions, inferences, and perceptions of the consequences of performance, in light of one's present perceptions, inferences, and perceptions of the consequences of performance. In this case, entitlement for the hypotheses that underwrite the challenge do not flow from

---

[23] Haugeland 1998 uses the concept of double-checking in the context of arguing for the thesis that commitment is a prerequisite for objective perception. He takes it for granted that double-checking is comprised of a more careful exercise of our 'primary recognition ability' plus an ability to tell whether the results come up differently than before. What I want to show here is simply that the 'primary recognition ability' involved in double-checking is experiential.

the attribution of other subjects but from the right connection between one's past and present *experiences*. When we double-check, we attempt to verify the hypotheses that underwrite a legitimate challenge by checking whether the commitments they involve are rationally responsive to the way things are. In this case, our assurance that this is so does not flow from the attribution of entitlement by other subjects but from one's *experience* (*Erlebnis*) – by checking whether the liquid actually *tastes* sour, or whether one actually *sees* the litmus paper turn red when dipped in the sour liquid, etc.

Now there is a way for Brandom to agree that the TOTE cycle, when used to double-check commitments, can confer entitlement on a challenge involving those commitments without need of an attribution of entitlement from other scorekeepers. The argument would be that entitlement is granted not by third-person attribution nor by first-person experience (*Erlebnis*), but by the inferential connections that are established between present and past *perceptual judgments*. So, in the case of double-checking the liquid, we acquire a perceptual judgment causally elicited by stimuli that covaries with sour things that is *compatible* with our prior commitments about acids. And when we double-check the result that the litmus paper turned red, we note the consequences of this performance by again having a *perceptual judgment* causally occasioned by stimuli that covaries with red things that is *incompatible* with our prior commitment that litmus paper dipped in acid turns blue. It is the checking of these compatibility and incompatibility relations that confers entitlement on the commitments involved in the challenge – not experience (*Erlebnis*). Double-checking is not based on experience (*Erlebnis*) but is rather simply a phase of a feedback-governed developmental learning process (*Erfahrung*).

But what confers entitlement on *these* perceptual judgments? What ensures that they are *rationally* constrained by *the way things are*? Certainly their being compatible or incompatible with one's prior commitments can't confer this status on them. That would make rational constraint the product of a 'self-contained game', one where it is generated by the relationship between thoughts and judgments rather than the relationship between judgments and the world such judgments are about. As we saw earlier, Brandom himself recognizes that this type of Coherentist account can't make sense of the "rational constraint 'constraint'." Indeed, this is precisely why he introduces reliability inferences. But such inferences are not the basis of double-checking. The basis, rather, is experience in the sense of *Erlebnis*.

Erlebnis and *Erfahrung*

But how can perceptual experience (*Erlebnis*) contribute to the rational constraint of experience (*Erfahrung*) without falling prey to the Myth of the Given? To conclude, I want to briefly give Dewey's answer to this question, recognizing that I shall have much more to say about it in Chapters 5 and 6.

Dewey makes a distinction between mind and consciousness. Mind "denotes the whole system of meanings as they are embodied in the workings of organic life" – i.e., in our beliefs, habits, feeling qualities, and emotions, while consciousness "denotes awareness or perception of meanings; it is the perception of actual events ... *in* their meanings" (LW 1, 230). While consciousness is "existentially intermittent and discrete, like a series of signal flashes or telegraphic clicks," conscious states, because they are funded by the meanings that comprise mind, nonetheless "involve a continuum of *meaning* in process of formation" (LW 1, 233). When do such meanings become the object of our conscious awareness? When the "system of meanings ... is undergoing re-direction, transitive transformation" (LW 1, 233) due to a disruption or crisis:

> Awareness means *attention*, and attention means a crisis of some sort in an existent situation; a forking of the roads of some material ... It represents something the matter, something out of gear, or in some way menaced, insecure, problematical, and strained ... Attention is a phenomenon of conflicting habits, being the process of resolving this conflict by finding an act which functions for all the factors concerned. (MW 4, 138)

For both Brandom and Dewey the inputting of something unexpected or surprising into experience (*Erfahrung*) leads to a type of reconstruction – to doxastic updating or to a process of resolving a conflict in one's habits. But for Dewey, unlike Brandom, this reconstruction involves an extended phase of attentive awareness in which we explore features of the environment that previously afforded fluid action. Sometimes reconstruction requires that we engage in an abstract and disembodied kind of reflection and deliberation. But in most cases, reconstruction is effected by perceptual experience itself. This is because of perception's functional interconnection with action.

Perception as a phase of a feedback-governed TOTE cycle is not a causal response to stimuli or a full-blown judgment. Rather, its nature is bound up with its functional role in the TOTE cycle. Dewey says two things about this role. First, perception is "not an instantaneous act of carving out a field ... but is a process of determining the indeterminate" (MW 7, 13). We should not think of perception as something that provides us with a photograph-like representation of the world, but as a temporally extended activity in which indeterminacies in the environment are made relatively determinate through exploratory sensorimotor activity.[24] Second, perception brings about a "functional transformation of the environment under conditions of uncertain action into conditions for determining an appropriate organic response" (MW 7, 19). If we bring these two roles together, we can say that perception determines an indeterminate environment so as to prepare the way for an appropriate organic response. Perception can achieve this result because it presents the environment "as it will be when modified by our reactions upon it." In other words, the content of perception, "*[w]hat* we perceive ... is not just the material upon which we *may* act, but material which reflects back to us the consequences of our acting upon it in this way or that" (MW 7, 13). Perception, therefore, presents the environment *as* an environment of things that will *afford* certain of our activities.[25] Because of this, perception "facilitate[s] ... choice ... since the act of appreciating in advance the consequences that are to accrue from incipient activities would surely affect our final action" (MW 7, 13).

For Dewey, environmental affordances are not Given because what affordances a creature directly perceives depends in part on prior processes of retention and habit that prime them to take the environment in certain ways and not others. As Dewey puts it, in "experience we come to recognize objects on sight. I see or note directly that *this* is a typewriter, *that* is a book, the other thing is a radiator, etc. ... But it is a product, mediated through certain organic mechanisms of retention and habit, and it presupposes prior experiences and mediated conclusions drawn from them" (LW 12, 146). To avoid the Myth of the Given, one does not need to reject experience understood as *Erlebnis*. One just needs to see that lived experience is mediated by, and mediates, the temporally extended learning process of which it is a part.

What makes perceptual experience rationally answerable to the world has nothing to do with the fact that it represents the world in an intrinsically credible fashion. Nor does it have to do with assessments of its

---

[24] For an extensive and detailed working out of this idea, see chapter 2 of Noë 2004, where he argues against what he calls the photograph model of perception.
[25] For the concept of an affordance, see chapter 8 of Gibson 1986. For an analysis of Dewey in light of Gibson's ecological account of perception, see Burke 1991.

reliability by other subjects. Rather, it has to do with the fact that the perceptual contents that help us, in advance, to unify our conflicting habits by finding an appropriate act are funded by what has been learned through past TOTE cycles. The content of perception, we could say, is *intelligent* because it is part of a feedback-governed learning process that corrects itself over time (*Erfahrung*). The key to perceptual answerability is not direct confrontation or intersubjectivity, but *self-correction* – the fact that in our exploratory sensorimotor activity, we continually adjust ourselves *to* objects – to their properties and typical behaviors – and these adjustments inform future perceptual-motor processes in a cumulative manner.

Of course, Brandom, in giving an account of *Erfahrung* in terms of the doxastic updating that happens in the TOTE cycle, wants to do justice to precisely this point. Due to surprising commitments non-inferentially elicited in perception, we must update our commitments, which is to correct them. But this correction is just stimulated or occasioned by perception; it does not itself involve an ongoing stream of perceptual experience that in being *sensitive* to changes in the environment in an ongoing way is able to *guide* future performance. This sensitivity and guidance cannot be accounted for by the fact that the perceptual phase of the TOTE cycle simply *causes* the performance phase, for this would simply bring back the atomism discussed earlier in the sections 'The Two-Ply Account of Action and The Myth of the Practical Given' and 'The TOTE Cycle: Atomism or Intellectualism'. Nor can it be accounted for by relations between full-fledged perceptual judgments, for this would just bring back the coherentism discussed at the end of the last section. Rather, perception guides future performance by presenting the world as affording this or that activity. Here, perception is not a causal response to stimuli or a full-blown judgment; it is an experience (*Erlebnis*).

CHAPTER 3

Communication, Perception, and Objectivity

Introduction

In this chapter, I examine two communicative-theoretic conceptions of objectivity – Brandom's and Davidson's – and compare them with a quite different conception of objectivity – namely, the perceptual-theoretic conception offered by Strawson and Evans. Both conceptions break with more standard accounts of objectivity. Their accounts are neither epistemic, concerned with what we must do in our inquiries to acquire an impartial view of things, nor ontological, concerned with what is 'there anyway' independently of our minds. Rather, both accounts of objectivity are transcendental in the sense of being concerned with the concepts that subjects must *grasp*, tacitly in practice or explicitly in being said, so as to be able to experience and think about a world of objects and properties that are independent of their thought and perception.[1]

Both conceptions agree that one can possess a concept, including that of objectivity, only if one grasps a range of related concepts that provides the context in which it is intelligible. However, they disagree on how to characterize the 'conceptual surround' of the concept of objectivity. Brandom and Davidson, on the one hand, think that it is best characterized in *communicative-theoretic* terms, meaning that the grasp of the concept of objectivity is made possible by a subject's taking part in interpersonal linguistic communication. It is participation in communication that gives a subject the capacities to grasp the fact that what is the case is the case independently of what they take to be the case. Strawson and Evans, on the other hand, account for the conceptual surround that makes grasp of

---

[1] In Stern's terms, they provide 'concept-directed' transcendental arguments rather than 'truth-directed' ones. See Stern 2000. I think that Davidson's work also contains a truth-directed transcendental argument, but I do not discuss it here. See Sachs 2009.

the concept of objectivity possible in *perceptual-theoretic* terms. Their argument is that the concept of objectivity is the result of an agent's grasp of the system of *spatial* concepts that informs their rudimentary 'theory of perception'. It is the use of these concepts that allows a subject to conceive of a world of objects and properties that continues to exist independently of its being perceived or thought about.

In this chapter, I argue that the communicative-theoretic conception of objectivity depends in a nonsymmetrical way on the form of objectivity that is identified by the perceptual-theoretic approach. The argument is not that the communicative-theoretic approach to objectivity is wrong *simpliciter* but that the type of objectivity that communication confers is constituted at a higher level than the type of objectivity conferred through our perceptual engagement with the world.

This chapter is an important hinge for the book, for here I not only critique new pragmatic strategies to rehabilitate the concept of objectivity but also begin to provide an alternative account. However, it is important to point out that the account given by Strawson and Evans is not, for me, the last word on objectivity. For they, I shall show, do not think that the content of the concept of objectivity is based in experience, but in forms of spatial reasoning made possible by one's simple theory of perception. In Chapter 4, I argue that this is wrong and show how the concept of objectivity emerges from experience.

Brandom's Account of Objectivity

In the last chapter, I claimed that Brandom's rejection of the concept of experience (*Erlebnis*) makes him incapable of giving an account of experience (*Erfahrung*) in which it is rationally constrained by the world. But Brandom has another account of objectivity, given in Chapter 8 of *Making It Explicit*, which claims that objectivity is "a feature of the structure of discursive intersubjectivity" (Brandom 1994, 599). On the account given there, it is communication and not experience that makes it possible for our thought and talk to be answerable to how things are. This account of objectivity is very complex, involving Brandom's intricate story about inference, substitution, and anaphora. It is not important for us to grasp all of the details of Brandom's account. What is important is to understand the main moves that underlie Brandom's strategy concerning objectivity and then to focus on whether it can deliver what his theory of experience (*Erfahrung*) could not – i.e., an account of our answerability to the objective world.

Two Conceptions of Objectivity

To begin, it is important to put Brandom's discourse-theoretic account of objectivity into proper context. Brandom's account of objectivity is part of a more general account of how, on inferentialist grounds, reference and representation are possible. This issue emerges for an inferential semantics because once it is postulated that the content of the concepts comprising our thought and talk are conferred through the inferences that such thought and talk entail or preclude, rather than through the reference of the singular and general terms that comprise our thoughts and utterances, then there is a question of how such contents can refer to, be about, or represent the world. The issue of objectivity concerns the further question of how the objective world can determine the correctness or incorrectness of a thought or judgment about it. Here is how Brandom puts the point:

> [A]n essential part of the representational dimension of our concepts – the way they purport to apply to an objective world – is that they answer for the ultimate correctness of their application not to what you or I or all of us *take* to be the case but to what actually *is* the case. Part of what it is for our concepts to be *about* an objective world is that there is an *objective* sense of correctness that governs their application – a sense of appropriateness that answers to the objects to which they are applied and to the world of facts comprising those objects. Even communally sanctioned takings or regularity of takings of what is correct concept application that are universal within a community can still be *mis*takings: even if all of us agree and always will agree that the mass of the universe is small enough that it will go on expanding forever, the possibility remains that we are all wrong. (Brandom 1994, 594)

Although Brandom runs them together, I think that we can tease out two distinct conceptions of objectivity in this passage. First, Brandom suggests that objectivity concerns the idea that the correctness or incorrectness of an application of concepts in a thought or judgment *transcends* all normative attitudes – what you, or I, or the community *takes* to be correct or incorrect. In arguing that what is correct transcends what even a whole community takes to be correct, Brandom rejects what he calls an I-we account of objectivity. According to an I-we account of objectivity, what the community takes to be correct, perhaps given certain idealizing conditions, *is* correct. We can imagine different idealizing conditions, for example, that the claims of the community, if they are to be counted as true, must be the product of open, unconstrained, and un-coerced inquiry and reason giving, or that the claims of the community are true only at the proverbial 'end of inquiry'. But even with these idealizing conditions in place, Brandom thinks this view is still mistaken because it can't make sense of the fact that whole communities can be in error, and remain in error, even when inquiry and reason giving are open and un-coerced, or even at the end of inquiry. This notion that what is the case can transcend what a whole community takes to be the case, even in ideal circumstances, is built into the concept of objectivity, and any account that cannot make sense of this falls short as an account of this concept.

The second conception of objectivity discussed in this passage concerns the fact that it is the objective world of objects and facts that determines the appropriateness of an application of concepts about it.[2] An application of concepts in a thought or judgment answers *to* this world, which stands as the authority for determining the correctness or incorrectness of this application. One might argue that this idea is not independent of the first, for if what is objectively correct is not settled by any given attitude, if it potentially transcends all attitudes, then what else other than the objective world could settle it? But this is not to give an *account* of how the objective world determines the appropriateness or correctness of an application of concepts – it is an assumption that it does. Brandom often simply takes it for granted that if we give an account of attitude transcendence we also, by default, give an account of how "the correctness of an application of a concept answers to the facts about the object to which it is applied" (Brandom 1994, xvii). But they are not the same. The first holds that what is objectively the case can always *transcend* what an individual or community takes to be the case; the second holds that what is objectively the case has *authority* with respect to the correctness or incorrectness of our thought and talk. To think that the first idea exhausts objectivity is therefore to miss a distinct "structure of *authority* and *responsibility*: ceding authority over the correctness of (some of) our claims to how it is with the things our claims count for that reason as being *about*, which is holding ourselves and each other *responsible to* those things *for* their correctness" (Brandom 1997, 198).

---

[2] Facts for Brandom are true claims – not in the sense that they are acts of claiming, but in the sense that they are true claimable contents. While these contents are the contents of our inferentially articulated claims, they are also, when expressive of facts, not "generally causally dependent on thinkers" (Brandom 2000d, 357). So thoughts that are answerable to the facts – thoughts that have true claimable contents – depend for their correctness or incorrectness on facts about objects that are not generally causally dependent on the thinker of those thoughts.

One might argue, as Wanderer has, that this second conception of objectivity is accounted for by the 'thickness', 'solidity', or 'world-involvingness' of the discursive practices in the TOTE cycle discussed in the last chapter.[3] Our concepts answer to the objects to which they are applied because, due to the surprising commitments that are inputted into our cognitive system through our sensorimotor engagement with the world, we are forced to continually update our commitments and entitlements. This account of discursive updating is all that Brandom needs, according to Wanderer, to make sense of the second conception of objectivity. But I don't think this account can be right, for it does not explain how states of the TOTE cycle can *be about* or *represent* objects. For the TOTE cycle to involve states that do not simply covary with objects, but are about them in a more robust sense, there needs to be in place a discursive structure that can make sense of the fact that the objects to which we cede authority, and to which we hold each other accountable, are objects of *representation*. This is made possible not through discursive updating itself, but through our moving back and forth between *social perspectives* in the intersubjective game of giving and asking for reasons. This structure is what allows us to *take* what is learned through the TOTE cycle to represent or be about independent worldly objects.

On my view, Brandom's account of objectivity has two levels over and above that of the account of the world-involvingness of the TOTE cycle: (1) an account of the discursive structure that institutes the authority of objects and our consequent responsibility to them and (2) an account of the discursive structure that institutes attitude transcendence. My main claim is that while Brandom can make sense of the second level in communicative-theoretic terms, he can't make sense of the first. But that is what is needed to understand the fact that it is *the world*, and not our take on the world, that determines whether a thought about it is appropriate or not appropriate, correct or incorrect.

---

[3] See Wanderer 2008, chapter 8. Habermas, in contrast, argues that the paucity of Brandom's account of the TOTE cycle in chapter 4 of MIE, and the fact that it is not in any way integrated with the account of objectivity given in chapter 8 of MIE casts doubt on whether the account of solidity is meant to be part of Brandom's objectivity argument (See Habermas 2003, chapter 3). If Habermas is correct and the account of objectivity in chapter 8 of MIE does not depend on what happened in chapter 4, then my argument in this chapter is necessary to demonstrate that Brandom's overall account of objectivity fails. If, on the other hand, Wanderer is correct, then my case is already made, as I showed in the last chapter that the account of solidity given in chapter 4 of MIE, and expanded in BSD, fails due to the lack of a theory of experience (*Erlebnis*).

Communication and Representation

Brandom argues that an explanation of the representational dimension of our thought and talk and its objectivity *falls out of* our "concern with explaining the possibility of *communication*" (Brandom 2000a, 167). If we can explain, in social-deontic terms, the possibility of communication, we will have all the resources we need to explain representation and objectivity. It is proper then to call his account of representation and objectivity a communicative-theoretic account.

Communication requires that two speakers *understand* each other's utterances. A subject achieves understanding when they are able to associate with their interlocutor's utterance a sentence that in their mouth expresses the claim embedded in that utterance. But the content of the claim expressed in the utterance, which is what one must understand for communication to happen, is, on a scorekeeping account, not separable from what inferences it is involved in, what commitments its endorsement entails and precludes, and this is only determinable relative to the collateral commitments and beliefs that a speaker already holds. But this entails that "a sentence in one person's mouth does not typically have the same significance as the same sentence emerging from another person's mouth, even where there is as much sharing of the language and as much mutual understanding as one likes" (Brandom 1994, 509).

For Brandom, the conceptual contents of our utterances are therefore *essentially expressively perspectival*, meaning that they can be "specified explicitly only from some point of view, against the background of some repertoire of discursive commitments" (Brandom 1994, 590). We cannot explain communication as the passing along of already formed common meanings, for there are none according to Brandom. Rather, we must conceive of it in terms of the ability of speakers to coordinate social perspectives, our own and others, in the intersubjective practice of deontic scorekeeping. "Mutual understanding and communication depends on interlocutors being able to keep two sets of books, to move back and forth between the point of view of the speaker and the audience, while keeping straight on which doxastic, substitutional, and expressive commitments are undertaken and which are attributed by the various parties" (Brandom 1994, 590). In keeping two sets of books, one can keep track of the different inferential significances of words, whether in one's own mouth or that of one's interlocutor, and this allows one to associate with one's interlocutor's utterance a sentence that expresses more or less the same claim made by that utterance.

What are some of the abilities necessary for a scorekeeper to keep two sets of books? First, one needs the ability to *interpret* utterances in Wittgenstein's sense – e.g., "to substitute one explicit expression of a claim for another" (Brandom 1994, 509).[4] Second, and more importantly for us, one needs the ability to track what an interlocutor is referring to, which depends on their ability to make *substitutional-inferential* commitments. This ability, in turn, is made explicit by the use of *de re* ascriptions of belief.[5] Let me elaborate on this latter package of abilities.

Classically, *de re* ascriptions are distinguished from *de dicto* ascriptions. A *de dicto* ascription of a propositional attitude is one that ascribes to another subject a belief in a dictum or saying, which is what is specified by a 'that' clause. A *de re* ascription, on the other hand, ascribes to a subject a belief about a *res*, an object. On the classical account, the difference between *de re* and *de dicto* ascriptions has to do with whether substituting singular terms within them potentially changes the truth-value of the ascription or not. In a *de dicto* attribution it might, while in a *de re* attribution it does not. Take the *de dicto* ascription 'Tom believes *that* the morning star is Venus'. Here one can't substitute 'evening star' for the 'morning star' and necessarily maintain the truth-value of the ascription because it may be the case that Tom does not know that the morning star is the evening star. Here, the point of the ascription is to "specify *how* things are represented by the one to whom the belief is ascribed. Thus only expressions that the believer acknowledges being committed to intersubstitute ... are intersubstitutable in these contexts, salva veritate" (Brandom 1994, 503). In a *de re* ascription like 'Tom believes *of* the morning star that it is Venus', on the other hand, one *can* substitute the 'evening star' for the 'morning star' and maintain the truth-value of the ascription. This is because the point of the ascription is not to get right what *Tom believes* about an object, but to get right the *object* that Tom is related to. Since *de re* "expressions serve to specify *what* is represented by a

---

[4] This ability is quite general, informing our use of pronouns and demonstratives, for example. To understand the statement, 'I am feeling sad today' when made by Jane, one must substitute 'Jane' for 'I', for otherwise it would claim that it is *me* who is feeing sad today, not *Jane*. Similarly, the ability to use an unrepeatable demonstrative requires the ability to substitute for it other demonstratives and pronouns, creating anaphoric chains that allow both speaker and hearer to track individual objects through the communicative exchange.

[5] In arguing that the explanation of the possibility of communication is the key for Brandom's account of representation and objectivity, I follow Loeffler 2005 and Prien 2010. However, both of these authors highlight the role of anaphora and recurrence commitments for explaining representation and objectivity and downplay the importance of substitutional inferences and of *de re* ascriptions. While recurrence commitments are very important, in this chapter, I highlight the importance of substitutional inferences and *de re* ascriptions for the question of objectivity.

belief rather than *how* it is represented, any singular term that picks out the right object is all right, one specification is as good as another" (Brandom 1994, 502). In specifying what is represented rather than how it is represented, *de re* ascriptions are the fundamental representational locution of natural languages.

Brandom translates this apparatus into scorekeeping terms. He argues that *de re* and *de dicto* ascriptions are *expressive* additions to deontic scorekeeping, meaning that in using them, a scorekeeper is able to explicitly *say* what they otherwise could only do. What it is that is made explicit by the use of these locutions? The "implicit capacity to keep and correlate multiple sets of books is made explicit in the availability of both *de dicto* and *de re* specifications of the contents of attributed discursive commitments" (Brandom 1994, 591). This implicit capacity to correlate two sets of books is made explicit by the use of these ascription types because in moving back and forth between them a scorekeeper is able to make explicit the different *social perspectives* from which the content of the commitment ascribed must be articulated.

To grasp this idea we need to make some distinctions. For Brandom, one *undertakes* a commitment whenever it is appropriate for others to attribute it to them. One can undertake a commitment in two ways; one either can *acknowledge* it or undertake it *consequentially*. One acknowledges a commitment when one self-ascribes it or when one uses it in reasoning, whether theoretical or practical. One undertakes a commitment consequentially, in contrast, when the commitment is entailed by other commitments that one acknowledges. In the former case, one is only committed to what one takes oneself to be committed to (or what one could take oneself to be committed to on sufficient reflection), while in the latter case, one is committed to whatever consequences follow from one's acknowledged commitments, whether one is aware of them or not.

The distinction is critical for keeping score on an interlocutor since keeping two sets of books, and therefore communicating, depends on getting clear about the difference between what one's interlocutor *takes themselves* to be committed to (by one's own lights), and what they are *actually* committed to (again by one's own lights).

Because the content of a commitment depends on what concomitant commitments are available as auxiliary hypotheses and collateral premises, to get clear about this difference requires putting the claim ascribed into two different deontic contexts; one articulated by the commitments that the other acknowledges (by one's own lights), and one articulated by the commitments that one oneself acknowledges. In case of a *de dicto* ascription, the content ascribed is determined in light of the concomitant commitments acknowledged by the one to whom the commitment is ascribed, while in a *de re* ascription it is the ascriber's commitments that stand as the basis for content ascription.

> When the specification of the content depends only on auxiliary premises that, according to the ascriber, the target of the ascription *acknowledges* being committed to, it is put in the *de dicto* position, within the 'that' clause. When the specification of the content depends on auxiliary premises that the *ascriber* endorses, but the target of the ascription may not, it is put in the *de re* position. (Brandom 1994, 506)

Now there is a basis for communication because one has a sense of what the content ascribed means in both one's own and one's interlocutor's mouth.

But what does this have to do with the ability to track what a speaker is referring to? We said earlier that *de re* ascriptions make explicit the ability to make what Brandom calls substitutional-inferential commitments. These commitments involve the ability to substitute, for the singular terms that have inferential consequences for one's interlocutor, singular terms that have consequences for oneself. If P acknowledges commitment to a claim involving the singular term x, then a scorekeeper is licensed to make the *de dicto* ascription (1) 'P claims *that* Φ (x)'. If according to the scorekeeper P also acknowledges that x is equal to y, then the scorekeeper can also attribute to P the claim (2) 'P claims *that* Φ (y)'. But if the scorekeeper acknowledges that x is equal to z, but P does not, they can still, in a *de re* ascription, substitute z for x, leading to the ascription (3) 'P claims *of* z that Φ'. In ascription (2) the substitution-inference is one acknowledged by P, whereas in (3) they are only committed consequentially to it. In moving back and forth between these two types of ascription a scorekeeper makes explicit

> whose substitutional commitments one is permitted to appeal to in specifying the consequences someone is committed to by acknowledging a particular doxastic commitment. Where in characterizing the commitment the ascriber has drawn out those consequences employing only commitments the ascriptional target would acknowledge, the content specification is *de dicto*. Where the ascriber has employed substitutional commitments the ascriber, but perhaps not the target, endorses, the content specification is *de re*. (Brandom 1994, 507)

The substitution-inferences made explicit by *de re* ascriptions are crucial for communication because to render the *inferential* consequences of an interlocutor's commitment, one must know what it is they are talking *about*. To illustrate, consider Brandom's example about a shaman's assertion, 'the seventh god has just risen'. If we parse this into a *de re* ascription, we get 'he claims of the seventh god that is has just risen'. If one does not have an equivalent to substitute for the seventh god, then one will not be able to generate inferential consequences of the commitment, either for oneself or for one's interlocutor. But suppose that one comes to know that the seventh god is equal to the sun. Then one could make a substitution inference and get the *de re* ascription 'he claims *of* the sun that it has just risen'. Through the substitution inferences made explicit in *de re* ascriptions, one can explore the inferential consequences of what is being talked *about*, the identified object, even though the meaning of the original assertion about this object has a different sense in the mouth of one's interlocutor. It is this that makes communication possible, for "[u]nless one has this substitutional interpretive capacity, which is expressed explicitly in *de re* specifications of the contents of ascribed commitments, one would not be able to understand what others were saying" (Brandom 1994, 513).

Communication and Objectivity

Brandom's goal, if we remember, was to show that an account of both the representational dimension of our thought and talk and its objectivity falls out of an explanation of the possibility of communication. How does the representational dimension of our thought and talk fall out of our ability to communicate?

As we just saw, to communicate requires making substitution inferences, which are expressed by *de re* ascriptions. But *de re* ascriptions specify *what* an interlocutor's claim represents *by* specifying its truth-conditions: "*De re* specifications ... are the specifications that present propositional contents in a form apt for assessments of *truth*. Thus the *information* a claim potentially communicates, its *representational* content in the sense captured by its truth-conditions, is what is expressed by *de re* specifications of propositional content" (Brandom 1994, 517). So in specifying what a claim is about one is specifying what "it must be *true of* if it is to be true at all" (Brandom 1994, 516), which is its representational content. The point is that if one can communicate by making substitutional inferences, one must already have a handle on the representational dimension of our thought and talk.

Objectivity falls out of our ability to communicate in a similar way. Here is how Brandom puts it:

> Our practical grasp of the objective dimension of conceptual norms – normative assessments of the objective truth of claims and objective correctness of applications of concepts – consists in the capacity to coordinate in our scorekeeping the significance a remark has from the perspective of the one to whom the commitment it expresses is attributed and its significance from the perspective of the one attributing it. This requires recognizing the different specifications of the same claim that correspond to extracting its inferential consequences and antecedents in the context of other commitments that are acknowledged as true by the scorekeeper, on the one hand, and extracting them in the context of other commitments acknowledged by the target of that scorekeeping, on the other. This is just the difference between employing as auxiliary hypothesis claims that are true (according to the scorekeeper) and employing as auxiliary hypothesis claims that are merely *held* true (according to the scorekeeper) by the interlocutor whose commitments are being assessed. Thus every scorekeeping perspective incorporates a distinction between what is (objectively) true and what is merely (subjectively) held true. (Brandom 1994, 598)

So to keep two sets of books on a commitment, which is necessary to communicate, a scorekeeper must practically grasp the distinction between what is objectively true and what is merely held to be true. So, again, the point is that if one can communicate, one must already have a handle on the difference between what is objectively the case and what is merely subjectively taken to be the case.

On this account, objectivity is a structural feature of any scorekeeping perspective. It is "a kind of perspectival *form*, rather than in a nonperspectival or cross-perspectival *content*. What is shared by all discursive perspectives *is that* there is a difference between what is objectively correct in the way of concept application and what is merely taken to be so, not *what* it is – the structure, not the content" (Brandom 1994, 600). This account must be distinguished from two others. The first sees objectivity as equivalent to non-perspectival contents that capture the way things really are. Here we would have a type of metaphysical realism in which certain contents or facts – primary qualities, microphysical particles, invariant laws, etc. – are posited as what is objectively the case. Brandom rejects this view because it depends on a correspondence theory of truth and a picture of reference in which representations are taken as semantically primitive.

The second account agrees with Brandom that we should think of objectivity in social-pragmatic terms, but it identifies what is true with a single privileged perspective, the perspective of the community. Here we come back to the I-we account of objectivity in which what is true is identified with what a community, perhaps given certain idealizing conditions, takes to be true. Brandom's perspectival view cannot be equated with this position because, for it, any perspective is, at most, *locally* privileged. Both scorekeeper and interlocutor – who, after all, is just another scorekeeper – are involved in a symmetrical I–thou relationship that involves, on both their parts, a practical grasp of the distinction between what is true and what is merely held true by their interlocutor. What *is* true is determined not by any perspective, including the communities, but by the

> messy retail business of assessing the comparative authority of competing evidential and inferential claims. Such authority as precipitates out of this process derives what from various interlocutors say rather than from who says it; no perspective is authoritative as such. There is only the actual practice of sorting out who has the better reasons in particular cases. The social metaphysics of claim-making settles what it means for a claim to be true by settling what one is doing in *taking* it to be true. It does not settle which claims *are* true – that is, are *correctly* taken to be true. (Brandom 1994, 601)

In light of this, I think we can say that Brandom's account of objectivity as a perspectival form that applies to any scorekeeping perspective can make sense of the first conception of objectivity discussed earlier – namely that what is correct in an application of concepts is attitude transcendent. But can it make sense of the second idea of objectivity – namely that it is the world that determines whether an application of concepts is correct or incorrect? Brandom's account of *de re* ascriptions is meant to give us an answer to this question. For, in making *de re* ascriptions, one specifies what another speaker "has in fact, willy-nilly, undertaken a commitment to – what object his claim is *about*, in the sense that matters for assessments of truth" (Brandom 1994, 595). In other words, one specifies "the objects that determine the truth or falsity – that is, the objective correctness – of the ascribed claim" (Brandom 1994, 595). So if one can make *de re* ascriptions, one practically grasps just the notion of objectivity for which we have been looking – i.e., that it is *objects* in the world that determine the truth or correctness of ascribed claims.

But this answer is too quick. As we saw, the *de re* specification of the objective content of a claim is the specification of its truth-conditions. A *de re* ascription specifies *what* an ascribed claim represents *by* specifying the entire claim or proposition's truth-conditions. But – and this is the key point – the specification of truth-conditions in a *de re* ascription is itself *perspectival* insofar as such ascriptions "express – *from the point of view of the interpreter attributing the commitment* – what would be required for the claim in question to be *true*" (Brandom 1994, 515, italics added). A *de re* specification of an interlocutor's claim depends on the interpreters auxiliary hypotheses, the commitments that she acknowledges and endorses. As such, "properly understanding truth talk ... requires understanding ... this difference of social perspective: between *attributing* a normative status to another and *undertaking* or adopting it oneself. This is just the distinction that underlies the use of *de re* ascriptions" (Brandom 1994, 515).

Brandom's claim is that the specification of truth-conditions in *de re* ascriptions makes explicit *the differences in social perspective* that scorekeepers must assume when they attribute and undertake commitments. The representational content expressed by *de re* ascriptions, content that was to underlie our practical grasp of the second idea of objectivity – i.e., that it is the world that is the standard which determines the correctness of our claims – is here interpreted in social-perspectival terms. What I want to argue now is that this social-perspectival rendering of the representational content made explicit in *de re* ascriptions cannot make sense of our grasp of this idea of objectivity.

Phenomenalism, Realism, and Idealism

To see why we must note that for Brandom this difference in social perspective must be cashed out in phenomenalist terms. Phenomenalism is the view that the normative proprieties or statuses that license or prohibit the inferential moves that confer content on our assertions are themselves instituted by the normative attitudes of deontic scorekeepers, attitudes of taking or treating others as committed and entitled to such proprieties. Deontic statuses are instituted by deontic attitudes because they are nothing but "consequentially expanded" (Brandom 1994, 596) deontic attitudes – i.e., expanded to include the consequential deontic attitudes that one *ought to acknowledge* given one's other acknowledged commitments. But as we know, what any given individual is really committed to, what consequential attitudes they ought to acknowledge, given their acknowledged commitments, is itself determined by the score kept on them by *other* scorekeepers in light of the commitments that *they* attribute and acknowledge. As such, the consequentially expanded attitudes that comprise deontic statuses are determined by other scorekeepers' immediate deontic attitudes – i.e., those that they are prepared to attribute and acknowledge:

> From the vantage point of any particular scorekeeper, what one is *really* committed to by an acknowledgement ... what *really* follows from a claim (and hence its objective content), is to be assessed by conjoining it with truths – that is statements of fact. But what plays this role for a scorekeeper is the set of sentences by the assertion of which the scorekeeper is prepared to *acknowledge*, and so undertake doxastic commitment. Thus immediate deontic attitudes determine consequential ones, and so deontic statuses, from each scorekeeping perspective. (Brandom 1994, 596–597)

Because the difference between what an interlocutor is really committed to and what they take themselves to be committed to is relative to the commitments that a scorekeeper is prepared to attribute and acknowledge, the distinction for that scorekeeper between what is objectively correct and what is merely taken to be correct can be rendered, by those interpreting the scorekeeping practice from the sideways-on, solely in terms of attitudes:

> [E]very scorekeeping perspective maintains a distinction in practice between normative status and (immediate) normative attitude – between what is objectively correct and what is merely *taken* to be correct ... Yet what from the point of view of a scorekeeper is objectively correct – what from that perspective another interlocutor is actually committed to by a certain acknowledgement – can be understood by us who are interpreting the scorekeeping activity entirely in terms of the immediate *attitudes,* the acknowledgments and attributions, of the scorekeeper. What appears to the scorekeeper as the distinction between what is objectively correct and what is merely taken to be or treated as correct appears to us as the as the distinction between what is acknowledged by the scorekeeper attributing a commitment and what is acknowledged by the one to whom it is attributed. The difference between objective normative status and subjective normative attitude is construed as a social-perspective distinction between normative attitudes. In this way the maintenance, from every perspective, of a distinction between status and attitude is reconciled with the methodological phenomenalism that insists that all that really needs to be considered is attitudes. (Brandom 1994, 597)

So from the point of view of we who are interpreting a scorekeeping practice from the sideways-on, a scorekeeper's sense of what is objectively correct is simply what *they* take to be correct concerning an interlocutor's commitment. So we interpreting this scorekeeping practice know that the distinction within each scorekeeping perspective between what is objectively correct and what is subjectively correct is actually *the social-perspectival distinction between what a scorekeeper takes to be correct about an attributed commitment and what their interlocutor takes to be correct*. The question is: can we ascribe to scorekeepers a practical grasp of what *we* grasp, namely that their perspective on what *is* correct is merely what they *take* to be correct, and that the difference between what is objectively correct and what is taken to be correct is just a social-perspectival difference in attitudes?

We might want to answer this question negatively and say that each scorekeeping perspective, at least when involved *in* scorekeeping, takes the distinction between objective and subjective correctness at face value. They grasp objective correctness to be what is correct independently of what anyone thinks, and they understand what is taken to be correct as falling short of that. But in this case scorekeepers are making a systematic error because their practical grasp is out of alignment with what *we* grasp, namely that what is objectively correct is *not* independent of what anyone thinks (of immediate normative attitudes) and that the distinction between objective and subjective correctness is really a social-perspectival difference in attitudes. They miss the fact that "[o]bjectivity ... is not intelligible in complete abstraction from our activities" (Brandom 1997, 198).

On this view, each and every scorekeeping perspective involves a *realist error* – the error of thinking that their grasp of objective correctness is a grasp of something independent of *all* normative attitudes, and the error of thinking that the distinction between objective and subjective correctness is not a social-perspectival distinction.

If, on the other hand, we answer the question affirmatively and ascribe to scorekeepers a practical grasp of what *we* grasp, then those subjects would be subject to a converse error. This is the *idealist error* of thinking that what one takes to be correct, one's acknowledged commitments, *determines* what is in fact correct. If what my interlocutor is really committed to, as opposed to what they take themselves to be committed to, is determined by *my* attributions, then my perspective on them is definitive for specifying the truth of the matter. If a scorekeeper generalizes this point, we get a view in which their perspective determines what is correct, and the thought 'It is possible that (I believe that p and it is not true that p)' (see Brandom 1994, 604) becomes senseless. But if one can't think this thought, then Brandom's argument that objectivity transcends all attitudes would collapse, for now there *is* a privileged perspective – not the community's, but one's own. This would "show that there is a problem with the *local*, perspectival privileging of each scorekeeper's repertoire of commitments that corresponds, in the *I-thou* rendering of discursive social practice, to the failure to account for the objectivity of conceptual norms that afflicts the *I-we* rendering of social-discursive practice in virtue of its *global* (or quantificational) privileging of the communal repertoire" (Brandom 1994, 604).

Brandom tries to avoid this idealist error, and complete his account of objectivity, by arguing that scorekeepers grasp that the distinction between what is correct and what is merely taken to be correct applies not only to the claims of other scorekeepers but to their acknowledged (in the sense of self-attributed) claims, *those they otherwise take to be objectively correct.* "Although grounded in essentially social, other-regarding scorekeeping ... the possibility of a distinction between how things actually are and how they are merely taken to be by some interlocutor remains a structural feature, even ... in the case of attributions to oneself" (Brandom 1994, 597). In other words, scorekeepers grasp that any commitment that they acknowledge as objectively correct might in fact not be correct, might not reflect how things are but merely how *they* take things to be. They grasp that they are not the final arbiters of their commitments and entitlements, that they can make mistakes, can fall into error. But it is hard to understand how one could grasp this with respect to one's present commitments, for one seemingly can't make *de re* attributions about such commitments. One can't because one has no way of ascertaining the commitments that one is currently consequentially committed to, and so the commitments that one *really* has. How can I distinguish between what I am really committed to and what I acknowledge being committed to when the only auxiliary hypotheses that I can access are acknowledged commitments?

Brandom's account stresses the fact that "ascriptional locutions make explicit the possibility of taking up hypothetically a sort of third-person scorekeeping attitude toward my own present commitments" (Brandom 1994, 605).[6] In other words, by taking part in scorekeeping, I grasp that not only am I keeping score on others, but others are keeping score on me. Insofar as I can track the difference between the claims that they avow and the claims that they are really committed to, given their other commitments, I am in position to appreciate that, from their point of view, this same distinction applies to me. This gives me a sense that I could really have commitments that I am not able to acknowledge (in the sense of self-ascribe). I could be ignorant of them. It also gives me a sense that I could

---

[6] Brandom's demonstration of how we come to take up this hypothetical third-person point of view is centered on showing, with respect to a commitment p, that two conditionals do not hold, the (1) The *no first-person ignorance* conditional: (p) [p —> (I claim that p)] and (2) The *no first-person error* conditional: (p) [(I claim that p) —> p]. Here, I just give the upshot of the argument not the details. See MIE 601–607.

be entitled to an *act* of self-ascription but not to the *content* of the claim or commitment that is ascribed by this act. I gain entitlement to self-ascriptions as a *kind* of act when scorekeepers in the space of reasons begin to take my first-person reports to be reliable.[7] Once this happens, others will take me, by default, to be immune to error through misidentification vis-à-vis my use of the first-person pronoun. But with respect to the content of the commitment that I self-ascribe, it is different. I can be in error about *what* I think I think because the content of a claim that I self-ascribe depends on its compatibility and incompatibility relations with other commitments (both acknowledged and consequential) to which I am entitled. But I am not in a privileged position to determine what these relations are, and so to determine the *objective contents* of the thought's I self ascribe. To determine the compatibility and incompatibility relations that a content *really* has requires that other *scorekeepers keep score on the content*. And from their point of view, and from mine when I hypothetically take it up, I can be entitled to an act of self-ascription but not to the content of the commitment ascribed.

With this, Brandom shows that I can grasp, from my perspective, that there is a potential distinction between (1) the commitments I really have (from the perspective of a scorekeeper keeping score on me) and those I acknowledge and take myself to have and (2) the acknowledgments (in the sense of self-attributions) that I am entitled to make, and the claims or commitments to which I am, in fact, entitled. In grasping this, I grasp that I am not the final arbiter of my commitments and entitlements. And to grasp this *is* to grasp that the distinction between what is objectively correct and what is merely held to be correct applies to my present commitments.

Two Conceptions of Objectivity Revisited

The difficulty that we were trying to avoid was this: if I understand implicitly in practice what those who view scorekeeping from the sideways-on grasp – i.e., that the difference between what is objectively correct and what is merely taken to be correct is really just the social-perspectival distinction in attitudes between what I acknowledge about an attributed commitment and what my interlocutor acknowledges – then I have reason to take my perspective to be the standard that determines

---

[7] Brandom's account of this is essentially the same as the one Sellars gives in his Myth of Jones. See Sellars 1997 and Chapter 1 of this work.

what is objectively correct. To avoid this idealist illusion Brandom shows how scorekeepers apply the distinction between what is objectively correct and what is merely held to be correct to their own perspective. Not only do I determine with respect to an interlocutor what they are really committed to as opposed to what they take themselves to be committed to; I also grasp that this difference applies to me.[8] It applies to me because I recognize that a scorekeeper keeping score on me determines the difference between what I am really committed to and what I take myself to be committed to. Since I now grasp that this distinction applies to myself in addition to any of my interlocutors, I now understand that the distinction applies to *all* perspectives. In other words, I now grasp "the possibility for *any* S and p that S believes that p but it is not true that p" (Brandom 1994, 604). But if I practically grasp what those who view scorekeeping from the sideways-on grasp, then we have to translate it into social-perspectival terms. In this case, the difference between what is objectively correct and what is taken to be correct is, for any S and p, the *social-perspectival distinction between what a scorekeeper acknowledges about attributed commitment p and what S acknowledges about it*. I practically grasp that the social-perspectival distinction between attributing and undertaking applies not just to my perspective on others but to all scorekeeping perspectives. But then while we grasp that what is objectively correct transcends any given scorekeeping perspective, including our own, we also grasp that what is correct is always relative to what *some* scorekeeper takes to be correct. We grasp that objectivity is not intelligible in complete abstraction from the attitudes involved in our collective scorekeeping practices, though we also grasp that it transcends any given attitude, even when that attitude is the collective attitude of a community.

But is what is practically grasped here equivalent to the second idea of objectivity that was our target – namely, one in which an application of concepts is correct or incorrect depending on whether the concepts 'answer to the objects to which they are applied'. Is it equivalent to the idea that it is the *world* that has the authority to settle whether a commitment is objectively correct or merely taken to be correct? It does not seem so. *To have a sense that what is objectively correct potentially transcends any given*

---

[8] It is important to see that this does not show that one can, in fact, distinguish, with respect to a *present* commitment, between *what* is objectively correct and what is merely taken (by oneself) to be correct, for it is still the case that one can't make *de re* attributions to oneself insofar as one still can't grasp from the first-person point of view one's present consequential commitments. Brandom's argument shows that we understand that this distinction applies to ourselves, not that we can in the present operationalize it. For much more on this, see Laurier 2005b.

attitude, although not attitudes in general, is not the same as having a sense that what determines the difference between what is correct and what is merely taken to be correct is not an attitude at all, but the world that we do not control.

In my view to make sense of objectivity, we must posit *two* distinctions – between what is objectively correct and what is taken to be correct – that are expressive of distinct practical understandings. According to the first, the difference between what is objectively correct and what is merely held to be correct is expressive of a practical grasp, on the part of each and every scorekeeper, of the difference in social-perspectives that can be taken on attributed and self-attributed commitments. The second involves a practical grasp of the fact that the correct epistemic status of an attributed or self-attributed commitment – one that is correct, as opposed to one that is merely taken to be correct – is settled *by what is objectively the case with the world and not by what is taken to be the case by any scorekeeper, whether oneself or another.* According to this distinction, what is objectively correct signifies the *norm* by which commitments, whether attributed to an interlocutor or undertaken by a scorekeeper, are judged, and what is merely taken to be correct signifies any content that falls short of that norm. This norm is not filled out by a cross-perspectival content that we can know in advance. I do not contest Brandom's idea that objectivity is a structural feature of each scorekeeping perspective. It is rather that the structural distinctions involved in a scorekeeping perspective are more complex than Brandom takes them to be, involving two distinctions between objective and subjective rather than one. One involves implicit grasp of the distinct social perspectives that can be taken on ascribed and undertaken commitments; the other involves implicit grasp of the idea that these distinct perspectives are objectively answerable for their correctness to a world that we do not control.

How does our grasp of this second structural distinction come about? Brandom never answers this question. Rather, he just assumes that we can get from the first social-pragmatic structural distinction to the second. I accept that Brandom's communicative-theoretic account articulates an important feature of the concept of objectivity. But, in not being able to explain the second structural distinction, he falls short of giving a satisfactory account of objectivity.[9]

---

[9] I read Lafont as making a similar claim at 2002, 194–195.

Davidson on Objectivity

I now want to take up Davidson's communicative-theoretic account of objectivity. Davidson's account starts with a datum that is not in question and works back to its conditions of possibility. The argument, therefore, has a transcendental structure. What is not in question for Davidson is the fact that subjects have objective thought, thought whose truth or falsity depends on the shape of the independent world. The question is how it is possible for subjects to entertain such thoughts. "Thought is objective, and we know that it is. But it is not obvious what it is about thought which makes this possible" (Davidson 2001b, 1). For Kant, as we know, objective thought is possible because of certain a priori conditions situated outside of space and time. For Davidson, in contrast, objective thought is made possible by a subject's taking part in a mundane practice – i.e., interpersonal communication with one or more persons, what he calls 'triangulation'. Entering into a communicative triangle allows a subject to (1) ascribe to their empirical thoughts a determinate content or meaning and (2) distinguish between subjective experiences and the objective world toward which those experiences are directed, between appearance and reality, seeming and being. Here, I focus only on the second capacity.

Error and Objectivity

A thought or proposition is objective when its truth or falsity depends on the shape of the independent world rather than on a subject's take on the world. But thought's objectivity also depends on a subject's awareness that this is so – and this because of the role that truth plays in determining content. For Davidson, the content of a thought or proposition is conferred by its truth conditions, the conditions under which it would be true. But to

> know the truth conditions of a proposition, one must have the concept of truth. There is no more central concept than that of truth, since having any concept requires that we know what it would be for that concept to apply to something – to apply truly, of course. The same holds for the concept of truth. To have the concept of truth is to have the concept of objectivity, the notion of a proposition being true or false independently of one's beliefs and interests. In particular, then, someone who has a belief, who holds some proposition to be true or false, knows that that belief may be true or false. In order to be right or wrong, one must know that it is possible to be right or wrong. (Davidson 1995, 10)

So in having a belief, the subject of that belief must already grasp the concept of objectivity. What we don't know is what makes this possible.

Davidson's answer focuses on error. If we can explain how subjects are able to appreciate that their thoughts and beliefs can be in error, then we will be in a position to explain how they are able to grasp that "truth is not in general guaranteed by anything in us" (Davidson 1995, 7). In grasping the possibility of error, one grasps that the world about which one thinks is potentially different from what one takes it to be, and so is independent of one's powers of thought. Through error, one is therefore able to appreciate "the contrast between true belief and false, between appearance and reality, mere seeming and being" (Davidson 1991, 209).

Davidson's goal is to demonstrate that awareness of error, and so objectivity, requires a communicative triangle between two or more creatures. This is not obvious. Jason Bridges, for instance, argues that communication is not necessary for having beliefs with objective purport because a creature by itself can come to appreciate their being in error. It acquires this appreciation through the frustration of its instrumental expectations about a recalcitrant reality. Bridges says, "Suppose an isolated creature regularly produces behavior B in and only in situations S and thereby receives reward R. Now the creature performs B in a non-S situation and R does not ensue ... Why isn't it in ... position ... to appreciate that it has made a mistake? The basis for that appreciation ... would be the thwarting of *its* expectations" (Bridges 2006, 294–295). Davidson is skeptical of this type of account. In his discussion of *surprise*, he explains why. To be surprised about something is to experience the fact that one's expectations about reality (if one performs B in situation S, R will result) and reality itself (if one performs B in non-S, R does not result) have come apart. So in Davidson's terms, Bridges' proposal is that an isolated animal could come to appreciate error by first being surprised that R does not result in non-S and then, based on "natural inductions," modify their future behavior. The modification of behavior is important because this is what demonstrates, in the absence of communication, that the *creature itself* appreciates their error and so appreciates that its expectations did not latch onto the way things are.

Davidson thinks that surprise *is* an essential concomitant of belief.[10] If a creature can be surprised it demonstrates that they grasp that truth is not guaranteed by their antecedently held beliefs, that their beliefs can be tested and found wanting in light of the way things objectively are. But

---

[10] See Cooke 2011 for much more on this.

while surprise is a concomitant of belief, it cannot account for our grasp of objectivity because it assumes what it means to explain. To be surprised is to have one's expectations thwarted. But to have expectations *about the way things are* is already to have propositional attitudes whose content is determined by truth-conditions, which requires a grasp of the concept of objective truth. "Surprise – the frustration of expectation – cannot explain our having the concept of objective truth, because we cannot be surprised, or have an expectation, unless we already command the concept. To be surprised is to recognize the distinction between what we thought and what is the case. To have an expectation is to admit that it may be faulted" (Davidson 1995, 7–8). Instead of explaining the awareness of error and therefore objectivity, Bridge's account assumes it, insofar as the capacity to be surprised, requires already having the concept of objective truth and so already having the awareness that one can be in error about the world.

From Precognitive to Cognitive Triangulation

In contrast to accounts that think an awareness of error is possible for a single creature coping instrumentally with the world, Davidson thinks that it comes about through a subject's taking part in a triangular communicative interaction with another subject about an object. So the question is why must there be this triangular interaction for an awareness of error, and how does the awareness of error arise out of it? Davidson's answer is complex because it involves two different levels of triangulation: a precognitive/prelinguistic form of triangulation and a cognitive/linguistic form. The first form sets out conditions necessary for the awareness of error, while the second provides sufficient conditions.

The first precognitive form of triangulation pertains to the behavior of prelinguistic children and animals. Here, the "basic situation is one that involves two or more creatures simultaneously in interaction with each other and with the world they share ...To put this in a slightly different way, each creature learns to correlate the reactions of the other with changes or objects in the world to which it also reacts" (Davidson 1997b, 128). These correlations can be hardwired in, as in a school of fish when each fish reacts instantly to the behavior of the school, or learned, as when a dog learns to respond to the ringing of a bell, or in a more complex case, when preverbal children learn to correlate more and more of the sounds they hear from others with features of the world.

The introduction of learned correlations is key because the correlation of learned mutual reactions sets up a proto-norm or standard that sets the bar for our mutual future expectations concerning the behavior of the other creature vis-à-vis the world. The *possibility* of error is introduced when these expectations are not met. Here is how Davidson puts it:

> Where do we get the idea that we may be mistaken, that things may not be as we think they are? Wittgenstein has suggested, or at least I take him to have suggested, that we would not have the concept of getting things wrong or right if it were not for our interactions with other people. The triangle I have described stands for the simplest interpersonal situation. In it two (or more) creatures each correlate their own reactions to external phenomena with the reactions of the other. Once these correlations are set up, each creature is in a position to expect the external phenomenon when it perceives the associated reaction of the other. What introduces the possibility of error is the occasional failure of that expectation; the reactions do not correlate. Wittgenstein expresses this idea when he talks of the difference between following a rule and merely thinking one is following a rule. (Davidson 1997b, 129)[11]

For subjects to have *expectations* about each other's behavior, there must already be enough overlap in their behavior to set up a baseline against which divergences can be distinguished. This baseline is set up by precognitive triangulation, and it is the violation of this baseline that makes space for the grasp of error. So the notion of error that informs thought and belief *does* emerge from the frustration of our stable expectations – but not instrumental expectations that are directly about the world (as it was with surprise) – but, rather, the mutual expectations about the behavior of another creature with respect to the world.

However, while precognitive triangulation is necessary for an awareness of the possibility of error, it is not sufficient:

> What is missing, one might say, is the idea of understanding. Introducing more than one creature does add something basic to the situation with one creature, for with the possibility that their actions may diverge we have introduced the gap needed to make sense of the notion of error. But the mere possibility of divergence, even when combined with sanctions to enforce conformity, does not introduce the sort of norm needed to explain meaning or conceptualization ... [O]nly social interaction brings with it the space in which the concept of error, and so of meaning and of thought, can be given applications. A social milieu is necessary, but not sufficient, for objective thought. (Davidson 2001b, 3–4)

---

[11] Davidson takes it that for there be enough overlap in expectations to generate the possibility of error, it is not, in general, necessary that agents act as others do because they are following the same rules. So, while he uses the language of rules when talking about Wittgenstein, he does not endorse the talk. Here we find a large difference between Brandom and Davidson.

While the divergence of an individual's behavior from that of another's makes space for the frustration of expectations, and so the grasp of error, it is not sufficient because this divergence in behavior can be explained by there being "two different dispositions at work" (Davidson 2001b, 5).

"What must be added in order to give an account of error is something that can count as recognition or awareness, on the part of those who share reactions, of each other's reactions" (Davidson 2001b, 5). In other words, for a grasp of error and so objectivity to be possible, creatures must not only share reactions to an object with another creature, they must *recognize* that they do so. This, Davidson argues, cannot be accounted for just by each creature *observing* each other's reactions in a third person manner; rather, it requires that they communicate second-personally with each other:

> Without one creature to observe another, the triangulation that locates the relevant object in a public space could not take place. I do not mean by this that one creature observing another provides either creature with the concept of objectivity ... [this] is at best a necessary condition for such a concept. Only communication can provide the concept, for to have the concept of objectivity, the concepts of objects and events that occupy a shared world, of objects and events whose properties and existence is independent of our thought, requires that we are aware of the fact that we share thoughts and a world with others. (Davidson 1990, 202)

But what is Davidson's argument here? As part of his campaign against the idea that the sociality of language is to be accounted for by shared rules or conventions, Davidson, in his later work, follows Grice in emphasizing "the central importance of intentions in communication" (Davidson 1992, 112).[12] On this account, successful communication happens not because both speaker and interpreter follow the same rule or convention but when the interpreter understands the speaker's utterance in light of the truth-conditions that the speaker *intends* the interpreter to assign to the utterance. On this account, "the point of language or speech ... is communication, getting across to someone else what you have in mind by means of words that they interpret (understand) as you want them to" (Davidson 1994, 120). So, according to the Griceian picture, communication involves my interlocutor not only forming certain beliefs that are imparted through my speech act, but also forming certain beliefs about my intention for them to form certain beliefs. Communication, therefore, has built into it a reflexive aspect: in communicating something to someone

---

[12] For the relationship between Davidson and Grice, see Avramides 2001 and Eilan 2007.

we intend for them to form correct beliefs not only about the something we are talking about but also about *our beliefs* about that something, which are the beliefs that we intend or want them to form. So when two creatures successfully communicate about something they mutually understand that they each intend the other to not only form beliefs about that something, but to form beliefs about the something *that the other intends them to form*. Here we have *two* forms of mutual recognition: of *each other* (as intending each other to form certain beliefs) and of each other as having beliefs about *a common object*. Here is how Davidson puts it:

> The only way of knowing that the second apex of the triangle – the second creature or person – is reacting to the same object as oneself is to know that the other person has the same object in mind. But then the second person must also know that the first person constitutes an apex of the same triangle another apex of which the second person occupies. For two people to know of each other that they are so related, that their thoughts are so related, requires that they be in communication. (Davidson 1992, 121)

Here we can seen why communication is necessary for mutual recognition, but why is this communication-enabled recognition necessary for a grasp of error, and hence objectivity? Above, Davidson said that what introduces the possibility of error into the triangular situation is that sometimes the reactions of two creatures to an object do not correlate. This upsets their expectations about how the world will be, based on their reading of the reactions of the other creature. The point is this: in the mutual recognition made possible by linguistic communication, each creature not only witnesses the other and their reactions to an object, they are also able to *compare* those reactions with their own and note *for themselves* whether they diverge from their expectations or not. It is this that allows the creatures, from *their point of view*, to grasp the concept of error. As Kirk Ludwig puts it, it is the "possibility of identifying a perspective which potentially contrasts with my own that gives content to the idea of error. The two perspectives minimally needed are my own and that of another whose thoughts are focused on the same world. The possibility of a contrast between the two gives scope for the concept of error, and so of objectivity" (Ludwig 2011, 73). The contrast of perspectives is necessary for grasp of error because in this contrast, one grasps that one's perspective on the world *is only one amongst others*. My perspective – i.e., the way things appear or seem to me – is a *partial* perspective on a world that transcends that perspective, and we are aware of this because we are aware that there are *other perspectives* on the same world. Because my perspective is only a partial perspective, it can be in error, for example, when I expect an object based on the reaction of the other creature, and no such object is forthcoming. My expectations have been frustrated, and I am aware that I am out of alignment with the other creature. I am aware that I, or the other creature, have made an error.

Objectivity and Points of View

So now we have given an account of why communicative triangulation between two creatures and the world is necessary for their awareness of the possibility of error. What notion of objectivity results? We can grasp the specific nature of objectivity at play in Davidson's thought by considering a proposal that he would reject. The proposal is that a single creature could come to be aware that there are contrasting perspectives on the world by *moving* to different perspectives consecutively and tracking their spatial position over time. The proposal, unlike the one given by Bridges earlier, accepts the need for triangulation, but claims that a single creature moving and plotting different spatial positions vis-à-vis an object can achieve it. Here, all the creature would need for a sense of objectivity are basic perceptual-motor skills and the ability to track and remember places.

The problem with the proposal, from a Davidsonian perspective, is that what is needed to grasp the concept of objectivity is the understanding of the fact that there are perspectives on an object that exist *concurrently* to one's own experience. What is needed is awareness of simultaneous perspectives on the world. Davidson gestures to this fact in the famous passage where he first mentions triangulation. He says,

> If I were bolted to the earth, I would have no way of determining the distance from me of many objects. I would only know they were on some line drawn from me towards them. I might interact successfully with objects, but I could have no way of giving content to the question of where they were. Not being bolted down, I am free to triangulate. Our sense of objectivity is the consequence of another sort of triangulation, one that requires two creatures. Each interacts with an object, but what gives each the concept of the way things are objectively is the baseline formed between the creatures by language. (Davidson 1982, 105)

In other words, while our free movement (our not being bolted down) is necessary for taking part in a form of triangulation in which a single creature marks different points with respect to a single object, our concept of objectivity emerges from 'another sort of triangulation' in which two creatures knowingly interact and communicate about an object in a shared world. In communicating with another subject about an object, subjects experience simultaneously to their present experience that there are other experiences of that object from other spatiotemporal perspectives. Movement of a single creature cannot account for this sense of objectivity; only linguistic communication can.

So Davidson's conception of objectivity is this: the concept that a subject has of objects and events whose nature and existence are independent of them is the concept of objects and events occupying a shared world, a world that is there for you as it is for me. Objectivity is here "traced to the intersections of points of view – for each person, the relation between his own reactions to the world and the reactions of others" (Davidson 1991, 218). The object, in being at the intersection of at least two points of view is now understood to be part of a shared or public world – i.e., an objective world. Here we can see that Davidson embraces "the Wittgensteinian intuition that the only legitimate source of objectivity is intersubjectivity" (Davidson 2001b, 13), the idea that the "concept of an intersubjective world is the concept of an objective world, a world about which each communicator can have beliefs" (Davidson 1982, 105).

But there is an obvious problem with this picture. If the concept of an objective world is the concept of an intersubjective or public world, then it follows that one could not grasp the distinction between one's perspective on the world and the world itself – between seeming and being, appearance and reality – without grasping that the world is there for others as it is for oneself. In other words, grasp of *our* having a perspective on the world is instituted by grasp of their being other potential perspectives on the world. But surely the very possibility of being aware of and comparing one's point of view on the world with another's concurrent point of view – which is what gives substance to error and so objectivity – is made possible by the fact that one *already has a point of view on a world that is distinct from oneself.* If one did not already have a point of view on something distinct from oneself, it would not be possible to compare one's point of view with the point of view of another creature, for one could not oneself have a point of view from which to make the comparison. Any sense of objectivity as publicness, of things available for others as they are for oneself, seems to depend upon on a more basic sense of objectivity.[13]

We can bring the point out in another way. The upshot of the notion of objectivity as publicness is this: we know that the world only seems or

---

[13] Strawson makes this argument in chapter 2 of Strawson 1959.

appears to us to be a certain way from our point of view because if we were located like the creature with which we communicate, it would seem or appear differently than it does. But the only way to generate this notion of 'seeming' or 'appearing' is to assume that we already have the *spatial concepts* necessary to account for our understanding that the other creature is differently located with respect to an object than oneself. The condition of possibility of comparing one's point of view to another's point of view on an object is that one can *simultaneously* grasp the location of the other creature with respect to the object and one's own location, and this requires that the subject place both positions within a *single spatial framework*. In other words, to communicatively triangulate an object with another subject requires, as its condition of possibility, that one already grasp that there is a common spatial context in which both subjects and the object are located. So to have a conception of objectivity, of an independent world to which thought answers for its truth or falsity, one needs to grasp that there is a common space in which oneself, other, and object are housed. This grasp is built into the very notion of a 'point of view'.

We can identify two distinct views of objectivity here: Davidson's communicative-theoretic view and what we could call a perceptual-theoretic view. Davidson's view involves the idea that perception itself cannot account for the concept of objectivity because "perception operates within the ambit of propositional thought, and so assumes that the perceiver is armed with the idea of an objective world and the concepts of truth and error" (Davidson 1999, 730). Before gaining the ability to triangulate communicatively, one has dispositions to respond to objects that are independent of oneself, but one cannot – because one does not grasp error and hence the appearance–reality distinction – perceive such objects *as* independent of oneself. The perceptual-theoretical account, in contrast, does not think that communication is necessary to grasp different perspectives on the same objective order. Rather, as John Campbell puts the point: "An account of communication must surely depend on the idea of different perspectives on the same temporal order; but the dependence appears to be asymmetric. No appeal to communication-theoretic notions seems to be needed in explaining what makes available the conception of the objective temporal order" (Campbell 1986, 161). In other words, communication depends on communicators already having a conception of an objective world (what Campbell calls an objective temporal order) upon which different perspectives can be taken – it cannot render that conception. As we are about to see, this conception does not need to wait on grasp of error because the conception of things as distinct from one's point of view is built into the spatial conditions of *veridical perception* itself.

The Perceptual-Theoretic Account of Objectivity

We can find a worked-out version of the perceptual-theoretical account in the neo-Kantian tradition of thinking about objectivity inaugurated by Strawson and Evans. This tradition agrees with Davidson that for a subject to have the concept of objectivity, they must be aware that there is a distinction between appearance and reality, seeming and being. They put the point this way: a subject must be able to distinguish between the objective order and their changing perspective or point of view on this order. "For the world to be conceived of as objective, it must be possible to distinguish between the order of perceptions occurring in one experiential route through it and the and relations which the objective constituents of the world independently possess" (Strawson 1966, 23). However, this tradition has a very different account of what makes grasp of this distinction possible, an account in which communication and error do not have explanatory priority.

Strawson and Evans take it that to perceive the mind-independent world, we cannot just be in casual contact with it; we must also *conceive* of it *as* independent of ourselves. They enumerate two conditions for our having this conception. First, subjects must be able to make certain 'primitive self-ascriptions' – i.e., be able to ascribe to themselves their spatial position and orientation, and changes in their position and orientation.

> Any subject at all capable of thought about an objective spatial world must conceive his normal experiences as simultaneously due to the way the world is and his changing position in it. The capacity to think of oneself as located in space, and tracing a continuous path through it, is necessarily involved in the capacity to conceive of the phenomena one encounters as independent of one's perception of them – to conceive of the world as something one 'comes across'. (Evans 1982, 176)

In other words, to grasp that one's spatial perspective on the world is not the same as the world it is a perspective on, the subject must be able to track their continuous movement through it so as to know what in their changing experience is due to this movement and what is due to the world.[14]

---

[14] The account of primitive self-ascription found in Strawson and especially Evans is bound up with a complex account of self-identification. We shall ignore this account here.

Second, subjects must be able to grasp what Campbell calls a 'modal datum': "that all the things around me might have existed, and might continue to exist, even if I simply had not been around to think about any of them" (Campbell 1993, 259). In other words, to grasp that one's experience is of a genuinely distinct and independent world requires not only understanding that certain particular objects would continue to exist independently of one's experience of them (would 'exist unperceived'), but that *all* the objects around one would continue to exist even if one had not been around to perceive them. What Strawson and Evans argue is that the only way to give substance to this idea is to conceive of the world as a *spatial world*. According to this view, the only way that one can have "the notion of an objective world is by having the notion of a spatial world" (Campbell 1985, 150).

We find this argument spelled out in Evans' paper "Things without the Mind." Here, Evans provides a defense of the Kantian thesis "that space is a necessary condition for objective experience" (Evans 1985, 250) by demonstrating that "the idea of space" is "implicitly involved in the very idea of existence unperceived" (Evans 1985, 260–261).[15] But why think that the idea of space is implicitly involved in the idea of existence unperceived? The idea of existence unperceived, of objects existing beyond what is perceptually present, is not one that can stand on its own without a surrounding theory for the simple reason that one cannot perceive something that exists unperceived, for it is precisely *unperceived*. As such, the content of this concept cannot come *from* perceptual experience itself. But this does not mean, as Berkeley thought, that there is no such concept. It just means that the concept of an object existing unperceived is a concept whose content is not, like an empirical concept, conferred *through* experience. But then how is its content conferred? For Evans, it is conferred through the spatial forms of reasoning that comprise what he calls our 'rudimentary theory of perception'.

> Now, the idea of existence unperceived, or rather the idea of existence now perceived, now unperceived, is not an idea that can stand on its own, stand without any surrounding theory. How is it possible that phenomena *of the very same kind as* those of which he has experience should occur in the

---

[15] As Cassam points out (in Cassam 2005), Evans does not focus on the *existence* of space as necessary for objectivity, or the *perception* of space. Rather, it is the *idea* or *conception* of space that is a necessary condition for grasp of the objective world. So his interest is in the "connection between the *idea* of an objective world and the *idea* of a spatial world" (Evans 1985, 249, my italics). However, once this connection is set up correctly, it comes to inform our perception or experience of things in space.

absence of any experience? Such phenomena are evidently *perceptible*; why should they not be perceived? To answer this question, some rudimentary theory, or form of a theory of perception is required. This is the indispensible surrounding for the idea of existence unperceived, and so, of existence perceived. (Evans 1985, 261–262)

In saying that the concept of existence unperceived is embedded in a rudimentary theory of perception, Evans does not mean to suggest that a subject, to entertain the concept, must *self-consciously* apply the theory. Rather, they simply must have a "conception of the world of sufficient complexity to enable [them] to understand why what is perceivable should sometimes be and sometimes not be perceived" (Evans 1985, 263). So the question is this: what conceptual resources must a subject possess to understand this? One understands that a perceivable object is sometimes not perceived when one understands that the perception of the object depends not only on the object but also on certain *enabling conditions of perception*. What are these conditions? They are the following: that one is correctly positioned with respect to an object so as to perceive it (that one is near enough and not too distant from the object); that one has the right orientation on the object; and that there is nothing in the way of our seeing it (see Evans 1985, 263). So these enabling conditions are *spatial*, involving the spatial concepts of position, nearness and distance, orientation, and relation.[16]

A subject's grasp of these enabling spatial conditions is key for their grasp of the notion that an object might continue to exist even when not perceived because it allows a subject to *explain* and so understand how they might fail to perceive an object – i.e., by not being appropriately located with respect to it, by not being correctly oriented, by there being something in the way, etc. In grasping that perception depends on these conditions and that these conditions can sometimes go unfulfilled, a subject grasps, in Eilan's words, "that everything that happens in the world is not automatically experienced," that there "are truths about the world which, if one is not correctly positioned, one will not have access to" (Eilan 1997, 244). In other words, by using spatial concepts to explain why objects are sometimes perceived and sometimes not, the subject grasps that there are truths about the world that transcend what is accessible from their current perspective and therefore exist unperceived. In this way, we understand

---

[16] A further condition is that one must meet these enabling conditions at the right time, for example, when the object is there to be perceived. Hence, these enabling conditions are also temporal.

that our perceptions concern a world of objects which are there independently of us. The independence of the particulars is grasped once the subject understands that perception of them requires not just their existence but the meeting of these further, enabling conditions of perception. The existence and character of the particulars is quite independent of whether these further conditions are met. (Campbell 1993, 260)

When the enabling conditions of perception are not met, one is *not* in error about the object; rather, one is simply not in the right spatial position to perceive it. One grasps when a perceivable object is not perceived that it does not go out of existence; rather, it continues to exist but in a spatial position not accessible to one now. The key point is that one grasps this within *veridical perception*. As such, our perceiving things as part of an independent world does not depend on our having thoughts that we know can be in error but simply on our ability to reason spatially by using the rudimentary theory of perception.

But while we have gone a good way towards explaining how a subject can grasp the modal datum, the account given so far is incomplete, for we have not ruled out the possibility that the spatial concepts that comprise the rudimentary theory of perception are *egocentric* spatial concepts – i.e., concepts that gain content solely through their relationship to a subject's perceptual-motor activity. If these spatial concepts were only egocentric, one would have the ability to understand, because the enabling conditions of perception sometimes are and sometimes are not met, why *particular* objects are unperceived. We will have explained how a "subject might entertain a thought about a position or region in egocentric space whether or not he is currently perceiving it. Consider, for instance, a subject who has placed a bottle of whiskey by his bed, and who thinks, in the dark, 'There's a bottle of whiskey *there*'" (Evans 1982, 161). But we will not have explained how one can grasp that *all* objects would continue to exist even if unperceived. To grasp this, Evans argues, a subject's rudimentary theory of perception must also include spatial concepts that are 'absolute' or 'objective'. In having such concepts, one can grasp the idea that space is an interconnected network of places and locations in which all unperceived objects can be housed. But how is grasp of such concepts possible?

For Evans, the difference between egocentric and absolute spatial concepts is this: while egocentric concepts gain content through being part of a system of spatial relations centered, roughly, on one's own body, absolute spatial concepts gain their content by being centered allocentrically on the spatial relations of a number of objects that make up a frame of reference. We should not think that we have here two different kinds of space; rather, we have two kinds of information about space that respectively inform two different ways of thinking about space (see Evans 1982, 157). With respect to egocentric space, the subject of thought "conceives himself to be in the center of a space (at is point of origin), with its co-ordinates given by the concepts 'up' and 'down', 'left' and 'right', and 'in front' and 'behind'" (Evans 1982, 153–154). This grasp of space is systematic: to have the demonstrative thought 'F is here' requires recognizing that this thought belongs to a "system of thoughts about places that also includes such thoughts as 'It's F *over there*', 'It's F *up there to the left*', 'It's F *a bit behind me*'" (Evans 1982, 153). Because the subject is at the center of this spatial field when they, for example, hear a sound, they specify it "in *egocentric* terms (he hears the sound as up, or down, to the right or the left, in front or behind). These terms specify the position of the sound in relation to the observer's own body" (Evans 1982, 155).

Egocentric space is only *roughly* centered on the body, however. This is because while some of the axes of egocentric space, for example, 'front' and 'behind', are centered on the body, some, like 'up' and 'down', cannot be determined by the position of the body. While 'up' is often coordinated with the direction of my head (and not my feet), this is not always the case (for instance, when I'm lying down or am upside down) (See Evans 1982, 156). So how do these axes, and the demonstrative thoughts based on them, get spatial content? Evans takes it that the spatial content of an egocentric thought is based in nonconceptual information rendered by the relation between experience (visual, auditory, or tactile) and behavior:

> Egocentric spatial terms are the terms in which the content of our spatial experiences would be formulated, and those in which our immediate behavioral plans would be expressed. This duality is no coincidence: an egocentric space can exist only for an animal in which a complex network of connections exists between perceptual input and behavioral output. A perceptual input ... cannot have spatial significance for an organism except in so far as it has a place in such a complex network of input-output connections. (Evans 1982, 154)

To be aware of an object's location in egocentric space – i.e., to the left, or above, or in front – requires having complex dispositions and propensities to respond to the object as to the left, or above, or in front. And to be perceptually aware of an object's shape, as round or cubical for instance, is to have disposition and propensities to act on the object in ways appropriate to that shape. So an awareness of spatial content in general is bound up with disposition and propensities to appropriately behave with respect to places and things. These dispositions will be enormously complex because there is no single way that one must respond to an object. But the point still holds that if a creature did not have disposition to act appropriately with respect to an object, one would not have grounds for ascribing spatial awareness of the object to them.

Absolute or objective spatial concepts, in contrast, are features of a more complex representational system, one that can represent space by forming a 'cognitive map'. In forming such a map, one has "a representation in which the spatial relations of several distinct things are simultaneously represented" (Evans 1982, 151). The representation is not centered on the body but on the *relations* between the objects that make up the frame of reference for the representation. As such, in this representation, "[e]ach place is represented in the same way as every other; we are not forced in expressing such thinking, to introduce any 'here' or 'there'" (Evans 1982, 152). Here we think of things spatially, not from our engaged point of view but from 'no point of view' – i.e., by having a representation of the simultaneous spatial relations of various objects to one another. While one can only entertain such a representation if one can recognize these objects and places, which makes reference to egocentric space, the *spatial content* of the representation need not refer to a subject's real or imaginary point of view on them.[17]

Evans' argument, which we will discuss next, is that for a thinker to be able to have a concept of an objective world, a world of objects existing independently of them, they must

> have the capacity to form and employ representations such as these ... To say that the fundamental level of thought about the spatio-temporal world – the level of thought to which all our other thinking directs us – is thought which would be sustained by a cognitive map of the world is to stress that our fundamental level of thinking is, in a certain sense, "objective". (Evans 1982, 151–152)

As Campbell points out, this notion of objectivity, if understood in a certain way, can cause a type of dizziness. For what it seems to demand "is that one should build up a synoptic picture of the world, one that wholly abstracts from one's place in the throng ... What is dizzying is the kind of complete objectivity, the degree of abstraction ... that is required" (Campbell 1994, 6). One response to this dizziness is to undertake what Campbell calls an 'empiricist-pragmatist' critique of objective space and deny that subjects can have an autonomous grasp of objective space at all.

---

[17] This objective way of thinking about space is not yet a geometrical way of thinking about space, though it provides the basis for the development of this way of thinking.

On the empiricist-pragmatist view, "all ways of representing space must be explicable in terms of their connections with perception and action, in terms of their relations to egocentric space" (Campbell 1994, 7). If one is to resist this critique, one must identify a type of spatial thinking that is not reducible to egocentric spatial thinking, but also one that does not induce dizziness by making objective spatial thought something not possible for subjects situated in the world to grasp.

Evans avoids the empiricist-pragmatist critique, while also avoiding the dizziness brought on by complete objectivity, by arguing that egocentric spatial thought itself would not be possible if it did not presuppose the ability to engage in this more fundamental level of thought:

> [T]he network of input-output connections which underlies the idea of an egocentric space could never be regarded as supporting a way of representing space (even egocentric space) if it could not be brought by the subject into coincidence with some such larger spatial representation of the world as is constituted by a cognitive map. For instance, the subject must be able to think of the relation in which he stands to a tree that he can see as an instance of the relation in which (say) the Albert Hall stands to the Albert Memorial. That is, he must have the idea of himself as one object among others; and he must think of the relations between himself and objects he can see and act upon as relations of exactly the same kind as those he can see between pairs of objects he observes. This means that he must be able to impose the objective way of thinking upon egocentric space. (Evans 1982, 163)

A subject must be able to impose objective ways of thinking on their egocentric modes of spatial thought because if a subject could not "make sense of the idea that *he* might be one of the points representable within his [cognitive] map" (Evans 1982, 163), he would simply *have* an egocentric position in space but would not be able to grasp *that* he has that position. But then it would not even be possible for him to represent egocentric space, for he would have no ability to place himself *in* space. To do this, he must locate his egocentric space within a wider field of spatial relations that are indifferent to the objects (including himself) that are placed within them.

If egocentric modes of spatial thought depend on objective modes, then the latter cannot be reduced to the former. This rules out the 'empiricist-pragmatist' position. But how does Evans avoid the dizziness induced by objective thought? Objective modes of spatial thinking do not cause dizziness because they must, to play a role in our cognitive lives, be *applied* to an egocentric world of places and spaces. As Evans puts it, "any subject who is able to think 'objectively' about space – any subject who can be credited with a cognitive map of a region – must know what is involved ... in imposing his knowledge of the objective spatial relations of things upon an egocentric space" (Evans 1982, 162). In other words, one must be able to form identities between one's location in egocentric space with positions in objective space and on that basis generate hypotheses about what one would perceive if one moved in such and such direction. It is by having "the capacity to find one's way about, and to discover, or to understand how to discover, where in the world one is" (Evans 1982, 162) that one evinces knowledge of objective and not just egocentric space.[18]

The upshot is that Evans avoids the empiricist-pragmatist reduction and the dizziness of complete objectivity by claiming that objective spatial thinking and egocentric spatial thinking are *interdependent* for creatures that grasp space in the way that we do. Because of this interdependence, the rudimentary theory of perception that we use to explain and so understand why a perceivable object is not perceived can be extended to explain why perceivable objects in general are not perceived. They are not because they are housed in spatial positions and connected by spatial relations that while unperceived, are connected to, and are of exactly the same kind as, the places and relations that comprise the egocentric space that I presently inhabit.

Brandom and Davidson Revisited

The interdependence of egocentric and absolute spatial concepts gives us the means to identify important limitations in both Brandom's and Davidson's views. Let's begin with Davidson. As we know, Davidson traces the concept of objectivity back to the 'intersection of points of view'. I know that the world is independent of my perspective because I grasp, through communication, that there are other simultaneous perspectives on it. This concept of objectivity, we can now see, assumes a spatial framework that is egocentric. When one is aware that the other creature has a point of view on the same object as oneself in triangulation, one is aware that 'this' (the 'common cause' of our perceiving) is being

---

[18] In Evans' jargon, one can locate a place p in public space only if "one can be credited with a knowledge of what it would be for '$\pi = p$' to be true – where π is a stand-in for any arbitrary *fundamental*, and hence holistic, identification of a place" (Evans 1982, 162). A 'fundamental identification' of a place is an identification that singles it out by pointing out its 'ground of difference' from other things of the same kind. The only way to identify the difference of one place from another is through being able to find one's way about.

perceived from both 'here' and 'there'. I can give sense to the fact that the other perceives 'this' from 'there' only because 'this' and 'there' are elements of *my* system of egocentric spatial concepts that is centered 'here'. To grasp this, I do not need to engage in a more objective type of spatial thinking in which all three positions – the other creature's, my own, and the object – are placed within an interconnected spatial world that *goes beyond the triangle we are in*. But without this more extensive understanding, one cannot account for the fact that we are able to grasp that all objects, including all those that transcend the triangle we are in, continue to exist even when not perceived.

On Davidson's view, grasp of objectivity is not grasp of something that is perspective independent. For if my grasp of error depends on comparing my perspective with another, then my grasp of the distinction between seeming and being, appearance and reality, always makes tacit reference to that other perspective. But while this tacit reference allows me to grasp that my subjective perspective on things is a partial perspective, and so not equivalent to the object it is a perspective on, it does not allow for grasp of the fact that all objects would continue to exist even if I did not exist and if there were *no* perspectives at all. But this is a critical part of the concept of objectivity: what is objective is that which would continue to exist even if there were no points of view on it – mine, my interlocutors, or anyone else's. What allows one to grasp this, even from within the perspective of consciousness, is the use of egocentric and objective spatial concepts as part of one's rudimentary theory of perception. Once again, we get the result that the perceptual-theoretic account of objectivity is more primitive than the communicative-theoretic account.

What about Brandom? If we remember, Brandom takes it that a subject grasps objectivity when they grasp that the difference between what is taken to be correct and what is correct applies to all social-scorekeeping perspectives, including their own. This is the basis of their grasp that any given commitment can be incorrect, even if endorsed by oneself or the whole community. I argued that this social-pragmatic account of objectivity overlooks one of its key features – namely that our sense that the correctness or incorrectness of an application of concepts is settled by the way the world is, not by differences in social-perspective. Brandom can't account for our grasp of this latter fact because he has no way of detaching the concept of objectivity from our horizontal social-practical relations to others. While social scorekeepers grasp that what is correct transcends not only those with whom they actually communicate but even all those with whom they could communicate, what is correct or not is still relative to *some* social-scorekeeping perspective. While what is correct transcends any given attitude, it does not transcend attitudes in general.

Even though the perceptual-theoretic account of objectivity has little to say about the correctness or incorrectness of our thought insofar as it locates objectivity at a more primitive level, it nonetheless can help us explain the basis of our sense that what is objectively correct is settled by the way the world is and not by the attitudes of scorekeepers. According to it, our grasp of objectivity depends on our understanding of the fact that the enabling conditions of perception sometime are and sometime are not met. Whether these conditions are met is dependent not on other scorekeepers but on our spatial position and, more importantly, on the way the world is spatially arranged. So in reasoning spatially to explain why perceivable objects are not perceived, we grasp not only that things can exist unperceived but also that our perceptual access to these things *depends on* the way the world is spatially arranged. Because we understand that our access to things depends on the antecedent and independent spatial arrangement of those things, we are in a position to also understand that experience and thought, if they are to get things right, must be answerable *to* those antecedent things, rather than the other way around. Of course, we have not explained *how*, on a pragmatist account, they are answerable to the world. This question we take up in the second half of the book.

PART II

CHAPTER 4

An Experiential Account of Objectivity

Introduction

In the last chapter I argued that Davidson's communicative-theoretic account of objectivity depends, in a nonsymmetrical way, on a conception of objectivity found in our perceptual point of view on things. I articulated this conception by calling upon Strawson and Evans' neo-Kantian account of objectivity. Through the use of the spatial concepts that comprise one's rudimentary theory of perception, concepts that detail the enabling conditions of perception, one is able to understand why things that are perceivable are sometimes not perceived. Because these spatial concepts are interconnected with absolute or objective spatial concepts, one grasps that all the things that are perceivable but which are not perceived are housed in a unified spatial world. When one grasps this, one grasps the concept of objectivity.

Strawson and Evans aim to articulate the *concept* of objectivity because if grasp of objectivity is grasp of existence unperceived, then it is not perceivable, and hence not experienceable. The understanding of objectivity that is at play in perception is something that we *bring to* our experience of objects through the use of a rudimentary theory of perception, it is not something based *in* our experience of them. The concept of objectivity has its origin off stage, as it were. What I want to show in this chapter is that this is incorrect, that our concept of objectivity is based in our *experience* of existence unperceived. But the notion of experience to which we shall trace this concept is not that of the classical empiricists, but the much richer notion given by James in *The Principles of Psychology* and other allied works.[1] As I mentioned in the Introduction, this is an account of *Erlebnis*.

In *The Principles*, James talks about 'thought', 'consciousness', and 'experience'. Thought is his generic term for any state of consciousness,

---

[1] In this chapter, I look primarily at *The Principles of Psychology* (1890), an unpublished chapter of *The Principles*, "The Object of Cognition and the Judgment of Reality" (1883–1884), and the paper "The Knowing of Things Together" (1894).

whether sensory or cognitive. For James, the contrast between sensory and cognitive states of consciousness is not that the former are phenomenal and the latter intentional. Both kinds of state have phenomenal and intentional properties. The contrast between the two

> is really between two *aspects*, in which all mental facts without exception may be taken; their structural aspect, as being subjective, and their functional aspect, as being cognitions. In the former aspect, the highest as well as the lowest is a feeling, a peculiarly tinged segment of the stream. This tingeing is its sensitive body, the *wie ihm zu Muthe ist*, the way it feels whilst passing. In the latter aspect, the lowest mental fact as well as the highest may grasp some bit of truth as its content ... From the cognitive point of view all mental facts are intellections. From the subjective point of view all are feelings. (James 1981, 452n)

Consciousness for James is not what it is for us – namely, the seat of phenomenal awareness. Rather, consciousness is understood functionally as "primarily *a selecting agency*." It brings "one out of several of the materials so presented to its notice, emphasizing and accentuating that and suppressing as far as possible all the rest. The item emphasized is always in close connection with some *interest* felt by consciousness to be paramount at the time" (James 1981, 142).

James's notion of experience encompasses both of these prior concepts. On the one hand, we experience, in the sense of undergo, thoughts as they pass in the stream of thought. Thoughts are pulses of consciousness that we experience as part of our personal consciousness, as constantly changing, sensibly continuous with other thoughts, and of objects. Thoughts are given in experience as having these characteristics; we *live through* them as they pass in time. But James also uses the term experience when he is keen to point out – as in chapters 11 and 13 of *The Principles* on attention and discrimination – that what we experience is not just the result of what is given to our senses but also on what is *taken* – on what one attends to, discriminates, and potentially conceptualizes – in light of one's biological and culturally reproduced interests and ends. The actualization of these selective powers does not introduce anything supersensible into experience. They rather emphasize, accentuate, and suppress features of what we are already vaguely acquainted with, making a portion of it relatively clear and distinct. As James puts it dramatically:

> [T]he moment one thinks of the matter, one sees how false a notion of experience that is which would make it tantamount to the mere presences

An Experiential Account of Objectivity

to the senses of the outward order. Millions of items of the outward order are present to my senses which never properly enter into my experience. Why? Because they have no *interest* for me. *My experience is what I agree to attend to*. Only those items which I *notice* shape my mind – without selective interest, experience is an utter chaos. Interest alone gives accent and emphasis. Light and shade, background and foreground – intelligible perspective, in a word. (James 1981, 380–381)[2]

In this chapter, I demonstrate that the concept of objectivity is grounded in experience in two basic ways. First, I argue that our concept of objects as existing independently of our minds is based in the fact that due to the selectivity of the mind, we experience objects as persisting, as staying the same through our changing experiences of them. James puts the experience of the Same at the center of his account of mind. But a full account of objectivity must go beyond this experience and explain how persisting objects can be understood to exist even when unperceived. Strawson and Evans are therefore right in thinking that grasp of existence unperceived is critical for a grasp of objectivity. It's just that their account of this grasp is overly intellectualized.[3]

Second, I argue that James's theory of spatial consciousness gives us the means to articulate an experiential-theoretic account of existence unperceived. We *experience* existence unperceived because in our consciousness of space we always 'know-together' presence and absence. But this

---

[2] This passage is misleading in two respects. First, it suggests that what one attends to is voluntary (is what 'I agree to'). But for James most of the selections that our mind makes are not voluntary but biologically entailed by the type of creature that one is. Second, in using the term 'chaos', James gives the impression that before the selective powers of the mind do their work, the sensory stream is a disorganized flux, something akin to Strawson's pure sense-data experience. But, as we shall see, this view – also suggested by James's famous claim that children originally experience the world "as one great blooming, buzzing confusion" (James 1981, 462) – is very misleading, as it assumes the kind of atomist picture that James strenuously rejects. James thinks that the world is originally experienced as chaotic not because the sensory stream is *intrinsically disorganized*, but because the stream includes an overabundance of information that a child, because of their undeveloped powers of attention and discrimination, is not able to properly accentuate or suppress. Once, however, a child develops these powers, what comes into focus in their perceptual consciousness are objects that already have objectivity, unity, and extent.

> In his dumb awakening to the consciousness of something *there*, a mere *this* as yet ... the infant encounters an object in which (though it be given in a pure sensation) all the "categories of the understanding" are contained. *It has objectivity, unity, substance, causality, in the full sense in which any later object or system of objects has these things*. (James 1981, 657)

For more on this, see Siegfried 1978.

[3] I therefore agree with Tyler Burge when, in Burge 2009, he accuses Strawson and Evans of giving an overly intellectualized account of perceptual objectivity. But, as will become clear in this chapter, I disagree with him that perceptual objectivity depends only on the activation of perceptual constancies.

knowing-together applies not only to intuitively given spatial fields but also to our conception of space as an infinitely continuous unit. James agrees with Strawson and Evans that we can't intuit space as an infinitely continuous unit; we can only have a conception of it. However, the content of this conception is not based in spatial reasoning but in two experiential conditions: the fact that as we move through space there is a continual oscillation between relatively clear and distinct experiences and those that are vague and indistinct; and the fact that through these changes we can reverse our attention at will and recover objects that have been lost from sight. The first condition, I argue, accounts for our grasp of space as an infinitely continuous unit in which all objects can be housed, and the second for our understanding that these objects, most of which are absent, are nonetheless available to be perceived and, hence, continue to exist unperceived.

Methodological Preliminaries

I begin with James's account of thought. As is well known, James's main opponent in *The Principles* is an atomistic account of the mind, which he thinks is the default view that underlies both empiricist and rationalist psychologies. He thinks it is their default view for two main reasons.

First, it is because of the difficulties of introspection. While for James introspection remains the main, though by no means the only, method by which psychology is done, it "*is difficult and fallible; and that difficulty is simply that of all observation of whatever kind*. Something is before us; we do our best to tell what it is, but in spite of our good will we may go astray, and give a description more applicable to some other sort of thing" (James 1981, 191). Atomist accounts go astray because while it is easy to introspect the relatively enduring 'substantive parts' of a thought – i.e., the images or sense-qualities that comprise its content – it is very difficult to isolate the rapidly changing relations that imbricate and connect such contents as thought moves through time. The attempt to introspectively grasp what James calls the 'transitive parts' of the stream of thought "is in fact like seizing a spinning top to catch its motion, or trying to turn up the gas quickly enough to see how the darkness looks" (James 1981, 237). Because of this difficulty, we overlook what James calls the stream of thought's transitive parts and think that it is comprised only of its substantive parts, which leads to atomism.

If to hold fast and observe the transitive parts of thought's stream be so hard, then the great blunder to which all schools are liable must be the failure to register them and the undue emphasizing of the more substantive parts of the stream ... Now such ignoring as this has historically worked in two ways. One set of thinkers have been led by it to *Sensationalism*. Unable to lay their hands on any coarse feelings corresponding to the innumerable relations and forms of connection between the facts of the world, finding no *named* subjective modifications mirroring such relations, they have for the most part denied that feelings of relation exist ... Substantive psychoses, sensations and their copies and derivatives, juxtaposed like dominoes in a game, but really separate, everything else verbal illusion – such is the upshot if this view. The *Intellectualists*, on the other hand ... have made the same admission that the feelings do not exist. But they have drawn the opposite conclusion. The relations must be known, they say, in something that is no feeling, no mental modification continuous and consubstantial with the subjective tissue out of which sensations and other substantive states are made. They are known, these relations, by something that lies on an entirely different plane, by an *actus purus* of Thought, Intellect, or Reason. (James 1981, 237–238)

The second reason why atomism is the default view in psychology has to do with the relationship of the psychologist to their object. The psychologist stands outside of the object they are studying – i.e., mental life. "Even when he introspectively analyzes his own mind, and tells what he finds there, he talks about it in an objective way" (James 1981, 183). But this can lead to a kind of objectivist misunderstanding of mental life. James calls this misunderstanding the 'psychologist's fallacy'. Overall, the fallacy involves the psychologist's *"confusion of his own standpoint with that of the mental fact* about which he is making his report" (James 1981, 195). But there are two varieties of the fallacy. The first involves the psychologist substituting their third-personal description of a mental state, which includes all that they know about the state, for the first-person experience of the state that is had by the subject. Based on this, the psychologist assumes that *"the mental state studied must be conscious of itself as the psychologist is conscious of it"* (James 1981, 195). This mistake, however, is based on another mistake, which gives us the second variety of the fallacy. Here is how James puts it:

> The psychologist ... stands outside the mental state he speaks of. Both itself and its object are objects for him. Now when its is a *cognitive* state (percept, thought, concept, etc.), he ordinarily has no other way of naming it than as the thought, percept, etc., *of that object*. He himself, meanwhile,

> knowing the self-same object in *his* way, gets easily led to suppose that the thought, which is *of* it, knows it in the same way in which he knows it. (James 1981, 195)

So the psychologist is apt to substitute their thought of the object for the thought of the object undertaken by the subject they are studying because they confuse *thought with objects generally.*

This tendency is grounded in the fact that the language that the psychologist uses to describe mental life in their introspections is a language of "outer things" (James 1981, 300). In other words, the psychologist does not yet have a vocabulary to accurately describe subjective life, and this absence leads them (and ordinary folk as well) to describe mental life using concepts that have their natural home in the description of the objects that comprise the outer world. "Naming our thought by its own objects, we almost all of us assume that as the objects are, so the thought must be" (James 1981, 194). In so doing, the psychologist comes to think:

(1) As objects in their reality stay the same, so do thoughts;
(2) As objects in their reality are composed of discrete parts, so are thoughts;
(3) As objects in their reality are discontinuous with other objects, thoughts are discontinuous with other thoughts; and
(4) As objects in their reality only have contingent and external relations to other objects, thoughts only have external and contingent relations to objects.

James tries to show, both through more accurate introspective descriptions of mental life and through indirect psychological and physiological considerations, that the psychologist is mistaken in their thinking. He argues that to avoid these mistakes we must carefully distinguish between: (1) thought understood as a conscious mental state, (2) the object of thought as it is experienced from within the thought, what James calls 'thought's object'; and (3) the object of thought as it exists in the psychologist's reality, which is a physical reality situated outside of the thought and its object (see James 1981, 184). In light of this, we can see that the second variety of the psychologist's fallacy consists in interpreting thought's object in terms that apply to objects as they exist in the psychologist's reality. If we stop committing this fallacy, we will be able to see that

(1) Thought is in constant change;
(2) Each thought is a unitary and singular pulse of consciousness that does not have parts, even if its object is complex and has parts;

(3) Each thought is sensibly continuous with other thoughts;
(4) Each thought refers to some object, what James calls thought's object, in an internal and necessary way.

Let us go through these more carefully.[4]

Thought and Its Characteristics

The first mistake that we make by modeling thought on objects as they exist in the psychologist's reality is that it leads us to overlook the fact that thought is constantly changing. "Now we are seeing, now hearing; now reasoning, now willing; now recollecting, now expecting; now loving, now hating" (James 1981, 224–225). It's not that these states don't have duration – they do – it's rather that, once past, they cannot recur in identical form.

> Every thought we have of a given fact is, strictly speaking, unique, and only bears a resemblance of kind with our other thoughts of the same fact. When the identical fact recurs, we *must* think of it in a fresh manner, see it under a somewhat different angle, apprehend it in different relations from those in which it last appeared. And the thought by which we cognize it is the thought of it-in-those-relations, a thought suffused with the consciousness of all that dim context. (James 1981, 227)

This idea that thoughts can never recur is resisted, according to James, for two reasons. First, in their zeal "to reduce complexity to simplicity," the atomist attempts to explain our continually changing thoughts as the "resultant effect of variations in the *combination* of certain simple elements of consciousness that always remain the same. These mental atoms or molecules are what Locke called 'simple ideas'" (James 1981, 225). So beneath the ceaseless change of thought, there are elementary mental atoms that 'remain unchanged amid the flow'. Second, this conclusion about unchanging mental atoms is corroborated by 'common experience' (i.e., common sense). For is it not obvious that when we experience the same patch of grass in the same light that we experience the same idea of

---

[4] This list is related to, yet not the same as, the list of the five characteristics of thought that James famously gives at the beginning of chapter IX of *The Principles*. That list is as follows:
1. Every thought tends to be part of a personal consciousness.
2. Within each personal consciousness thought is always changing.
3. Within each personal consciousness thought is sensibly continuous.
4. It always appears to deal with objects independent of itself.
5. It is interested in some parts of these objects to the exclusion of others, and welcomes or rejects —chooses from among them, in a word—all the while. (James 1981, 225)

green on both occasions? Is it not obvious that "thought of the object's recurrent identity is" nothing but "the identity of its recurrent thought" (James 1981, 194)? James's answer is no:

> What is got twice is the same OBJECT. We hear the same *note* over and over again; we see the same *quality* of green, or smell the same objective perfume, or experience the same *species* of pain. The realities, concrete and abstract, physical and ideal, whose permanent existence we believe in, seem to be constantly coming up again before our thought, and lead us in our carelessness, to suppose that our 'ideas' of them are the same ideas. (James 1981, 225)

So here is why common experience confuses thought and object. Common experience has the "habit of not attending to sensations as subjective facts, but of simply using them as stepping-stones to pass over to the recognition of the realities whose presence they reveal" (James 1981, 225). But if we could stop passing over the subjective facts, if we could attend to them, we would be able to see that it is not the successive states or thoughts that are the same green or the same smell, but the *object* of those states, and that our thoughts of these objects are constantly changing.

Modeling thought on objects as they exist is the psychologist's reality has a second baleful effect, this one involving a view of the composition of thought. In assuming that 'as objects are, so thought must be', we assume that "the perceptions of multiplicity, of coexistence, of succession, are . . . brought about only through a multiplicity, a coexistence, a succession of perceptions." In thinking this the "continuous flow of the mental stream is sacrificed, and in its place an atomism . . . is preached, for the existence of which no good introspective grounds can be brought forward" (James 1981, 194–195). In other words, in modeling thoughts on objects, one comes to assume that a complex object involving coexistent, multiple, or successive parts, can only be cognized by a thought that is itself comprised of such parts (be they simple atomic impressions or ideas). James's contrary view is this: "*There is no manifold of coexisting ideas*; the notion of such a thing is a chimera. *Whatever things are thought in relation are thought from the outset in a unity, in a single pulse of subjectivity, a single psychosis, feeling, or state of mind*" (James 1981, 268). How does James establish this?

James challenges the atomist picture by asking whether such a view can make sense of the unity of consciousness necessary to experience a complex object *as* a single thing. For, on the face of it, a multiplicity of impressions is not by itself a perception of a multiplicity, coexistent impressions are not a perception of coexistent things, and a *"succession of feelings, in and of itself, is not a feeling of succession"* (James 1981, 591). The atomist claims that a complex of ideas can add up to a thought of a single complex thing because the "'series of states' *is* the 'awareness of itself'" in the sense that "if the states be posited severally, their collective consciousness is *eo ipso* given" (James 1981, 164n). In other words, the atomist claims that if you have a number of discrete states given severally (as a multiplicity, a coexistence, or a succession) that those severally given states add up to an awareness of all the states together. But if each item is "shut up in its own skin, windowless, ignorant of what the other feelings are and mean" (James 1981, 162) – i.e., if they are truly 'discrete' and 'separate' from one another as the atomist thinks – then it is unclear how this registering of the severally given states as a unity is possible. James nicely illustrates the problem for successive thoughts with this example:[5]

> Take a sentence of a dozen words, and take twelve men and tell to each one word. Then stand the men in a row or jam them in a bunch, and let each think of his word as intently as he will; nowhere will there be a consciousness of the whole sentence. (James 1981, 162)[6]

To understand James's alternative account of the unity of consciousness, consider the thought, 'the pack of cards is on the table'. James says:

> [T]he thought has time-parts ... Now I say of these time-parts that we cannot take any one of them so short that it will not after some fashion or other be a thought of the whole object "the pack of cards is on the table." They melt into each other like dissolving views, and no two of them feel the object just alike, but each feels the total object in a unitary undivided way. This is what I mean by denying that in the thought any parts can be found corresponding to the object's parts. Time-parts are not such parts. (James 1981, 269)

To have a unified thought of this complex object, we don't have a thought that contains, as distinct atomic parts, the idea of the cards, the idea of the table, the idea of their relation, and so on. Rather we have a single unified thought, 'the pack of cards is on the table', that is of the complex yet unified object the-pack-of-cards-is-on-the-table.

---

[5] James has similar arguments for non-successive thoughts. See James 1981, 163.
[6] James recognizes that Kant and his followers also had "little trouble in showing that such a bundle of separate ideas would never form one thought at all," which led them to think "an Ego must be added to the bundle to give it unity, and bring the various ideas into relation with each other" (James 1981, 267). But if one denies in the first place the idea that complex thoughts are composed of atomic impressions and ideas, as James does, then there is no reason to posit the Kantian "elaborate internal machine shop" (James 1981, 344) to bring order to the manifold.

But how can we say that a thought of a complex object is a single thought if the thought of it has different time-parts moving through the stream of consciousness? The answer begins by pointing out that time-parts are sensibly continuous with one another; "they melt into each other." Because they are sensibly continuous, the nature of each time-part involves the other time-parts, those just past and those just to come. Because of this, even if each part "feels" the object in a slightly different way as consciousness moves through time, they feel the object "in a unitary undivided way."

But even if this is so, why think that the time-part 'the pack of cards' and the time-part 'is on the table' comprise a single thought rather than two thoughts that are themselves sensibly continuous? We can establish their identity, James thinks, only by seeing that each sensibly continuous time-part is of the same 'total' object – i.e., is self-transcendent to the same object. To establish the unity of the time-parts of a single thought, a single pulse of consciousness, we must therefore have in view the self-identical object to which they refer. As such, the unity of consciousness necessary to think of a complex object as a unity is accounted for not by the laws of association, as the empiricist thinks, nor by the fact that there is a self-identical subject who unifies the disparate parts of the complex thought, as Kant thinks, but by the fact that the sensibly continuous time-parts of a single thought intend the same object:

> [The] sense of identity of the knowing subject is held by some philosophers to be the only vehicle by which the world hangs together. It seems hardly necessary to say that a sense of identity of the known object would perform exactly the same unifying function, even if the sense of subjective identity were lost. And without the intention to think the same outer things over and over again, and the sense that we were doing so, our sense of our own personal sameness would carry us but a little way toward making a universe of our experience. (James 1891, 434–435)

The third mistake that is made by modeling thought on objects is that it leads us to overlook the sensible continuity not just of the time-parts of a single thought but of the stream of multiple thoughts as they unfold through time. To illustrate, take James's example of a sudden contrast in the successive parts of the stream, for example, a thunderclap. While one might think that this rends or interrupts the continuity of consciousness, one only thinks this because, once again, one is confusing "thoughts themselves, taken as subjective facts, and the things of which they are aware" (James 1981, 233). While a thunderclap rends nature and introduces into it a chain of "discrete and discontinuous" (James 1981, 233) spatiotemporal events, the coming and going of these events is given continuously, with no breaks. These events "no more break the flow of the thought that thinks them than they break the time and space in which they lie ... The transition between the thought of one object and the thought of another is no more a break in the *thought* than a joint in a bamboo is a break in the wood" (James 1891, 233–234). So in confusing thought and objects we are prone to

> overlooking, even when the things are contrasted with each other most violently ... the large amount of affinity that may still remain between the thoughts by whose means they are cognized. Into the awareness of thunder itself the awareness of the previous silence creeps and continues; for what we hear when the thunder crashes is not thunder *pure*, but thunder-breaking-upon-silence-and-contrasting-with-it. Our feeling of the same objective thunder, coming in this way, is quite different from what it would be were the thunder a continuation of previous thunder. The thunder itself we believe to abolish and exclude the silence; but the *feeling* of the thunder is also a feeling of the silence as just gone. (James 1981, 234)

Hearing the thunder involves the feeling of the silence just gone because the silence is retained and intermixes with the hearing of the thunder, making the thunder-feeling distinct from what it would be in a different context. So although the feeling of thunder is a single pulse of consciousness, a pulse that has no atomic parts, the nature of this pulse partly depends on the relations it has to other thoughts in the stream.[7]

But it is not only the thought of the thunder that is sensibly continuous with the thought of the silence. There is also continuity in the *object thought about*. The *thunder that is heard* is continuous with the *silence that was heard*. As James puts it, "all our concrete states of mind are representations of objects with some amount of complexity. Part of the complexity is the echo of objects just past, and, in a less degree, perhaps, the foretaste of those just to arrive" (James 1981, 571). Here the *object of thought*, the thunder, involves, as part of *its* sense, objects just past and objects to come. This object, which James calls *thought's object*, is manifestly not the same as the thunder as it exists for the psychologist who stands outside of the

---

[7] This is reflected in our experience of time. In having a thought of the thunder, we do not experience it as if on a knife-edge, as something that is present at a single now point. Rather, we sit perched, looking "in two directions into time. The unit of composition of our perception of time is a *duration*, with a bow and a stern, as it were – a rearward- and a forward-looking end. It is only as parts of this *duration-block* that the relation of *succession* of one end to the other is perceived" (James 1981, 574). We are aware of the duration block 'thunder-overtaking-silence' precisely because the nature of the feeling of the thunder involves the retained silence and the anticipated more to come. For more on this, see Gurwitsch 1966b.

thought. The thunder that exists in the psychologist's reality is a physical event that is discrete and discontinuous with the silence just past, and has parts that can be literally decomposed. When we incorrectly model thought on objects, it is discrete objects like this that we model it on. But there is another concept of object in James: thought's object. Here, the object is not 'thunder' but nothing short of 'thunder-breaking-on-silence', all in hyphens.

James famously characterizes the stream of consciousness in this way:

> Like a bird's life, it seems to be made of an alternation of flights and perchings. The rhythm of language expresses this, where every thought is expressed in a sentence, and every sentence closed by a period. The resting-places are usually occupied by sensorial imaginations of some sort, whose peculiarity is that they can be held before the mind for an indefinite amount of time ... [T]he places of flight are filled with thoughts of relations, static or dynamic, that for the most part obtain between the matters contemplated in periods of comparative rest. *Let us call the resting-places the 'substantive parts', and the places of flight the 'transitive parts', of the stream of thought.* (James 1981, 236)

But this passage is misleading in two respects. On the one hand, it makes it seem as if we go from having completely non-relational sensorial qualities and images to having thoughts and feelings of relation and then back again. But this would make the stream a 'chain' or 'train' rather than a stream. What we should say is that as consciousness moves through time, we move from substantive states of consciousness imbricated by feelings of relation, to feelings of relation in which sensorial qualities and images are at a minimum, to new substantive experiences shot through by feelings of relation, and so on. On the other hand, the passage is misleading because it does not indicate that the stream has *depth*. The stream not only includes the back and forth between the substantive and transitive parts, it also includes the relations between these parts and *their object*. The substantive parts of the stream cognize things in which properties and relations, static and dynamic, interpenetrate. The transitive parts of the stream, in contrast, just "cognize the relations rather than the things" (James 1981, 249n). Corresponding to the transitive parts of the stream are all of the relations that we cognize: spatial, temporal, logical, etc.

As we mentioned in the section on 'Thought and Its Characteristics', the transitive parts of the stream are often overlooked because, unlike the relations they are about, they are 'in flight'. But, James argues:

> If there be such things as feelings at all, *then so surely as relations between objects exist in rerum natura, so surely, and more surely, do feelings exist to*

which these relations are known ... If we speak objectively, it is the real relations that appear revealed, if we speak subjectively it is the stream of consciousness that matches each of them by an inward coloring of its own. (James 1981, 238)

James often illustrates by discussing logical relations: "We ought to say a feeling of *and*, a feeling of *if*, a feeling of *but*, and a feeling of *by*, quite as readily as we say a feeling of *blue* or a feeling of *cold*" (James 1981, 238). These feelings, unlike the substantive feelings of blue or cold, are

> bare images of logical movement ... psychic transitions, always on the wing, so the speak, and not to be glimpsed except in flight. Their function is to lead from one set of images to another. As they pass, we feel both the waxing and waning images in a way altogether peculiar and a way quite different from the way of their full presence. (James 1981, 244–245)

The stream of thought includes another important kind of transitive part, what James calls 'feelings of tendency'. Feelings of tendency are also 'in flight'. But they, unlike feelings of relation, do not have a definite object. Feelings of tendency are feelings in which we anticipate something but when there is no determinate object in mind that we are anticipating. So in having a feeling of tendency there is an emptiness or an absence in one's consciousness. But we should not say that there is an absence *of* consciousness, for as James says, "the feeling of an absence is *toto coelo* other than the absence of a feeling" (James 1981, 243). It is a feeling, indeed an intensely active feeling, but one that does not have a definite object. It is a nonrepresentational state. Yet because it is anticipatory *of* something, it nonetheless is an intentional state, a state that goes beyond itself by pointing to 'something' (something absent in this case) that is not itself.

James gives a plethora of examples. In trying to recall a forgotten name, we have a sense of the direction we need to go in to fill the gap in our minds, yet we have no definite object in mind. Or take the experience of hearing someone say 'wait', 'hark', 'look'. In this case, we have a sense of anticipation, a sense that our experience is about to be fulfilled, whether it is eventually fulfilled or not. Or take the most common of examples, human speech itself: "The truth is that large tracts of human speech are nothing but *signs of direction* in thought, of which direction we nevertheless have an acute discriminative sense, though no definite sensorial image plays any part in it whatsoever" (James 1981, 244). Often, when we are speaking we have a sense of the direction of our speech without having any sensorial images 'in mind' to undergird that sense. Instead we have a "rapid premonitory perspective views of schemes of thought not yet articulate"

(James 1981, 245), a perspective that while not actually present, nonetheless guides one's current activity.

If there are feelings of relation and tendency, then the empiricist idea that all mental states are images of a perfectly definite nature that only 'know' substantive sense-qualities is exploded.

> What must be admitted is that the definite images of traditional psychology form but the very smallest part of our minds as they actually live. The traditional psychology talks like one who should say a river consists of nothing but pailsful, spoonsful, quartpotsful, barrelsful, and other moulded forms of water. Even were the pails and pots all actually standing in the stream, still between them the free water would continue to flow. It is just this free water of consciousness that psychologists resolutely overlook. Every definite image in the mind is steeped and dyed in the free water that flows around it. With it goes the sense of its relations, near and remote, the dying echo of whence it came to us, the dawning sense of whither it is to lead. The significance, the value, of the image is all in this halo and penumbra that surrounds and escorts it, – or rather that is fused into one with it and has become bone of its bone, and flesh of its flesh; leaving it, it is true, an image of the same *thing* it was before, but making it an image of that thing newly taken and freshly understood. (James 1981, 246)

In saying that every image is fused with a halo or fringe of free water (feelings of relation and tendency), James aims to reinstate "the vague to its proper place in our mental life" (James 1981, 246). There are two types of vagueness here. On the one hand, the nature of a conscious state is never completely clear to the subject who undergoes the state. This is because the content of a conscious state is partly determined by the vague halo or horizon that imbricates and surrounds it. When we momentarily focus on a portion of the vague horizon, making it the focal point of our attention, a new horizon forms around it that is itself vague. While one can for a moment make *a* portion of the horizon clear and distinct to oneself, there is simply no way to make the whole of one's experience such. The vagueness of the free water always remains. On the other hand, the *object* of such states is also vague. For the fringe of relations and tendencies is also "part of the *object cognized* – substantive *qualities* and *things* appearing to the mind in a *fringe of relations*" (James 1981, 249n). In other words, corresponding to the fringe of feelings is a fringe of *relations felt*. Of most of an object's relations, "we are only aware in the penumbral nascent way of a 'fringe' of unarticulated affinities" (James 1981, 250). These relations surround and imbricate the object of thought, making *what* we attend to in experience always part of a larger inarticulate field.

The final mistake that results from modeling thought on objects as they exist in the psychologist's reality is thinking that thought's reference to an object is always an external and contingent affair. That James thinks that thought's relation to some objects is internal and necessary comes out in his distinction between the 'object of thought' and the 'topic of thought':

> In popular parlance the word object is commonly taken without reference to the act of knowledge, and treated as synonymous with individual subject of existence. Thus if anyone ask what is the mind's object when you say 'Columbus discovered America in 1492', most people will reply 'Columbus', or 'America' ... They will name a substantive kernel or nucleus of the consciousness, and say the thought is 'about' that – as indeed it is – and they will call that your thought's 'object'. Really that is usually only the grammatical object, or more likely the grammatical subject, of your sentence ... or you may call it the 'topic' of your thought, or the 'subject of your discourse'. But the *Object* of your thought is really its entire content or deliverance, nothing more nor less ... It is nothing short of the entire sentence, 'Columbus-discovered-America-in-1492' ... with hyphens between all its words. (James 1981, 265–266)

Thought's object is "neither more nor less than all that the thought thinks, exactly as the thought thinks it" (James 1981, 266). But this includes not only *what* is thought about, but also the manner in which it is thought about, including the halo of obscure relations in which it is bathed. In phenomenological language, which is helpful here, thought's object is the *object-as-it-is-intended*.[8] Clearly this cannot be determined without reference to the thought that intends it. But neither can the thought be determined without reference to the object thought about. This is because, as we saw earlier with the pack of cards example, the sensible continuity of the time-parts of the thought cannot specify, by itself, whether such parts comprise a single thought of something or two sensibly continuous thoughts of it. What is also needed is that these time-parts are of the same 'total object', which is the object-as-it-is intended by that thought. In light of this, we can understand what it means to say that the reference of thought to thought's object is internal and necessary: the identity conditions of the thought depend on the object meant or intended by the thought.

The topic of thought, we could say, is the referent of thought. It is the *object-which-is-intended*. But we can view the topic of thought in two ways. First, we can view it from the psychologist's point of view. From this point

---

[8] See Gurwitsch 1966a and Wilshire 1968.

of view, the topic is the *empirical referent* of the thought – which exists in what, for the psychologist, is *objective reality*. This object is externally and contingently related to the thought that is of it. This is the object of which James speaks in papers like "The Function of Cognition." There he gives an account in which thought's relation to its empirical referent is nothing magical, a matter of thought 'jumping' or 'transcending' the divide between mind and world and hitting upon the right object. Rather, reference is determined by "the procession of mental associates and motor consequences that follow on the thought, and that would lead harmoniously, if followed out, into some ideal or real context, or even into the immediate presence, of the [object]" (James 1975b, 34). Reference to an object depends not on meanings that the thinker of the thought ascertains from within their experience, but on whether the associates of the thought *in fact* lead to the object "*through a context which the world supplies*" (James 1975b, 35).[9]

But the topic of thought can also be viewed from within the stream of thought. From this point of view, the topic is a *higher-order thought's object*. James says of this object that is in one way "less than the thought's object ... in another way it may be more" (James 1981, 266). It is less than thought's object because while the topic understood in this way denotes the object thought about, it still does not specify *what is thought* about it. The object of thought specifies this. The topic is more than the object of thought, however, because within the stream we "as a rule ... are fully aware that we have thought before of the thing we think of now. The continuity and permanency of the topic is of the essence of our intellection" (James 1981, 454). In other words, the topic of thought is required to make sense of the fact that from within the stream of thought, different thoughts – for instance, 'Columbus discovered America in 1492' and 'he was a daring genius' – can nonetheless intend the same thing. They can intend the same thing because it is of the essence of thought that the "'*same matters can be thought of in successive portions of the mental stream, and some of these portions can know that they mean the same matters which the other portions meant*'. One might put it otherwise by saying that '*the mind can always intend, and know when it intends, to think of the Same*'" (James 1981, 434). This ability of different thoughts to intend the same is, for James, "the most important of all the features of our mental structure" and

---

[9] For this theory, see Jackman 1998.

"is the very keel and backbone of our thinking" (James 1981, 434).[10] So the topic of thought is more than thought's object because it denotes not just an object of a single thought but an object potentially intended as the same by a multitude of distinct thoughts.

Unity and Objectivity

As we have seen, for James the unity of a thought depends on its sensibly continuous time-parts intending the same object, which gives us a basis to individuate those parts as part of a single thought instead of two thoughts. Similarly, the unity of the stream of thought depends on the fact that thoughts are sensibly continuous, involve one another in their temporal unfolding, and can intend the same object (the topic as higher-order object). So, in both cases, sensible continuity and the ability to intend the same are interconnected features of mental life. But James's account of the unity of the stream of consciousness has another component, namely that the stream involves a backward-facing *learning process* in which we come to increasingly *know-about* the object of our acquaintance. James's account of *Erlebnis*, we could say, involves an account of *Erfahrung*.

This stands out most clearly in an important unpublished chapter of *The Principles*, "The Object of Cognition and the Judgment of Reality" (1883–1884).[11] In this chapter, James takes up the question of whether "there are any states of mind which inform us only of their own immediate presence" (James 1988a, 264). James answers negatively. All states of mind, even those that common sense does not take to be cognitive of things other than themselves (pains, emotions, and moods) involve "the peculiar relation of self-transcendency" by which a state of mind has "revealed to it or through it the existence of something else" (James 1988a, 264). But the concept of self-transcendence, in accord with his distinction between empirical referent and object of thought outlined earlier, has two distinct meanings in James: (1) the self-transcendence by

---

[10] James lays out this feature of mental life in chapter XII of *The Principles*, "Conception." But, as we shall see, the principle applies not just to conceptual acts of consciousness but also to intuitive acts: sensory, perceptual, and orectic.

[11] Much of the material of this chapter is included in *The Principles* or in "The Function of Cognition," but not all of it. James set this chapter aside for two reasons. First, it was thought, in the words of Alice James, to be "superseded by other stuff" (James 1988a, 498). But I don't think this is the case. The chapter includes original material and connects, in an illuminating way, concepts that are mostly kept apart in *The Principles*. The second reason James set it aside is that he meant *The Principles* to avoid metaphysical questions concerning the relation of mind and world. This chapter directly takes up such questions, and for that reason was abandoned.

which a thought is of *reality*, of something that exists in the spatiotemporal world (of the psychologist) and (2) the self-transcendence by which a thought is of its *object*, which is "equivalent to the mental content, or deliverance or matter of consciousness, whether it reveal a reality recognized as such by us psychologists or not" (James 1988a, 265). James's question is this: what are the conditions by which a state of mind, a feeling, *knows* or is *cognitive of*, a reality that stands outside of the feeling in which it appears?

To answer this question, James begins with an account of the simplest possible pulse of consciousness, a feeling of fragrance, and asks us, contrary to fact, to consider it in isolation from the rest of a subject's cognitive architecture, from its relation to other pulses of consciousness, and from the mind's ability to intend the same.[12] In being acquainted with it one knows not a single fact "*about* the fragrance – knows not that it is a fragrance, not that there is a feeling other than itself knowing it, not that it is a quality, so-called ... that it will ever recur and be cognized by other acts of feeling and receive a name, nor that it is an item in the phenomenal world" (James 1988a, 269). Now one might assume under these conditions that the feeling of fragrance is not knowledge. For knowledge requires a feeling that contemplates "some phenomena whose existence is not bound up with its own, but lasts when it is gone ... a feeling whereby from out of its own passing existence it grasps something *other* than that passing existence itself" (James 1988a, 268). Having "an intrinsic, immanent quality" (James 1988a, 268) of fragrance within consciousness does not seem to fit the bill. But James has an externalist account here that vindicates the potentially cognitive nature of this feeling. "The 'nub' of this vindication of the cognitive function for the first feeling, lies ... in the discovery that the fragrance *does* occur elsewhere" (James 1988a, 269). In other words, if, as a matter of empirical fact, there is "fragrance in the world, and if there be a feeling of that fragrance, then the feeling is knowledge, of the acquaintance type" (James 1988a, 274). While in James's thought experiment, the subject of the feeling does not *know* that their feeling opens them up to a feature of the world, it *in fact* opens them up to it, something that is only ascertainable from an outside point of view.

But James recognizes that such a single isolated state, even if it were possible, would be almost less than nothing. While it might provide a momentary revelation of outward truth, that revelation would be

---

[12] As he does in the "The Function of Cognition," James illustrates the point by using Condillac's example of a statue suddenly endowed with sensations.

extinguished the moment the mental state ceased. We need an account of how the minimum of knowledge provided by this mental state can "grow into something more" (James 1988a, 274). So James asks us to imagine, again, contrary to fact, not one but two mental states, a feeling of fragrance and a feeling of sweetness. For an account of how knowledge grows, we cannot think of these states as "each shut up in its own skin and cognizant during the moment it lasts of nothing but its own content" (James 1988a, 274). For if these feelings are taken in this atomistic way, then "the fragrance" would be "non-existent when the sweetness exists" (James 1988a, 275). Here, "the feeling of sweetness simply as such throws no backward light on the feeling of fragrance, nor ... does anything remain form the feeling of fragrance to modify our perception of the feeling of sweetness" (James 1988a, 274). How, then, are these states related?

As we have already seen, the feeling of sweetness is sensibly continuous with the feeling of fragrance. But now James adds to this characterization by saying that it is *self-transcendent* to this prior state. Later states of consciousness, he argues, are not merely acquainted with a present content but also *know-about* prior states of consciousness *and* their objects, which now are part of the overall *object* of that later state.[13] As James puts it:

> To make [the feeling of sweetness] in any degree equivalent to a perception of the having-been of the fragrance, or of the fact that it is itself different from the fragrance, we must assume it to be a totally different psychic fact from the simple sweetness we began by postulating. We must equip it with a full intellectual outfit, and give it a function of cognitive self-transcendency – not only to the extent of knowing the quality of sweetness which is its own content, but to the extent of knowing another feeling, dead and gone, and *its* content; – and we must give it the power of comparing its own present existence with that of this dead and gone feeling, and of stating the relation between the two. Such 'gifts' as these on our part are, however, the sole conditions upon which our first minimum of knowledge can be expected to 'grow into anything more'. If a mind with any structure is to come, the second feeling must be a fact with an altogether different sort of an inward constitution from that of the first. Its object can be no simple quality, but must be complex, involving the previous sensation and its quality, *plus* the sense of its difference from the new simple quality now perceived to be on hand. Such a feeling as this is altogether different from the feeling of the new quality pure and simple. That would have been bald *acquaintance*; this is knowledge *about*. (James 1988a, 275)

---

[13] We should not think that later thoughts introspect earlier thoughts. Introspection is usually effortful and voluntary while the knowing-about described here takes almost no effort and is not voluntary.

Every state of consciousness in the stream of consciousness is therefore both immediate and mediate: immediate insofar as it acquainted with a quality (the quality of sweetness); and mediate insofar as this quality is know-about as part of a complex object that includes the past feeling and its content ('sweetness-other-than-and-later-than-fragrance'). Insofar as a present thought feels the content with which it is acquainted as part of this more complex object, it *mediates* and is *mediated by* the contents that have just past. In this way, the later thought develops and makes explicit what is nascent in the earlier content, and in so doing comes to be "of more and more complicated objects as time goes by" (James 1988a, 276).

For current thought to be cognitive of an object, "it is requisite that [a subject] must believe his earlier feeling to *mean* or *point* to an objective truth which the present feeling also *points to and means*. In other words, he must not only remember something as experienced in the past, but he must *identify* it with something experienced now" (James 1988a, 283). This 'synthesis of identification' is requisite because if one were not able to grasp that the object just gone is the same as the object with which one is currently acquainted, one would not be able to grasp the continuity of objects through time, and therefore their increasing complexity.[14] This synthesis allows us to run "back and forth, like spiders on the webs they weave," and "feel ourselves to be constantly working over the same materials and thinking them in different ways. And this feeling of the self-sameness of an object filling two different times, forms a far higher and more valuable principle of synthesis for us than the mere sense of the continuity of time" (James 1988a, 285).

The ability to work over the same material in different ways at different times is a higher and more valuable synthesis than the continuity of time because it is the experiential basis of our belief in mind-independent objects. Here is how James puts it:

> The reason why we all believe that the objects of our thoughts have a duplicate existence outside, is that there are *many* human thoughts, each with the *same* object ... The judgment that my own past thought and my own present thought are of the same object is what makes *me* take the object out of either and project it by a sort of triangulation into an

---

[14] 'Synthesis of identification' is Husserl's term. See the "Second Meditation" of the *Cartesian Mediations* (Husserl 1950).

independent position, from which it may *appear* to both. *Sameness* in a multiplicity of objective appearances is thus the basis of our belief in realities outside of thought. (James 1981, 262)[15]

The point here is that *within experience* we grasp the difference between the temporally streaming multiplicity of experiences of an object and the object that stays the same throughout those experiences. Because we "intend the same," we experience objects *as* persisting beyond our experiential glimpses of them.[16] This is the experiential basis of our belief that persisting things are *real*, are things that exist in the mind-independent world.

We have been asking about the conditions by which a thought can know or be cognitive of a reality that stands outside of it. It is important to point out here that James's discussion only answers this more limited question: how is it possible for a subject *to take* their thought to be cognitive of an objective reality. This is because for James the fact that "the mind can mean the Same is true of its *meanings*, but not necessarily of aught besides" (James 1981, 435). In other words, our intending the same, which is the basis of our belief in outer realities, is a psychological or phenomenological principle, not an ontological one. While our intending the same is necessary for meaningful thought, our so doing does not entail that that thought actually corresponds to the way things are. This limitation is consistent with my purposes in this chapter because I am only interested in explaining, on experiential-theoretic grounds, grasp of the concept of objectivity, not how our thought can, in fact, be objective.

Here we have gone some way toward giving an account of our grasp of objectivity. But while belief in persisting mind-independent objects is necessary for grasp of objectivity, it is not sufficient. It is not sufficient because a full account of objectivity must explain how we grasp that these objects continue to exist when unperceived. To explain this, we need to discuss James's account of spatial consciousness.

---

[15] Husserl makes a similar point: "The fact that a re-perception, a renewed perception of the same thing, is possible ... characterizes the fundamental trait of transcendent perception, alone through which an abiding world is there for us" (Husserl 2001, 47). For another account along these lines, but one that highlights the importance of imagination for the kind of triangulation James mentions, see Church 2013.
[16] See chapter 8 of Campbell and Cassam 2014 for an experiential account of persistence.

Sensation and Spatial Consciousness

For James, spatial consciousness is sensory. But James uses the term 'sensation' in at least three distinct ways.[17] First, James use this term to refer to the sensory atoms posited by both empiricist and rationalist psychologies. Second, James talks of sensations as items that are, through discrimination, abstracted out of the thick world of colored and shaped physical objects in space and time. For James, what are originally given to consciousness are objects in space and time that have *sensory properties*, and what atomist philosophers mistakenly call sensations are the product of quite complex mental operations performed on these given objects.

> The "simple impressions" of Hume, the "simple ideas" of Locke are both abstractions, never realized in experience. Experience, from the very first, presents us with concrete objects, vaguely continuous with the rest of the world which envelops them in time and space, and potentially divisible into inward elements and parts. These objects we break asunder and reunite ... [T]he elements with which the traditional associationism performs its constructions – "simple sensations," namely – are all products of discrimination carried to a high pitch. (James 1981, 461)

Understood in this way, sensations are not sensory atoms out of which experiences are constructed but are rather the result of abstractive mental acts that operate on already given objects. While sensations understood as sensory atoms are mythical, experiences of sensory qualities that are the result of discriminative attention are not.

Third, and most importantly for us, James speaks of sensations as distinct and unique pulses of consciousness by which we originally become *acquainted* with the world's basic qualities and relations. Sensations here are "*first things* in the way of consciousness. Before conceptions can come, sensations must have come; but before sensations come, no psychic fact need have existed" (James 1981, 656). As first things, sensations are not qualia or intransitive states of consciousness. For from the very first, sensations "cognize an objective world" (James 1981, 651) and "perceive ... an *immediately present outward reality*" (James 1981, 652). Sensations are not intrinsically subjective states that must be made objective through certain kinds of objectifying acts; rather they signify a primitive form of world-openness. "[A]t their very first appearance quite as much as at any later date are they cognizant of all those qualities which we end by extracting and conceiving under the names of *objectivity,*

---

[17] See Linschoten 1968, 88, and High 1981, 473.

exteriority, and extent" (James 1981, 689).[18] They are cognizant of these qualities because, just as sensations contain as a native part of their content qualities like intensity, they also, James argues, include as part of their content a feeling of extent or voluminousness. "In the sensations of hearing, touch, sight, and pain we are accustomed to distinguish from among the other elements the element of voluminousness. We call the reverberations of a thunderstorm more voluminous than the squeaking of a slate-pencil; the entrance into a warm bath gives our skin a more massive feeling than the prick of a pin" (James 1981, 776).[19]

The feeling of voluminousness is "a simple vague consciousness of vastness" (James 1983, 66). It is vague in two ways. On the one hand, in having a sensation, we "take in at one glance ... an undivided *plenum*" (James 1983, 66), one that has "no subdivisions *ab intra*, nor precise limitations *ab extra*" (James 1981, 969). On the other hand, each sensation acquaints us potentially with a different plenum, for example, the mouth cavity felt by the tongue or the mountains seen in the distance. These plenums are originally unordered and do not comprise a single homogeneous space. So there is a question about how the vague senses of vastness with which our sensations acquaint us become part of a single spatial order. James's answer is this: while the sense of vastness is native to our sensations, the perception of spatial order is a product of a learning process in which attention and discrimination play a central part.[20] "[T]his form of sensibility – this quality of extension or spatial *quale*, as I have called it – exists at the outset in a simple and unitary form. The *positions* which ultimately come to be determined within it, in mutual relation to each other, are later developments of experience, guided by attention" (James 1983, 62–63).

James's view here contradicts what we could call the received view of spatial consciousness in the late nineteenth century, which says that

---

[18] James also says:

> So far is it from being true that our first way of feeling things is the feeling of them as subjective or mental, that the exact opposite seems to be the true. Our earliest, most instinctive, least developed kind of consciousness is the objective kind; and only as reflection becomes developed do we become aware of an inner world at all. (James 1981, 679)

[19] James thinks that this point also applies to bodily sensations:

> The sensations derived from the inward organs are also distinctly more or less voluminous. Repletion and emptiness, suffocation, palpitation, headache, are examples of this, and certainly no less spatial is the consciousness we have of our general bodily condition in nausea, fever, heavy drowsiness, and fatigue. Our entire cubic content seems then sensibly manifest to us as such, and feels much larger than any local pulsation, pressure, or discomfort. (James 1981, 777)

[20] For much more on this, see Klein 2009.

because sensations are devoid of all native spatiality, that synthetic acts of the intellectual are needed to bring about spatial awareness.[21] Acts of the intellect are necessary for spatial awareness because "the starting-point of their whole industry, in endeavoring to *deduce* space, lies in their regarding as the fundamental characteristic thereof the fact that any one spatial *position* can only be defined by its relation to other positions, and in their assumption that position, until thus defined, is not felt at all" (James 1983, 62). To be aware of something as having a position in space requires being aware of it as part of a system of relations, and to be aware of a system of relations requires synthetic acts of the mind to relate intrinsically spaceless sensory atoms.[22] The received view is therefore not the Berkeleyian view that the awareness of depth requires the association of sensory and kinesthetic sensations but the more radical view that *any* awareness of space, including of things in two-dimensional space, requires the synthesis of a manifold by acts of the intellect. But, James cogently asks, how can the synthesis of intrinsically spaceless items add up to an awareness of space? Why think that the mind has the power to *make* space out of completely spaceless ingredients?

Instead of having to explain how the perception of spatial order is built out of nonspatial mental atoms, James has the task of explaining how we get from an originally vague *sensation* of extent-ness to a *perception* of a unified spatial order – one in which there is position, shape, size direction, and distance.[23] James agrees with the received view that the perception of

---

[21] There were others who rejected the received view – for example, Hering, who had a large influence on James. The received view includes both empiricist (Mill, Bain) and neo-Kantian accounts of spatial consciousness (Green, Helmholtz, Wundt, and Peirce). See High 1981, chapter 4 of Myers 1986, Girel 2003, and Klein 2009. In my view, much present-day philosophy of perception (Evans, Noë, Hurley, Schellenberg) and cognitive science (Rock, Marr) is still within the orbit of the received view.

[22] For James, in contrast, spatial relations are not a product of synthetic acts of the mind but are themselves given in sensation.

> But just as, in the field of quantity, the relation between two numbers is another number, *so in the field of space the relations are facts of the same order with the facts they relate. If these latter be patches in the circle of vision, the former are certain other patches between them*. When we speak of the relation of direction of two points toward each other, we mean simply the sensation of the line that joints the two points together. *The line is the relation*; feel it and you feel the relation, see it and you see the relation. (James 1981, 791)

[23] While for James, sensation and perception are unique and distinct pulses of consciousness, they are nonetheless "not ... different sorts of mental *fact*" (James 1981, 651), meaning that perception is still a *sensory* act. In sensation, one has a vague awareness of something, of qualities surrounded by a fringe of dim relations, while in perception we, through attention, explore these relations and discriminate them from others, gaining a clearer intuitive knowledge-about them. "*Sensation*" therefore, "*differs from Perception only in the extreme simplicity of its object or content*. Its function

spatial order requires the development and actualization of certain acts of mind – attention and discrimination, as well as imagination, association, and memory. For to add up to "what we know as the real Space of the objective world," the "primordial largenesses which the sensations yield must be *measured and subdivided* by consciousness, and *added* together" (James 1981, 787). But in bringing about these operations, these acts do not *introduce* spatiality into sensations, nor do they add anything supersensible to the vastnesses given by them. Rather, they organize and subdivide what is already vaguely given in the spatial plenums with which we are acquainted:

> In these operations, imagination, association, attention, and selection play a decisive part; and although they nowhere add any new material to the space-data of sense, they so shuffle and manipulate these data and hide present ones behind imagined ones that it is no wonder if some authors have gone so far as to think that the sense-data have no spatial worth at all, and that the intellect, since it makes the subdivisions, also gives the spatial quality to them out of resources of its own. (James 1981, 787)

Let us briefly run through these operations. First, the spatial units yielded by our sensations are subdivided by selective attention. We attend to and discriminate objects and their positions within these units, and map out the relations between these objects and positions.[24] We are motivated to do so for primarily two reasons. First, we attend to objects that provoke our interest. "Emotional interests are the great guides to selective attention. One retinal position . . . could hardly be singled out from any other before an interesting object had come to occupy it" (James 1983, 75). Second, attention is awakened by the motion of impressions across our sensory receptors that comes about due to our perceptual exploration of things:

> [I]n the education of spatial discrimination the motions of impressions across sensory surfaces must have been the principle agent in breaking up our consciousness of the surfaces into a consciousness of their parts . . . In exploring the shapes and sizes of things by either eye or skin the movements of these organs are incessant and unrestrainable. Every such movement draws the points and lines of the object across the surface, imprints them a hundred times more sharply, and drives them home to the attention. (James 1981, 814)

---

is that of mere *acquaintance* with a fact. Perception's function, on the other hand, is knowledge *about* a fact, and this knowledge admits of numberless degrees of complication" (James 1981, 651–652).

[24] The discrimination of places requires the discrimination of objects in those places, and the discrimination of objects requires our already being vaguely acquainted with places in sensation. Place and object discrimination are therefore interdependent.

The second operation involves submitting different pulses of sensory consciousness to a common spatial measure. This happens in two steps. First, due to a 'natural norm' internal to our perceptual system we are able to distinguish, within the changing impressions falling on our sensory surfaces, between a perceived object's 'real' size and its merely 'apparent' size:

> *Out of all the visual magnitudes of each known object we have selected one as the* REAL *one to think of, and degraded all the others to serve as its signs.* This "real" magnitude is determined by aesthetic and practical interests. It is that which we get when the object is at the distance most propitious for exact visual discrimination of its details. This is the distance at which we hold anything we are examining. Farther than this we see it as too small, nearer too large. And the larger and the smaller feeling vanish in the act of suggesting this one, their most important *meaning.* (James 1981, 817)

Although the size of an object that appears due to the motion of impressions across our sensory surfaces is continually changing, we do not – because of this natural norm entailed by our practical and aesthetic interests – [25] experience the object *itself* as changing with respect to its size. The way the object *appears* to us continually changes as we or it moves, but it does not appear that the object itself, the *real* object, changes. Here we have an account of size constancy in which the same appears through difference.[26] We intend the Same through difference because of the mind's interest-guided selectivity, which is exercised passively in response to impressions falling across our sensory surfaces.

Second, single objects can be superimposed on the different spatial units given by our sensations. So, for example, the same object may be perceptually explored by touch or by vision, each modality marked by constancy effects. The 'real' size given by each modality can then be compared with

---

[25] Interests, according to James, "are the real *a priori* element in cognition" (James 1978, 11n). A creature's basic interests are 'subjective', not in the sense that they are the result of individual choice but in the sense that they are brought to the world by the subject, whether due to natural selection or a cultural learning process. Human creatures have two basic biological interests: a practical interest in coping with and mastering the environment to ensure survival, and an aesthetic interest in beholding and understanding it. It is in our practical interest to, for example, dissociate different types of plants, to know which ones can be eaten and which ones cannot, etc. But we also have aesthetic interests in plants, which can take the form of a desire to behold particulars in their uniqueness, or of a desire to understanding a plant as part of a system of plants.

[26] James gives a similar account of shape constancy at James 1981, 870–871. See Rock 1990 for an account of James's theory of the constancies, which insightfully compares it to Merleau-Ponty's. See also Burge 2009 for an account of the constancies that sees them as the central requirement for perceptual objectivity. My view is that constancy effects are necessary but not sufficient for perceptual objectivity.

each other. In this comparison our practical and aesthetic interests again determine what is real and what is appearance. For "*when two sensorial space-impressions, believed to come from the same object, differ, then* THE ONE MOST INTERESTING, *practically and aesthetically,* IS JUDGED TO BE THE TRUE ONE" (James 1981, 818).

The third and most important operation concerns the adding together of the various spatial units given by our sensations. This operation also involves two steps. First, James posits 'a basic law of mental economy' in which we take what is given in space by our different sensations to cluster around 'one and the same real thing'. In other words, we

> simplify, unify, and identify as much as we possibly can. *Whatever sensible data can be attended to together we locate together. Their several extents seem one extent. The place at which each appears is held to be the same with the place at which the others appear. They become, in short, so many properties of* ONE AND THE SAME REAL THING. This is the first and great commandment, the fundamental "act" by which our world gets spatially arranged. (James 1981, 821)

Here we have another version of 'the most important of all the features of our mental structure', namely that different thoughts, in this case pulses of sensory consciousness, can intend the same thing.[27] This is the fundamental act by which our world gets spatially arranged because if the different sensory places yielded by our sense organs about a place could not be "attended to together all at once" (James 1981, 822), then the spatial field of view would not have a figure-ground structure.

But, secondly, we not only add together spaces that are intuitively present *within* a field of view, we also add present spatial fields to fields not present. This addition gives us a sense of space as an infinitely continuous unit. Contra Kant, James does not think that we have an intuition of space as an infinitely continuous unit. He agrees with Strawson and Evans that we only have a conception of it. But he argues that the content of this conception has *experiential origins*.

Conceptions for James are 'teleological instruments' that help us, in light of our interests, to practically handle the sensory much-at-once-ness. Conceptions help us practically handle the much-at-once-ness by *identifying* items that concern us, *discriminating* them from other items, and *grouping* them with similar items that are not now present. "Each act of conception results from our attention singling out some one part of the

---

[27] For more on this, see chapter 3 of Cobb-Stevens 1974.

mass of matter-for-thought which the world presents, and holding fast to it, without confusion ... [T]he conceptual function requires, to be complete, that the thought should not only say 'I mean this', but also say 'I don't mean that'" (James 1981, 436–437). The identification through differentiation that concepts enact can be brought about in multiple ways: by enumerating an item's necessary and sufficient characteristics, by making explicit its practical effects, or it can be done with "no *connotation*, or a very minimum of connotation attached." Simply calling something "'this' or 'that' will suffice" (James 1981, 437). The key point for conceptualization does not have to do with connotation but with time and memory: to be considered a conceptual singling out of an item, the singling out has to be held fast to over some amount of time. For with the "belief that things recur in time and that the same reality can fill both *now* and *then*, we have already made a good step onward towards the possibility of translating our experience into conceptual form" (James 1988a, 285). The final step needed for this translation is connecting, in imagination, a temporally recurring reality to similar realities not now present. We take this step because, once again, we have both a practical and an aesthetic interest in understanding the *kinds* of things that can recur in time. For by picking out "the items which concern us, and connecting them with others far away, which we say 'belong' with them, we are able to make out definite threads of sequence and tendency; to foresee particular liabilities and get ready for them; and to enjoy simplicity and harmony instead of what was chaos" (James 1979, 95 and 1981, 1231n).

We already know how we identify and discriminate spatial positions and relations. But how do we gain the ability to grasp that the same spatial reality can 'fill both now and then', and how do we connect the space that is present here to spaces that are 'far away' and so not present? Here is James's explanation. We experience successive fields of view through movement. The "original sensible totals" given by our sensations are "united with other totals ... through the agency of our own movements, carrying our senses from one part of space to another" (James 1981, 461). In moving through space, we experience the fact that different spatial fields are *limited* yet *overlapping*. They are limited because even though their margin is vague, to perceive one field entails that another goes out of view. They are overlapping because an object that we intend as the same can exist in both fields. For example, in one spatial field, the same object can be to the left and in another to the right, at ground level in one field and at eye level in another, the focus of one's attention in one field and at the fringe of another. Here is how James puts it:

> Every single visual sensation or "field of view" is limited. To get to a new field of view for our object the old one must disappear. But the disappearance may be only partial. Let the first field of view be A B C. If we carry our attention to the limit C, it ceases to be the limit, and becomes the center of the field, and beyond it appear fresh parts where there were none before: A B C changes, in short to C D E. But although the parts A B are lost to sight, yet their image abides in the memory; and if we think of our first object A B C has having existed or as still existing at all, we must think of it as it was originally presented, namely, as spread out from C in one direction just as C D E is spread out in another. A B and D E can never coalesce in one place (as they could were they objects of different senses) because they can never be perceived at once: we must lose one to see the other. (James 1981, 823)

But our grasp that the same spatial reality can recur in time, and of space as an infinitely continuous unit, requires more than movement and retention of past fields, it also requires the ability to *reverse our attention* and bring back past objects. "We can usually recover anything lost from sight by moving our attention and our eyes back in its direction; and through these constant changes every field of seen things comes at last to be thought of as always having a fringe of *other things possible to be seen* spreading in all directions round about it" (James 1981, 823). This ability operates within and between fields of view. If a field of view is comprised of A B C, we can focus on A, making B and C horizontal, and we can then focus on B, making A and C horizontal, and then back to A, etc. When we change our field of view to C D E from A B C, in the process losing A and B, but gaining D and E, we can, at will, reverse our attention and regain A and B. We can then reverse the reversal and regain D and E, and so on. This is what gives us a sense that the spatial realities A B and D E can recur at different times, and that A and B continue to exist when we perceive C D E, and that D and E continue to exist when we perceive A B C. In light of this, "we conceive that their juxtaposed spaces must make a larger space. A B C + C D E must, in short, be imagined to exist in the form of A B C D E or not imagined at all" (James 1981, 823). This is the basis of our conception of space as an infinitely continuous unit.

The Experience of Objectivity

James often refers to Kierkegaard's idea that we live forward but understand backwards.[28] This means several things for James, but in the context

---

[28] See, for example, James 1976, 65n and 121, and James 1975a, 107.

of our discussion it refers to the unity and continuity of the stream of thought. On the one hand, we live forward because the stream of thought is pregnant with expectation insofar as it is characterized by an incessant alteration between the transitive and substantive parts of the stream of consciousness – which is an alteration between relatively empty experiences involving a sense of what is to come and future experiences in which this sense is either fulfilled or frustrated, and experiences that are relatively vague and indistinct and experiences that are relatively more clear and distinct. Here is how James puts it:

> The rush of our thought forward through its fringes is the everlasting peculiarity of its life. We realize this life as something always off its balance, something in transition, something that shoots out of a darkness through a dawn into the brightness that we know to be the dawn fulfilled. In the very midst of the alteration our experience comes as one continuous fact. "Yes," we say at the moment of full brightness, *this* is what I meant. No, we feel at the moment of the dawning, this is not yet the meaning, there is more to come. In every crescendo of sensation, in every effort to recall, in every process toward the satisfaction of desire, this succession of an emptiness and fullness that have reference to each other and are one flesh is the essence of the phenomenon. In every hindrance of desire the sense of ideal presence of what is absent in fact, of an absent, in a word, which the only function of the present is to *mean*, is even more notoriously there. And in the movement of thoughts not ordinarily classed as involving desire, we have the same phenomenon. When I say *Socrates is mortal*, the moment *Socrates* is incomplete; it falls forward through the *is* which is pure movement, into the *mortal*, which indeed bare mortal on the tongue, but for the mind, is *that mortal*, the *mortal Socrates*, at last satisfactorily disposed and told off. (James 1978, 77)

We understand backwards, on the other hand, because the objects of our thought get more and more complex due to the fact that the stream of thought as it presses into the future is sensibly continuous and involves a backward looking synthesis in which we come to know more and more about the objects of our acquaintance. This knowledge-about, in turn, informs the expectations that guide us in our forward living, and so our experiential encounter with future objects of acquaintance. As such, "our mental reaction on every given thing is really a resultant of our experience of the whole world up to that date" (James 1981, 228). The relation of acquaintance that we have with objects is therefore not Given, but is funded by past experience.

What I am going to argue is that our grasp of objectivity, our sense that all things continue to exist even when unperceived, has its origin in the fact that these two temporal dynamics of consciousness imbricate our spatial consciousness. Because of this, our consciousness of space is always a

An Experiential Account of Objectivity

consciousness of both presence and absence, not only in intuitively given spatial fields but also in our conception of space as an infinitely continuous spatial unit.

An account in which the consciousness of presence necessarily coexists with that of absence can be found in James's 1894 paper "The Knowing of Things Together." There, James considers the question of how our thought can be of an object that is not present. In accord with the view developed in "The Function of Cognition," he rejects the idea that a thought is of a *reality*, of a physical thing outside, through its being intentionally inexistent in the thought (see James 1978, 73). The thought is not 'self-transcendent' to the reality in the sense that the reality is present *in* the thought. But while he disowns this notion of 'presence in absence' when it comes to the relation of a thought to a reality, he *accepts* the idea when applied to the relation of thoughts to other earlier thoughts, which, as we saw in the section on 'Unity and Objectivity', comprise part of its *object*.

The undergoing of a single thought involves a kind of presence in absence because "past and future are already parts of the least experience that can really be" (James 1978, 78).[29] In other words, the content of single thoughts involve a feeling of what has just been and a feeling what is to come, even though what has just been and what is to come are not strictly speaking present *in* the thought. The thought involves

---

[29] In "The Knowing of Things Together" (1894), James famously changes his mind as to whether thoughts can have parts or not. But I think that there is much less than meets the eye here. On the one hand, in *The Principles*, James already admits that there is a way to view thoughts as having parts.

> I know that there are readers whom nothing can convince that the thought of a complex object has not as many parts as are discriminated in the object itself. We, then, let the word parts pass. Only observe that these parts are not the separate "ideas" of traditional psychology. No one of them can live out of that particular thought ... In a sense a soap-bubble has parts; it is the sum of juxtaposed triangles. But these triangles are not separate realities; neither are the "parts" of the thought separate realities. Touch the bubble and the triangles are no more. Dismiss the thought and out go its parts. You can no more make a new thought out of the "ideas" that have once served than you can make a new bubble out of triangles. Each bubble, each thought, is a fresh organic unity, *sui generis*. (James 1981, 268–269n)

In "The Knowing of Things Together," James said this:

> I am willing ... henceforth that mental contents should be called complex, just as their objects are, and this even in psychology. Not because their parts are separable, as the parts of objects are; not because they have an eternal or quasi-eternal individual existence, like the parts of objects; for the various "fields" of which they are parts are integers, existentially, and their parts only live as long as *they* live. Still *in* them, we can call parts, parts. (James 1978, 88)

While James here admits that thoughts can have parts, he is still keen to avoid the idea that parts are mental atoms that have a self-sufficient existence. The stress on a thought being an organic whole is kept. It's simply that, from a *descriptive* point of view, we can identify within such organic wholes various parts, for example, its time-parts.

them because these absent feelings and their content are part of the thought's complex object. So within a thought we have an experience of self-transcendency, of knowing-about things that are absent (feelings of the past and future), alongside something that is strictly speaking present (the object with which we are presently acquainted). "Here, then, inside the minimal pulse of experience," we have "that absolute and essential self-transcendency which we swept away as an illusion when we sought it between a content taken as a whole and a supposed objective thing outside," and the "original of presence in absence" (James 1978, 77).

But the conclusion that presence and absence are "known together" applies not only when an object is temporal but also when it is comprised of things experienced simultaneously. "The field of view, the chord of music, the glass of lemonade ... the gist of the matter is always the same – it is always knowing-together. You cannot separate the consciousness of one part for that of all the rest. What is given is pooled and mutual" (James 1978, 78). In other words, just as one cannot, in a single pulse of consciousness, separate the consciousness of the present from the consciousness of past and future, one cannot – if we focus on the spatial case – separate in a field of view the consciousness of one spatial part from another, separate focus from fringe, or the vividly present from what is horizontal, vague, and receding into absence.

What James calls the 'field of view' is not equivalent to the vague spatial plenums made present by sensory pulses of consciousness. Rather, the field of view is an object of spatial perception. Here is how James describes it in one of his unpublished lectures on psychology:

> That field is an experience of physical things immediately present, of "more" physical things "always there" "beyond" the margin, of my personal self "there," and of thoughts and feelings belonging to that self ... Of the various items some, as fully realized, are "sufficients"; others, the physical things "beyond" ... come as insufficients – they connect themselves with the marginal "more." (James 1988b, 256)[30]

---

[30] James also says in this passage that the field involves experience of "'other' thoughts and feelings connected with what I call 'your' personal selves" (James 1988b, 256). Here, I only focus on the 'physical more' beyond the margin and not this 'mental more'. For there is a critical difference between them: the 'physical more' beyond the margin is usually retrievable through movement and a reversal of our attention, while this is not the case with the thoughts and feelings of other selves. In this respect, the account of the experience of objectivity that I give in this chapter is incomplete. In Chapter 6, I discuss a pragmatic account of objectivity that builds in intersubjectivity.

It is critical to see that for James what is physically beyond the margin is *not* something "beyond the *experience*."[31] Rather, the "'more' is more than the vividly presented or felt; the 'beyond' is beyond the center of the field" (James 1988b, 256). The marginal more *is a part of consciousness*, but it is not *represented as an object* in consciousness. Rather, it is the 'free water', the transitive feelings of relation and tendency that make up the vague halo or horizon of any given state of consciousness.

Due to our ability to shift our attention, there is within a field of view constant interaction between the marginal more and the vividly present. We make explicit the field's vague halo of relations, in the process making what was vague vivid and what was vivid vague and marginal. Here there is constant movement from insufficient to sufficient, from emptiness to fullness, and vice-versa. The experience of absence in a transitive experience anticipates being fulfilled, and the experience of presence or fullness is one that is pregnant with expectations of future emptiness. We could say that, through time, absence and presence *haunt* the experience of each other. It is not as if we go from a complete consciousness of emptiness to a completely fulfilled consciousness. It is rather that, as we move our attention through a field of view, we *simultaneously* experience something vividly present and something vague and receding beyond the margin, but in different ratios as we move from fullness to emptiness and back again. In this way, emptiness and fullness, absence and presence, are always 'known-together'.

But we are aware not just of spatial fields of view but also of the fact that these fields are part of an infinitely continuous spatial unit. The grasp of objectivity, grasp that all things continue to exist even when unperceived, comes about because the 'knowing-together' of presence and absence applies not only to intuitively given fields of view but also to our conception of space as an infinitely continuous unit. As we saw in the last section, this conception has two experiential conditions.

First, in moving through space, we can experience the same object as parts of different fields of view. In one field, the object is vividly present; in another, it is part of the vague marginal more, which calls on us to make it present. So the emptiness–fullness structure applies not just to changes of attention within a field of view but also to our experience of temporally successive spatial fields. We experience our present spatial field as related to wider fields that are not present because our fulfilled experience of an object in one field and our empty experience of it in another have

---

[31] For a James-inspired account of the 'marginal more' of consciousness, see Gurwitsch 1985.

'reference to each other and are one flesh'. Second, we can at will reverse our attention and recover something that has been lost from sight in a prior field of view. This allows us to grasp that objects 'beyond the margin' not just of our current spatial field but also spatial fields not present are still available to us. Even though they are not present now, they are *available to be made present* by our moving and attending to them. This is what gives us a sense that things that are not perceived *are still perceivable*. This is the experiential basis of our grasp that objects continue to exist even though unperceived.

But notice that both of these features of our experience of successive spatial fields – i.e., that it has an emptiness–fullness structure and that we can bring back things seen in prior fields – depend on our ability to intend, and know that we intend, the same object through different experiences of it. If this ability were not in place, then there would not be single objects experienced as the same through different fields of view, giving us a sense of their interconnection, and there would be no recovery of anything from a past field of view, but just the continual discovery of new things in new fields. So our grasp of objectivity depends not only on our knowing presence and absence together in and between spatial fields, but also on our ability to build up a view of the world in which, like 'spiders on the webs they weave', we go over and gain an enriched understanding of the spatial properties and relations of the objects that pass in and out of presence. It is now easy to see why for James this is 'the most important of all the features of our mental structure'. For it is what underlies our grasp of the concept of objectivity, and so the possibility of objective thought.

CHAPTER 5

Pragmatism, Experience, and Answerability

Introduction

This book is primarily interested in two questions about objectivity. The first concerns our *grasp* of the concept of objectivity, the concept of a world of objects and events that continue to exist when not perceived or experienced. The second concerns the question of whether the content of the empirical thoughts and judgments undertaken in light of this grasp are *in fact* constrained by, and answerable to, the mind-independent world. The last chapter was meant to address the first question from a pragmatic perspective. I tried to show how for James the content of the concept of objectivity is constituted in experience. But, to motivate the second question of objectivity, we could pose this question to James: why think that an account of objectivity that traces it back to experience, even understood in James's robust way, can go beyond what a subject *takes* in experience to be objective? Why think that the thoughts and judgments that we develop on the basis of experience are, in fact, answerable to the way things are rather than just to how we experience them to be?[1]

In my view, James, in and after *The Principles*, develops some resources to answer this question. The view of James as a subjectivist who completely disregards the constraint on thought by the world is in my view not accurate.[2] I am not, however, going to focus on James in the final two chapters. I am instead going to examine Dewey's approach to the second question of objectivity because I think that his philosophy is centrally concerned with it, with the question of how thought, via experience, can be constrained by, and rationally responsive to, the way things are. This thesis cuts against the interpretive grain, for as many interpreters of Dewey

---
[1] I agree with Sacks 2000, 125–126, when he argues that James's account of thought in *The Principles* cannot by itself answer the second question of objectivity. I don't agree with him, however, that a revamped neo-Kantian view can.
[2] For my argument to this effect, see Levine 2014.

point out, he is critical of the idea that there is a ready-made antecedent reality to which our thought corresponds, and he claims that objects of knowledge are constructed rather than discovered by our reflective thought processes. For many interpreters, this signals that Dewey rejects the core realist idea that thought is constrained by, and answerable to, a world that is independent of it.[3]

In this chapter, I want to resist this reading of Dewey, but not by examining the details of Dewey's engagement with early twentieth century realists and idealists, or by examining his account of the object of knowledge. I come back to these topics in the next chapter. Rather, here I want to show that these interpretations do not properly grasp the *context* in which Dewey arrives at his view. To illuminate this context, I examine Dewey's early work on logic, specifically the transition from his early Hegelian logic to the instrumental logic that stands at the heart of his experimental empiricism.[4] This may seem a strange place to look for an account of thought's answerability to the world, but it is in fact here, in this transition, that the contours of his account stand out most clearly.[5]

In the Introduction to this book I said that to understand the connection between objectivity, thought, and experience, we need to go beyond the account of experience found in McDowell's minimal empiricism to the more robust account of experience found in the pragmatic tradition. In this chapter, I begin to cash this thought out. The account of objectivity that one finds in Dewey's experimental empiricism is motivated by his attempt to get beyond a 'seesaw' that he sees taking as place between idealism/coherentism and a kind of empiricism that accepts the Myth of the Given. His strategy depends on developing an account of experience in which it can stand as a 'tribunal for thought' by being independent of, yet homogeneous with, thought.[6] The motivation for Dewey's theoretical strategy is therefore strikingly similar to McDowell's in *Mind and World*, though they end up in quite different places. They do so because Dewey expands his account of experience to include bodily doings: experience is not just what we undergo, or even what we undergo due to an

---

[3] Such interpreters include McGilvary, Cohen, Russell, Santayana, Murphy, and more recently Misak.
[4] In calling Dewey's empiricism an experimental empiricism, I follow Tiles 2010.
[5] Dewey's Hegelian influenced logic can be found in his papers "Is Logic a Dualistic Science?" (1890), "The Logic of Verification" (1890), "The Present Position of Logical Theory" (1891), and "How Do Concepts Arise from Percepts?" (1891). His instrumental logic was first outlined in the four papers that comprise Dewey's contribution to the 1903 *Studies in Logical Theory*, included in *Essays in Experimental Logic*, and elaborated in the rest of papers found in *Essays in Experimental Logic* (1916) and *The Influence of Darwin on Philosophy and Other Essays in Contemporary Thought* (1910).
[6] The only paper I have seen that motivates Dewey's thinking in this way is Brodsky 1969.

actualization of conceptual capacities; it is what we undergo due to our simultaneous acting on, and being acted upon, by the world. In this chapter, I aim to show, based on this expansion, that Dewey's experimental empiricism is not a Promethean philosophy that eschews external constraint but, rather, a position that tries to account for it within an action-oriented context.

Hegel, Logic, and Science

It is often thought that Dewey denies that the question of the mind's answerability to the world is one that needs to be answered. For even in his early work, Dewey argued that the dualism on which this question is based – i.e., that between "subject and object, mind and matter" – is expressive of "points of view and of practical conflicts having their sources in the very nature of modern life" (EW 5, 6). If we can get at the roots of these practical conflicts through a kind of historical-therapeutic critique, we can liquidate the significance of this dualism for both our practical and theoretical lives and thereby stop worrying about how the mind is answerable to the world. But while Dewey often does pursue a historicist-therapeutic strategy to get past dualism, this strategy, in my view, rests on a prior *logical* strategy. For Dewey

> never for a moment denied the *prima facie* working distinction between "ideas," "thoughts," "meanings" and "facts," "existences," "the environment," nor the necessity of control of meaning by facts ... What is denied is not the genuineness of the problem of the terms in which it is stated, but the reality and value of the orthodox interpretation. What is insisted upon is the relative, instrumental, or working character of the distinction – that it *is* a *logical* distinction, instituted and maintained in the interests of intelligence with all that intelligence imports in exercise of the life functions. (Dewey 2007, 120–121)

The fact that the distinction between idea and fact, thought and existence, is a logical distinction is a difficult one for the contemporary reader to understand, for two reasons. First, how can logic have anything to do with the distinction between ideas and facts, much less the control of one by the other, when logic, post-Frege, is concerned with formal deductive systems?[7] Second, how can a logical distinction be *instituted* when logical forms are a priori, and how can it be *relative* when logical

---

[7] For excellent accounts of how Dewey's logic relates to post-Fregian logic, and of the place of logic in Dewey's thought overall, see Sleeper 1986 and Burke 1994.

forms are necessary and universal?[8] Dewey's central argument in logical theory aims to cut through both of these questions. For he thinks that the main error made by logical theory is that it categorically distinguishes logical form and matter.[9] While he accepts that we can make a local distinction between logical form and matter, he does not think, in general, "that thought has a nature of its own independent of facts or subject-matter; that this thought, *per se*, has certain forms, and that these forms are not forms which the facts themselves take, varying with the facts, but are rigid frames, into which the facts are to be set" (EW 3, 128). If logical forms are the forms that the facts themselves take, they are not a priori; if they vary with the facts, they are not universal; and if they are not rigid frames into which the facts fit, they are not necessary. How does he articulate this thought?

Dewey calls the logic that thinks that thought has a nature independent of its subject matter 'scholastic logic'. This is a 'logic of argument', which aims at self-consistency, not truth. Dewey, in contrast, thinks of logic as the 'logic of science', one that "has for its essential problem the consideration of the various typical methods and guiding principles which thought assumes in its effort to detect, master, and report fact" (EW 3, 126). Logic aims at truth not in the sense that it directly grasps fact but in the sense that it is helps us regiment, understand, and improve the rules of inference internal to the stages of inquiry so that *it* can better grasp fact. So like Peirce, Dewey thinks that logic considers all forms of inference that aim at truth, including induction and abduction, not only deductive inference. As Dewey will put it later, logic is an inquiry into inquiry.

If logic is primarily the logic of science rather than argument then, Dewey thinks, the "especial problem of logic, as the theory of scientific method, is the relation of fact and thought to each other, of reality and ideas" (EW 3, 126). Both empiricist and Kantian accounts of logic can't make sense of this relation, according to Dewey. Empiricist logic – for example, that of Mill's – is an advance on scholastic logic insofar as it thinks that logic is concerned with synthetic and not just deductive inference. But in thinking that the thought-forms found in synthetic inferences are applied *to* what is given by experience, rather than being actualized within experience, it excludes thought "from all share in the

---

[8] There is a third question that is often asked here: how can logical distinctions and relations have anything to do with the life-function, for does that not give rise to psychologism? See Chapter 6, note 14.

[9] In taking this to be the central point of Dewey's logic, and perhaps the keystone for his thinking generally, I follow Sleeper 1986.

gathering of material. The result is that this material, having no intrinsic thought side, shrinks into a more or less accidental association of more or less shifting and transitory mental states" (EW 3, 131). Kant agrees with the empiricist that what is given to thought is accidental and transitory sensory material. But for him, unlike Mill, logic is not an empirical science that identifies psychological patterns of reasoning that we, in fact, happen to employ. Rather, logic is concerned with universal and necessary a priori forms that do not come from experience, though they apply to it. "Kant never dreams ... of questioning the existence of a special faculty of thought with its own peculiar and fixed forms. He states and restates that thought in itself exists apart from fact and occupies itself with fact given to it from without" (EW 3, 135). So in Kant: "we have two elements, both existing in isolation, and yet both useless for all purposes of knowledge." However, if we "[c]ombine them ... presto, there is science" (EW 3, 135).

Now, in one way, this dualist reading of Kant is naïve, for it does not seem to recognize that for transcendental logic, unlike general logic, logical forms, via the pure forms of intuition, are not isolated but essentially object related – even if still a priori. But Dewey intimates in this paper, and spells out in others, a reading of Kant in which there is, as it were, two Kants: a dualist Kant who can't make sense of science, and a Kant who in positing the object-relatedness of logical forms begins a line of thought that leads past dualism – a line of thought developed and completed by Hegel.[10] It is the dualist "Kant who does violence to science, while Hegel (I speak of his essential method and not of any particular result) is the quintessence of the scientific spirit" (EW 3: 134).

Hegel is the quintessence of the scientific spirit because for him there is "no special apart faculty of thought belonging to and operated by a mind existing separate from the outer world" (EW 3, 137).[11] He therefore rejects the idea that there is a categorical distinction between a priori and a posteriori, logical form and matter. Thought on Hegel's account is intentional, always beyond itself, immersed in a subject matter. Indeed, Hegel has the view that "all thought is objective, that relations of thought are

---

[10] For this two-Kant reading, see "Kant and Philosophical Method" (EW 1) and "Experience and Objective Idealism" (MW 3).

[11] It is important to note that while Dewey in his 1886 papers on philosophical method, "The Psychological Standpoint" and "Psychology as Philosophical Method," as well as in his 1897 *Psychology*, was a partisan of so-called neo-Hegelianism, in the papers I am looking at, he rigorously distinguishes Hegel from neo-Hegelianism, which he thinks is really a kind of neo-Kantianism that has not genuinely overcome 'apart-thought'. Here I agree with Good 2006. For three of the many instances where Dewey makes this distinction, see EW 3, 97, 137 and Dewey 2007, 66.

forms of the objective world; [and] that the process of thinking is simply following the movement of the subject matter itself" (Dewey 2010, 96). But sometimes it loses its hold on a subject matter because contradiction arises within it (the subject matter). In this case thought is forced to reflect on the form of thought that has been used to get hold of the subject matter so as to see how it is and is not adequate to it. But this reflection is not on a priori forms resident in a distinct faculty of thought, but on relations of thought *arrived at in and through experience itself*. Logical forms are not

> separate forms. Relations of thought are ... the typical forms of meaning which the subject-matter takes in its various progressive stages of being understood. And this is what *a priori* means from a Hegelian standpoint. It is not some element *in* knowledge; some addition of thought to experience. It is experience itself in its skeleton, in the main features of its framework. (EW 3, 137)

For Hegel, what is a priori is what is relatively enduring *in* experience; it is not brought to experience by thought which has its seat elsewhere. Here we should be reminded of James's idea that relations, logical and otherwise, are not imposed on a sensory manifold by a subject situated outside of experience, but are found in experience as already imbricating the sensory stream.[12] While these relations are *constitutive* for how the framework of experience is structured at a particular stage of its progress, insofar as they are found in experience there is no a priori basis on which to hold them to be universal or necessary.[13] They can be changed if our ability to think the object of thought in a coherent way necessitates it.

To posit, as Kant does, "*a priori* elements somehow entering into the fact from without and controlling it" is, according to Dewey, "to give up the very spirit of science."

> For if science means anything, it is that our ideas, our judgments may in some degree reflect and report the fact itself. Science means, on the one hand, that thought is free to attack and get hold of its subject matter, and, on the other, that fact is free to break through into thought ... Apriorism of this sort seems like an effort to cramp the freedom both of intelligence and of fact, to bring them under the yoke of fixed, external forms. (EW 3, 136)

To posit a priori thought-forms that are universal and necessary is to give up the spirit of science because it means that we somehow know, in

---

[12] Dewey thought Hegel and James were united in this view. See his May 6, 1891, letter to James quoted in Good 2006, 146.
[13] We could say, using contemporary language, that here we have a concept of the *relative a priori*. See Friedman 1999.

advance, that the inquiries or learning processes that we engage in based on these forms could never yield results requiring the revision of those very forms. But to attack and get hold of a subject matter is to develop concepts and categories *out of* the subject matter itself, concepts and categories that in their content are answerable *to* the subject matter, which requires that the facts can break through into thought – i.e., can lead us to revise our concepts and categories in light of what has been learned about the facts. But we should not think that the facts break through to thought by being Given, for the way that the facts are *taken* is predetermined by the concepts and categories that one already has. In this way thought can get hold of its subject matter. The "facts by which [a] theory" or conceptual scheme "is to be verified or disproved are not a fixed, unchangeable, body; if a theory gets its verification through the facts, the facts get a transformed and enlarged meaning through the theory ... Both idea and 'facts' are flexible, and verification is the process of mutual adjustment, of organic interaction" (EW 3, 87). Scientific method is the process by which this mutual adjustment is arrived at, and Science (*Wissenchaft*) is the systematic body of knowledge that is the result of this process having been set free.[14]

Dualism, Coherentism, and the Myth of the Given

The critique of Kantian dualism that underlies Dewey's early Hegelianism also stands at the heart of the essays that comprise *Studies in Logical Theory* and *Essays in Experimental Logic* more widely. But in this context the critique leads to instrumentalism, not idealism.

Dewey's critique of Kantian Dualism is based on the question, familiar from German Idealism, of how, once we separate thought from its matter, they can ever come to be related again:

> How can thought relate itself to the fragmentary sensations, impressions, feelings, which, in their contrast with and disparity from the workings of constitutive thought, mark it off from the latter; and which in their connection with its products give the cue to reflective thinking? Here we have ... the same insoluble question of the reference of thought-activity to a wholly indeterminate unrationalized, independent prior existence. (Dewey 2007, 67)[15]

---

[14] For an account of science that notes both of these sides of the concept, see Dewey's paper "Logical Conditions of a Scientific Treatment of Morality" (MW 3).
[15] I have de-italicized a few words of this passage. In this passage, Dewey directs the dilemma at Lotze, whose *Logic* is the main critical target of *Studies in Logical Theory*. See Lotze 1887. However, the problem that he finds in Lotze that gives rise to this dilemma is exactly the same one that he finds in

Sensation, on the dualist account, "is given *to* thought ... free from all inferring, judging, relating influence." Sensation is "the immediate, the irreducible" (Dewey 2007, 73). But if sensations are truly *independent* of thought, are prior existences free of all inferring, judging, or relating, how can they be *homogeneous* enough with thought so as to solicit, or give the cue for, the right or correct thought? And if they are homogeneous enough with thought to solicit it, how can we say that they exist prior to thought, as is necessary if they are to constrain thought from the outside? Here we have two explanatory desiderata that pull apart: if one stresses independence, as seems necessary to explain constraint by the world, then one can't make sense of homogeneity, and if one stresses homogeneity, as is necessary to explain the solicitation of the correct thought, then one can't make sense of independence.

Dewey argues that if one tries to meet these desiderata on dualist grounds one will be led into "the same continuous seesaw" (Dewey 2007, 67) between idealism/coherentism and the Myth of the Given that McDowell identifies in *Mind and World*. Here is how Dewey characterizes the seesaw. The coherentist, on the one hand, thinks that because "thought is separate from the matter of experience," that "its validity is wholly its own private business" (Dewey 2007, 85). If validity is the private business of thought, then we don't need an account of how sensation solicits thought, for if only thought can be a reason for thought then sensation cannot rationally bear on thought at all. The problem with this view is that "every one knows that ideas may be self-consistent, and yet untrue, or even highly absurd" (EW 3, 83). So if we are to have a "test of objectivity" for our ideas, then we must move beyond "the thoroughly unsatisfactory and formal one of their own mutual consistency" (Dewey 2007, 84). To have such a test, we might seesaw to the Myth of the Given, where thought is directly constrained by "the original matter given in the impressions themselves." This at least seems to give us "an objective and external test by which the reality of thought's operations may be tried; a given idea is verified or found false according to its measure of correspondence with the matter of experience as such." But, in fact,

> now we are no better off. The original independence and heterogeneity of impressions and of thought is so great that there is no way to compare the results of the latter with the former ... The standard or test of objectivity is so thoroughly external that by original definition it is wholly outside the

Kant on the dualist reading. For a comparison of Lotze with Kant on the dualism issue, see Dewey 2007, 76.

realm of thought. How can thought compare meanings with existences? (Dewey 2007, 84)

In other words, if sensations are *existences* that are given to thought from the outside, then we have no way of understanding how they can so much as bear on the *meanings* that comprise thought, which is necessary to verify them.

The partisan of the Given tries to overcome this problem by holding that sense impressions are given to thought free of all inference and relation, and so are independent, yet are still intrinsically meaningful and so able to rationally bear on thought, to justify it. As Given, impressions are immediate existences that as meaningful are nonetheless empirical knowings – or items that can justify such knowings. As such, our thoughts can be tested or verified by comparing them with the facts directly and immediately made manifest by these impressions. Now impressions and thought are sufficiently homogeneous to allow for the comparison needed for correspondence as the test of objectivity.

Dewey's critique of this view, which is the basis of his lifelong critique of the correspondence theory of truth, depends on pointing to the temporal nature of thought and inquiry. If the facts are available because impressions are Given, then the facts are *already* known. But if "we already know the facts, it certainly seems a waste of energy and of time to ... elaborate ideas simply for the sake of going through the meaningless process of seeing whether or not they agree with a truth already perfectly known" (EW 3, 84). It is clear that we only develop ideas not when we are "in possession of the truth," but "when we are in search of it" (EW 3, 84). In this case, what is available to one is not the "real facts but the fact as they *seem* to be" (EW 3, 84). But then the facts cannot serve as a standard to test our ideas after all, for "it would certainly be a curious operation to test out theory by a standard whose discrediting had led to the formation of the theory" (EW 3, 84). Dewey sums up the problem thusly:

> If the standard by which we are to test our ideas is the real fact, the actual truth, then, by the necessity of the case, the standard is unknown; if the standard is facts as they seem to be, as already apprehended, it is worthless. The only standard of value is out of reach; the attainable standard is no standard at all. In either case, verification would seem to be an impossible process. (EW 3, 84)

If the standard by which we are to test our ideas against the facts is out of reach or worthless, then perhaps the standard is internal to thought. Here we seesaw back to coherentism. But that has already been shown to fail to account for the control of ideas by facts and so, for the mind's answerability, the world. So now we are stuck in McDowell's seemingly interminable oscillation.

The Tribunal of Experience: The Conceptual Account

In *Mind and World*, McDowell famously escapes this oscillation by articulating a minimal empiricism in which experience stands as a tribunal for our empirical thought. I want to canvas this view as it illuminates Dewey's alternative account of how experience can be a tribunal.

Experience is a tribunal for thought because it is the means by which the layout of reality is able to exert a rational influence on what we think. To be a tribunal experience must meet the two desiderata enumerated previously: experience must be independent of thought so that it can constrain it from the outside, yet it must also be homogeneous enough with it so as to be able to stand as a reason for it.[16] But it is hard to think these two desiderata together. One straightforward way to get constraint into the picture is to see experience as bringing objects into view through the direct causal affection of our senses. Because we have no control over how the world affects our senses, and so no control over the sense impressions we thereby undergo, we can be sure that experience is not the product of our thought and cognitive attitudes. But to be a reason for an empirical thought or judgment requires that experience be more than undergone sense impressions, for experience can only stand as a reason for our thinking that something is so-and-so in a normative context. In other words, to judge that there is a pink ice cube in one's vicinity *because* one has an experience of a pink ice cube requires – if the 'because' is rational and not merely causal – that the experience must be able to *speak in favor* of there being a pink ice cube in the vicinity. Sense impressions that are merely the product of natural transactions do not have this power. To think that they do is to fall prey to the Myth of the Given, the empiricist myth that immediately Given nonconceptual sense impressions can by themselves justify or be reasons for thought independently of language learning, concept acquisition, the development of habits, etc.

One way to avoid this myth – the way taken by Rorty, Brandom, and Davidson – is to say that sense experience *causally* constrains the mind, but does not *rationally* constrain it. As Davidson puts it, "although sensation

---

[16] For illuminating takes on these two desiderata, see DeVries and Triplett 2002, xxxvi–xxxvii, and Sachs 2014, 15.

plays a crucial role in the causal process that connects belief with the world, it is a mistake to think that it plays an epistemological role in determining the content of those beliefs" (Davidson 1988, 46). It is a mistake because for it to play an epistemological role "requires that both relata have propositional content" (Davidson 1997c, 136). In light of the fact that sensations don't have such contents, Rorty, Davidson, and Brandom accept a coherentism in which "nothing can count as a reason for holding a belief except another belief" (Davidson 1983, 141). But then a natural question emerges: how does causal constraint by the world *relate* to the rational constraint on belief provided by one's other beliefs? As we have seen, Rorty, Davidson, and Brandom all argue that this is a question we ought not feel compelled to answer, for to do so is to cross a line that ought not to be crossed, namely between reasons and causes.[17] But if one can't answer this question then, McDowell argues, one has no account of how thinking is not 'spinning in its own void' – i.e., no account of how it is rationally answerable to something outside of itself. In light of this mystery one is tempted to oscillate back to the Myth of the Given, which at least accounts for constraint. But then one again has the problem of understanding how sense impressions can stand as reasons.

McDowell argues for the idea that experience can be a tribunal in this way: experience is independent of thought in the sense that it is brought about by the affection of worldly objects, not by thought. It is homogeneous with thought, however, because what is brought about in this way is an "an actualization, in sensory consciousness, of conceptual capacities" (McDowell 2009b, 127). For something to be perceptually present, conceptual capacities must be drawn on *within* sensory consciousness prior to judgment. The conceptual capacities drawn upon are not innate, but acquired in the normal course of their coming to maturity. Because this is so, experience, which inextricably involves their actualization, is not Given. Nonetheless, it can be a tribunal. The actualization of conceptual capacities in experience provides them with propositional content. Experience is an experience of things as thus and so, and judgment is a noninferential endorsement of this content. Because sensory experiences and judgments have the same propositional content, an experience of a pink ice cube is able to stand as a reason for one to think that there is a pink ice cube in the vicinity. But how then are experiences differentiated from thought so as to provide constraint? They are differentiated because in

---

[17] One can also see this strategy at work in Price, for example in chapter 2 of Price 2013, where he recommends that we keep i-representations and e-representations separate.

experience we are 'saddled with' content – meaning that the actualization of conceptual-capacities in sensory consciousness is out of a subject's control – while the endorsement of this content in thought or judgment is a rational self-conscious activity within their control.

In his later papers, most importantly "Avoiding the Myth of the Given," McDowell relaxes the homogeneity and strengthens the independence requirement. States of sensory consciousness are no longer seen as having propositional but *intuitional* content. Although sense-experience is still seen to involve operations of the Understanding, such operations actualize in sensory consciousness a form of togetherness that results in a type of intuitive content. This content, though not propositional, is conceptual in the sense that "it is already suitable to be the content associated with a discursive activity" – even "if it is not – at least not yet – actually so associated" (McDowell 2009c, 264). So intuitive content is conceptual in the sense that it has a togetherness that makes it *amenable* to be the content of an act in which concepts are in fact actualized in a judgment, even if such concepts are not so actualized.[18] Because experience has intuitive content rather than propositional content made explicit by discursive activity, it is independent of thought and judgment. But because sense-experience already has a content that displays a form of togetherness that makes it amenable to being associated with a content made explicit by discourse, it is homogeneous enough with thought or judgment to be a reason for one to think that something is thus and so.

Dewey also avoids the seesaw between coherentism and the Myth of the Given by positing an account of experience in which it is a tribunal due to the fact that it involves both receptivity and spontaneity. And like McDowell, Dewey has two versions of this thought, the second of which also strengthens the independence condition. In this section, I look at the first version, which is found in his earliest papers on logic, while in the next two sections I will look at the version given in *Essays in Experimental Logic*.

In his earliest papers on logic, Dewey is committed to the idea that "logical processes enter equally into both perception and conception" (EW 3, 77–78). Logical processes enter into conception because to conceive of something, to make a judgment about it, is both to distinguish the subject of the judgment from other objects and to connect it to other, like objects. Predication is a product of analytical and synthetic operations undertaken

---

[18] Judgment for McDowell is a species of discursive activity because judgments are "inner analogues to assertions" (McDowell 2009c, 262). So thought and judgment, as well as overt speech, are discursive.

by the Understanding. Logical processes also enter into the perception of the facts. For "as soon as we give up the view," as we should, "that objects are presented to the mind already distinguished from others and united into cohering wholes" (EW 3, 78–79), then we need to posit logical processes to both distinguish and unify the manifold of sense. As such, "in the most elementary recognition of an object processes of analysis and synthesis of very considerable complexity are involved" (EW 3, 78). Perception therefore involves both receptivity and spontaneity, is a passive taking in of how things are that nonetheless involves logical processes.

Because perception and conception both involve logical processes, they are homogeneous. To perceive an object can justify our making a judgment about it because the judgment utilizes the same analytic and synthetic operations as the perception. But how then is perception independent of conception? Here is Dewey's answer: in perception, "we are not *consciously* aiming at truth and there is no *conscious* criterion or standard which controls the mental process" (EW 3, 79), whereas in conception, "its logical character is brought to consciousness, is rendered explicit, and is thus used as a criterion, or a standard ... by which the false and the irrelevant may be excluded" (EW 3, 82). So the difference between perception and conception is that the formation of a conceptual judgment is a self-conscious process controlled by logical and rational requirements, while in perception these processes are unconscious and so "uneconomical, imperfect, incorrect: they contain irrelevant material and leave out what is really coherent" (EW 3, 78).

But it is clear in this early work that the independence of perceptual experience does not really receive its due. For when we develop a conception of an object by self-consciously utilizing the logical processes that both it and perception involve, we gain "knowledge of what the real object is ... [The] concept means complete knowledge of an object – knowledge of it in its mode of genesis, and in its relations and bearings; while the percept means incomplete (that is, 'abstract' in the true sense of abstract') knowledge of an object – knowledge of the object in its qualitative, spatial, and temporal limitations" (EW 3: 144–145). Perception is not independent of conception because it is just confused conception, while conception is perception clarified and understood.

Primary Experience

In *Essays in Experimental Logic*, Dewey does not disown the idea that experience, prior to thought or judgment, involves both receptivity and spontaneity. But, like McDowell's second account, he tries to de-intellectualize the processes that passively organize experience.

Experience involves receptivity because "[s]ensory qualities *are* forced on us" (Dewey 2007, 74) whether we wish it or not. But sensory qualities are "*not*" forced on us "at large" because the

> sensory data of experience always comes *in a context;* they always appear as variations in a continuum. Even the thunder which breaks in upon me ... disturbs me because it is taken as thunder: as part of the same space-world as that in which my chair and room and house are located; and it is taken as an influence which interrupts and disturbs, *because* it is part of a common world of causes and effects. (Dewey 2007, 74)

The sensory data of experience always comes in a context because experience, to use McDowell's vocabulary, involves a type of togetherness that is brought about in our receptivity. Because of this, thunder is prepredicatively taken as thunder, as part of a single space-world, as something that is caused and that causes other things, etc. All predicative thought and judgment takes place in this already unified context. As Dewey puts it, "reflective thought grows organically out of an experience which is already organized" (Dewey 2007, 66).

But in his attempt to distance himself from so-called Neo-Hegelianism, a position that thinks that "the organization out of which reflective thought grows is the world of thought of some other type – of Pure Thought, Creative or Constitutive Thought" (Dewey 2007, 66), Dewey attempts, in light of his prior work on the reflex arc, to de-intellectualize his account of togetherness, holding that the operations that organize experience are not primarily cognitive but practical or teleological. In other words, the passive organization of experience is not primarily for the sake of representing or knowing objectively present objects in space and time but, rather, for the sake of organizing a context in which our purposes and projects can be forwarded. What Neo-Hegelians and his own earlier intellectualist view overlook is that "things and qualities are present to most men most of the time as things and qualities in situations of prizing and aversion, of seeing and finding, of converse, enjoyment and suffering, of production and employment, of manipulation and destruction" (Dewey 2007, 5). To illustrate, Dewey asks us to think about the difference between a perception of water when it is part of an experience of quenching our thirst and a perception of water in a context where knowing the nature of water is the controlling interest of the experience (see Dewey 2007, 4). In the first experience, the water, which is perceptually present as something to be used or enjoyed, is swallowed up in the larger experience of quenching one's thirst, while in the later experience the water is present as a disinterested object of knowing.[19]

Dewey calls experiences in which we primarily cope with objects rather than cognize them 'non-reflectional', 'non-cognitive', or 'primary' experiences.[20] Such experiences, Dewey says, are *had* rather than *known*.[21] In a primary experience, we are absorbed by our activity in such a way that the thing with which we are dealing does not appear as an object standing over against a discrete thought of it. "[P]rimary experience is innocent of the discrimination of the *what* experienced and the *how*, or mode of experiencing. We are not in it aware of the seeing, nor yet of the objects *as* something seen. Any experience in all of its non-reflective phases is innocent of any discrimination of subject and object" (Dewey 2007, 78n). The point is not that such an experience does not have an object, or that the experience is not focused in a certain direction rather than another; it is rather that the object is not taken *as* an object, and the experience is not taken to be *a kind* of experience. One is absorbed in one's activity such that the object of the activity is, as it were, telescoped into it. The having and the had in the experience are not distinct objects. They become distinct objects through the work of reflection. The "discrimination of something experien*ced* from modes of experien*cing,*" emerges with "the work of reflection" (Dewey 2007, 78n).

Dewey admits that "some element of reflection or inference may be required in any situation to which the term 'experience' is applicable in any way which contrasts with, say, the 'experience' of an oyster or growing bean vine" (Dewey 2007, 5). In other words, what makes a primary experience a "*conscious* experience" (Dewey 2007, 5), one consciously

---

[19] Dewey thinks that philosophers have had a tendency to overlook the former experience and privilege the latter because they commit what he calls the 'philosopher's fallacy', the fallacy of reading into the relation that subjects have with the world the relation that *they* have with it, which of course is cognitive. Since the philosopher is interested in getting knowledge, and he

> does not think about knowledge except when he is *thinking*, except, that is, when the intellectual or cognitional interest is dominant, the professional philosopher is only too prone to think of all experiences as if they were of the type that he is specially engaged in, and hence unconsciously or intentionally to project *its* traits into experiences to which they are alien. (Dewey, 2007, 5)

If we stop committing this fallacy, we will be able to see that knowing is one specialized modality of experience alongside other modalities, and not equivalent with experience overall. This is an epistemological version of James's psychological fallacy.

[20] For a rich account of primary experience that emphasizes its aesthetic dimension, see Alexander 1987.
[21] By 'known', Dewey means here 'object of reflective attention'.

undergone rather than just undergone, is the fact that it involves "a certain taking of some things as representative of other things" (Dewey 2007, 5). So while the perception of the water as something to be used or enjoyed does not involve our taking it as a something to be understood or known in a disinterested way, it nonetheless involves our 'naturally' or 'spontaneously' taking it *as* something, something that can quench our thirst. In this case something that is *strictly speaking* not present – the use to which water can be put – is made present. Here, the "spontaneous inference" brings "before the agent absent considerations to which he may respond as he otherwise responds to the stimulating forces of the given situation" (Dewey 2007, 212). Because primary experience is embedded by such inferences, the world as it is given in it is teeming with implications for future perception, action, and thought.

It is critical to note two things at this point. First, the inferences that primary experiences involve always remain set in a qualitative context that pervades the whole experience. Here, "the intellectual element is set in a context which is non-cognitive and which holds within it in suspense a vast complex of other qualities and things that in the experience are objects of esteem or aversion, of decision, of use, of suffering, of endeavor and revolt, not knowledge" (Dewey 2007, 5). We shall come back to this qualitative context in the section on 'The Unboundedness of the Situation'. Second, the nature of the "spontaneous inference[s]" that one makes "depends very largely upon the habits of the individual in whom inferring takes place" (Dewey 2007, 215). It is habits that are the primary organizer of primary experience, not inference:

> [O]rganization of some sort exists in every experience ... [But] this organization ... is not the work of reason or thought, unless "reason" be stretched beyond all identification ... Experience always carries with it and within it certain systemized arrangements, certain classifications (using the term without intellectualistic prejudice), coexistent and serial ... As *organizations*, as established, effectively controlling arrangements of objects in experience, their mark is that they are not thoughts, but habits, customs of action. (MW 3, 134–135)

Within primary experience, what is spontaneously actualized in our receptivity are not mental concepts and logical rules of synthesis but psychophysical habits and skills. Habits and skills are part of our receptivity because they operate outside of direct conscious control in response to environmental solicitations. In so doing, they automatically "effect and perpetuate modes of reaction and of perception that compel a certain grouping of objects, elements, and values" (MW 3, 134). But they actively bring about these modes of reaction and perception because, as we saw in

Chapter 2, they are propulsive and invested with a kind of rational intelligibility by past acts of reflection. In this sense, they are part of our spontaneity.

There are two ramifications of this for our view of primary experience. First, experience can no longer be identified with consciousness. While experience includes the stream of conscious thoughts, perceptions, and desires, it includes more than this. "Experience is no stream, even though the stream of feeling and ideas that flows upon its surface is the part which philosophers love to traverse. Experience includes the enduring bank of natural constitution and acquired habits as well as the stream. The flying moment is sustained by an atmosphere that does not fly, even when it most vibrates" (LW 1, 370). So experience not only has spatial and temporal breadth it also has depth, it includes what Dewey calls our 'subconscious', which involves "the immense multitude of immediate organic selections, rejections, welcomings, expulsions, appropriations, withdrawals ... of the most minute, vibratingly delicate nature. We are not aware of the qualities of many or most of these acts; we do not objectively distinguish and identify them. Yet they exist as feeling qualities, and have an enormous directive effect on our behavior" (LW 1, 227). This fringe of vague organic selections and qualities, both native and acquired, have a directive effect on our behavior because our flying conscious states and their objects not only shade off into them but are *bathed* by them. In other words, these organic selections are the bodily origin of the qualities that pervade the situation in which we live.

There is a second ramification. As we know, Dewey agrees with Kant that experience involves spontaneity and receptivity, and he agrees with McDowell that we must see spontaneity as actualized not just in overt judgments but also in our receptivity. But in making this latter actualization one of bodily habits and skills rather than concepts, Dewey comes to think of experience as involving *bodily doings*:

> The nature of experience can be understood only by noting that it includes an active and a passive element peculiarly combined. On the active hand, experience is *trying* – a meaning which is made explicit in the connected term experiment. On the passive, it is *undergoing*. When we experience something we act upon it, we do something with it; then we suffer or undergo the consequences. (MW 9, 146)

Primary experience goes beyond the given by involving an action or experiment that attempts to cope with the undergone consequences of a prior doing. This experiment, if successful, results in new behaviors and new habitual routines, which changes what we undergo vis-à-vis the environment going forward. In other words, these changes are the basis of new 'modes of reaction and of perception'. If these modes of reaction and perception allow for embodied coping, if we have relative equilibrium in our simultaneously active and passive interaction with the world, then we have primary experience.

These changes in the concept of experience make answering the question of how it can stand as a tribunal for thought difficult. For in making sensorimotor habits rather than concepts the main organizer of primary experience, we now cannot credit such experiences with conceptual content, either propositional or intuitive, that either is or can be homogeneous with thought or judgment. In giving examples of the habits and skills that organize primary experience, Dewey mentions the psychophysical visual habits of the Greeks, the locomotive habits of our bodies by which we plot space, and the ways of perceiving and imagining the world brought about by social institutions and political customs (MW 3, 134). Let us take as our example the plotting of space necessary to reach for a glass of water. To do this, one must have a grip on the spatial relations that pertain to one's body as well as the glass, and must coordinate visual and haptic activity in light of that grip. This coordination can fail if one grasps these relations incorrectly. The motor-intentional experience, therefore, has correctness conditions, and in so doing can be said to have content – in this case spatial. But this content is not conceptual.

On the one hand, the experience does not have propositional content. For we get a grip on the spatial relations necessary to coordinate the movement of our eyes, arm, wrist, fingers, etc., not by actualizing spatial concepts (in our receptivity) that *represent* the space in which these activities happen, but by actualizing habits and skills that, due to past training and practice, involve an embodied practical sense of these relations.[22] In our embodied actions, we do not primarily represent space; we inhabit it. On the other hand, the experience does not have intuitional content – content that, according to McDowell, could figure in discursive activity, even if it does not so figure.[23] Why not? We can, of course,

---

[22] For more on this, see Chapter 2, and Levine 2015b.
[23] McDowell's development of the concept of intuitional content could be read as an admission that there is nonconceptual content. It depends on what one means by nonconceptual content. If one means by it that the contents that are had in a given experience are not *composed* of concepts (are not Fregian senses, let's say), then it seems that McDowell accepts the notion. Intuitional contents are not on his conception composed of concepts. If, on the other hand, one means by nonconceptual content contents that one can entertain without *possessing* concepts that could be associated with

conceptualize the spatial relations at play in a motor-intentional experience after the fact, but then they are *known* and not *had*. For McDowell, when an intuitional content figures in discursive activity one makes "that content – that very content – explicit in speech or judgment" (McDowell 2009c, 264). For Dewey, in contrast, when the content of a motor-intentional experience is made explicit by discursive activity, it is fundamentally *transformed*. In being known rather than had, it is no longer the same content. Furthermore, even in experiences that have conceptual content, there are always nonconceptual contents that are *had* in the background of the experience. Dewey thinks this because he follows James in accepting the thesis that experience is inextricably fringed:

> The scope and content of the focused apparency have immediate dynamic connections with portions of experience not at the time obvious. The word which I have just written is momentarily focal; around it there shade off into vagueness my typewriter, the desk, the room, the building, the campus, the town, and so on. *In* the experience, and in it in such a way as to *qualify* what is shiningly apparent, are all the physical features of the environment extending out into space no one can say how far, and all the habits and interests extending backward and forward in time, of the organism which uses the typewriter and which notes the written form of the word only as temporary focus in a vast and changing scene. (Dewey 2007, 6)

We can, of course, conceptualize any feature of the fringe of our experience by attending to it with a conceptual act, making what was vague sharp. But then other contents will necessarily recede into being vague and indistinct, yet still present as contents *in* the experience. These contents are not composed of concepts, even if they can become the object of conceptual activity. For Dewey, this signals that any experience that we undergo, even those that have conceptual content, involves contents that are nonconceptual.[24]

In thinking that primary experience has nonconceptual content, Dewey strengthens its independence and weakens its homogeneity vis-à-vis thought. But how can experience be a tribunal for thought if experience

---

that content, then it is clear that he does not accept the notion. For these two different ways of thinking about nonconceptual content, see Speaks 2005 and Crowther 2006. McDowell almost always has in mind the latter way of thinking about nonconceptual content, which is what accounts for his denial of it even after the introduction of intuitional content. For this, see his debate with Peacocke (McDowell 1996a and 1998b and Peacocke 1998 and 2001).

[24] For a worked out argument along these lines, though in a phenomenological vein, see Siewert 2005.

does not either have, or potentially have, a content that is the same as thought or judgment itself?

The Tribunal of Experience: The Experimental Account

Dewey's answer is to introduce temporal considerations into the relationship between experience and thought. Thought does not come about primarily to endorse an already given experiential content, as it does for McDowell; rather, it comes about *when there is no clear content to be had*, when one does not know what to think. In this case, one must *do* something, for to say that something "is to be found out, is to be ascertained or proved or believed, is to say that something is to be done" (Dewey 2007, 209). On this conception, thought is a creative process that "occupies an intermediate and mediating place in the development of an experience" (Dewey 2007, 4). Thought begins with an experience that cannot be made sense of and it ends – if all goes well – with a warranted judgment, one that is expressive of the fact that the experience, now reconstructed by thought, has a coherent and unified sense. But even though this reconstructed experience is influenced by thought, it nonetheless can, Dewey argues, stand as a tribunal *for* thought. For thought depends "upon a consequent experience for its final test" (Dewey 2007, 92). Let me explain how this works.

As we know, primary experience is an experience in which there is equilibrium in our simultaneously active and passive interaction with the world. Experience remains non-reflective when the adjustments needed to maintain equilibrium do not necessitate reflective steering. But sometimes experience, in its temporal unfolding, comes across a recalcitrance with which the adjustments that flow from our standing habits cannot cope. Our experience, up to now 'in the flow', has become 'conflicted' or 'indeterminate'. Here "an experience previously accepted comes up in its wholeness against another equally integral; and ... some larger experience dawns which requires each as a part of itself and yet within which the required factors show themselves as mutually incompatible." In this larger experience, we have a "situation which is organized or constituted as a whole, yet which is falling to pieces in its parts – a situation which is in conflict within itself" (Dewey 2007, 62).

According to Dewey, the conflicted situation is both objective and subjective. It is objective in two senses, existential and logical. It is existentially objective because "[i]t is there; it is there as whole; the various parts are there; and their active incompatibility with one another is there"

(Dewey 2007, 63). The conflicted situation is conflicted not because an experiencing agent *takes it* to be conflicted, but because its parts have, in fact, come apart.[25] It is a recalcitrance that stops experience in its tracks and which takes us by surprise. As such, it "has to be reckoned with" (Dewey 2007, 87). Surprise is essential for Dewey because, as he puts it in his later work, "[e]xperience teaches . . . by means of a series of surprises. It is through the conflict of our expectations with what happens in actuality that we learn" (LW 11, 423). Surprise teaches not only in the sense that it spurs us on to engage in reflective learning processes, but also in the sense that it teaches us that we are not in control of experience. As Dewey says, "surprise . . . indicates interaction between the self and the world and so disproves every subjective idealism" (LW 11, 423).

Although in experience there is never a raw confrontation with the Given (insofar as it is pre-predicatively organized), our undergoing of a surprising recalcitrance indicates to us, *within experience*, that experience and reality have slipped out of phase. Here the second logical sense of objectivity emerges, because with this indication, the conflicted situation "effects a transition into the thought-situation . . . The conflict has objective worth because it is the antecedent condition and cue of thought" (Dewey 2007, 63).

The conflicted situation is subjective, on the other hand, because its indeterminacy brings about a feeling of uncertainty that motivates the subject in this situation to do something to get out of it. "The situation, the experience as such, is objective . . . But just *what in particular* is objective, just what *form* the situation shall take as a organized harmonious whole, is unknown; that is the problem . . . Viewed from this standpoint of uncertainty, the situation as a whole is subjective. No particular content or reference can be asserted off-hand" (Dewey 2007, 64).

---

[25] Here we already find the sentiment that Dewey expresses in his *Logic* when he says: "It is the *situation* that has these traits. *We* are doubtful because the situation is inherently doubtful . . . Consequently, situations that are disturbed and troubled, confused or obscure, cannot be straightened out, cleared up and put in order, by manipulation of our personal states of mind" (LW 12, 109–110). Many, for example Russell 1996, read this point as a kind of illegitimate anthropomorphizing of the situation. Is it not persons who doubt in light of some interest or purpose, not situations? But the point can be domesticated in this way: to have doubt in a situation that is not doubtful, that does not *call for* doubt, is to form what Peirce calls "paper doubt," which according to Dewey is "pathological." (To put doubts to oneself so as to advance inquiry is to have a reason to doubt, and so is not pathological). For doubt to be motived, it must flow from the *situation's being doubtful*, which depends on its parts actually conflicting. This does not mean that the situation can be doubted without there being a "subject" who doubts. But this subject does not doubt from a position removed from the situation; rather, they themselves are *part* of the doubtful situation.

We can begin to find out what is objective and what is not because even in a conflicted situation, there are, due to the legacy of past experience, features that are not indeterminate:

> There is somewhat which is untouched in the contention of incompatibles. There is something which remains secure, unquestioned. On the other hand, there are elements which are doubtful and precarious. This gives the framework of the general distribution of the field into "facts," the given, the presented, the Datum; and ideas, the *Quaesitum*, the conceived, the Inferential (Dewey 2007, 70)

Facts for Dewey are logical and not psychological items, meaning that they are not equivalent to the raw and immediately sensory materials posited by empirical psychology. Rather, facts are something *taken* by reflection in its controlled attempt to isolate stable features of the indeterminate situation.[26] While they are given, they are not Given. Ideas, on the other hand, are meanings that are used as hypotheses to guide inferences that go beyond what is present in the situation. These inferences are not natural and spontaneous but considered and deliberate. Ideas too are logical instruments rather than psychic items. "[A]n idea, intellectually, cannot be defined by its structure, but only by its function and use. Whatever in a doubtful situation ... helps us to form a judgment and to bring inference to a conclusion by means of anticipating a possible solution is an idea" (LW 8, 224).

Ideas and facts are not original and separate existences that must be brought together to produce experience. For as Dewey will put it later, experience "recognizes in its primary integrity no division between act and material, subject and object, but contains them both as an unanalyzed totality. 'Thought' and 'Thing' ... refer to products discriminated by reflection out of primary experience" (LW 1, 18–19).[27] They are derivative instruments that "arise only within reflection" (Dewey 2007, 63) to help us deal with a conflicted experience.[28] They are therefore "divisions of labor, cooperative instrumentalities, for economical dealing with the

---

[26] We could say that data is doubly mediated insofar as the sensory data that are taken and interpreted in reflective inquiry to make sense of an indeterminate situation are already part of a primary experience that while disrupted for the moment has been pre-predicatively organized by habits that are the result of past experience.

[27] This follows from the fact that Dewey always accepted Hegel's critique of 'apart-thought', even after he was no longer a Hegelian strictly speaking.

[28] On this point, Dewey's view is similar to Heidegger's insofar as for Heidegger the representation of 'present-to-hand' objects, which brings about the subject–object distinction, is a modification of a prior way of being-in-the-world, one where we cope in an absorbed way with what is 'ready-to-hand'. See Blattner 2008.

problem of the maintenance of the integrity of experience" (Dewey 2007, 71). Here is how Dewey sums up the point:

> All the distinction discovered within thinking, of conception over against sense-perception, of various modes and forms of judgment, of inference ... all these distinctions come within the thought-situation as growing out of a characteristic antecedent typical formation of experience; and have for their purpose the solution of the peculiar problem which respect to which the thought-function is generated or evolved: the restoration of a deliberately integrated experience from the inherent conflict into which it has fallen. (Dewey 2007, 68)

We restore the integrity of experience by thinking, by undertaking a process of reflective inquiry that utilizes these instrumentalities in a cycle of perception, suggestion, reasoning, action, and perception. Here is a brief schema of this process: (1) we attempt to determine, through observation, the facts of the case – what in the indeterminate situation is settled and what is not; (2) we try, on that basis, to identify and define what exactly is indeterminate in the situation, turning an indeterminacy into a defined problem; (3) we then, on that basis, form ideas, suggestions, or hypotheses for solving the problem that go beyond what is strictly speaking present; (4) then, through reasoning, we trace the consequences of these ideas in light of our background concepts and theories, revising them in light of those envisaged consequences; (5) then we make an inference beyond the given by trying, in a controlled way, to experimentally institute these revised ideas in experience, and finally (6) we note in perception the consequences of this attempt.[29] If the consequences of the experiment are such that they 'reconstruct' the experience, allow it to go forward fluidly, then we can say that the idea that brought about these consequences 'works'. It is objectively valid.[30] In this case we can exit inquiry by issuing a warranted judgment. If the idea does not 'work' then we must modify it by revisiting prior stages of the inquiry and going through the process again.

---

[29] For an excellent account of the stages of inquiry, and some of the different versions that Dewey gave at various points in his career, see Brown 2012.
[30] As I mentioned in the Introduction, there is a question about whether an objectively valid belief is a true belief. While Dewey sometimes seems to answer this question in the affirmative, I think we must answer it negatively. A true belief is one that would stand up to all evidence, questioning, reason-giving, etc., while an objectively valid belief is one that we have good reason to think is true because it is *properly based in experience*. But what is objectively valid can turn out to be false, and hence cannot be identified with what is true.

It is critical to see that this account is the result of Dewey's attempt to avoid the seesaw between idealism/coherentism and the Myth of the Given. His view avoids idealism/coherentism because the assertion of a warranted judgment is the product of an experimental intervention into the world that exits the realm of concepts. "If we exclude acting upon the idea, no conceivable amount or kind of intellectualistic procedure can confirm or refute an idea, or throw any light upon its validity" (Dewey 2007, 122).[31] An empiricism that endorses the Myth of the Given is closer to the truth because it correctly grasps that thought must be verified by something beyond thought, i.e., experience. Empirical thought is verified by its correspondence with the facts immediately Given in experience. The problem with this view is that when we are engaged in inquiry, the question of *what facts are experientially given is precisely what is at issue*. What the facts are has become indeterminate. So it can't be the case that the experienced facts stand as the tribunal for thought, for in inquiry these facts have become *seeming facts*. The only alternative is to say that what stands as the tribunal for thought is not the given facts but the facts as they exist in a reconstructed experience that *eventuates* from our acting on a hypothetical idea. In this way we

> can understand how validity of meaning is measured by reference to something which is not mere meaning; by reference to something which lies beyond it as such, viz., the reconstruction of an experience into which it enters as a method of control ... [T]he test of objectivity is everywhere the same: anything is objective in so far as, through the medium of conflict, it controls the movement of experience in its reconstructive transition. (Dewey 2007, 87)

One might think that this move undercuts any claim Dewey can make about the objectivity of thought. For if the tribunal for thought is the experience that eventuates from thought's reconstruction of experience, then it seems that the tribunal for thought is not independent of thought. How is this not idealistic? But it is critical to see that while for Dewey

---

[31] One difficulty that many interpreters have with Dewey is that it seems that certain domains of knowledge – mathematics, for example – do not involve experiment or action. But Dewey's account of experimental action is capacious, involving not only actual actions but also imaginative actions that have consequences for future practice. Dewey's account of mathematics, for example, involves mapping functions. But even if a mathematician does not engage in actual mapping, part of what they are doing in reasoning mathematically is imaginatively doing so, which has consequences for their future mathematical practice. "[I]n mathematics every inference means at least a changed attitude toward mathematical terms, a different way of treating them henceforth" (MW 10, 92). This change would count as an example of action for Dewey.

an idea "controls an action to be performed ... the consequences of the operation determine the worth of the directive idea; the directive idea does not fix the nature of the object" (LW 4, 230). In other words, it is the *consequences* that eventuate from our acting, the *connections* between things in the world that emerge from the interaction between our doing something and our undergoing the consequences of so doing, that determines the worth or validity of the idea acted upon. 'Spontaneity' is involved here insofar as in experiment we attempt to push the world in a certain way in light of a certain idea. Paraphrasing Kant, we put nature to question in light of our already acquired understanding of things. But 'receptivity' is also inextricably involved, for while we "do something to the thing ... it does something to us in return" (MW 9, 146). It is *how the world pushes back* on our doing, whether it allows for a reconstructed experience or not, that determines whether an idea about the world has objective validity or not. Without an actual test, in which idea and world existentially clash through the medium of action, thought would merely spin in its own void and so could not be said to answer to the objective world.

Dewey takes the fact that the reconstructed experience that validates thought is not completely independent of the thought that reconstructs it to be a feature of the theory rather than a bug. For this is how he explains the *homogeneity* of experience and thought. As we saw earlier, primary experience is independent of thought because it is organized not by concepts but by sensorimotor habits and skills. But these habits and skills are not completely independent of thought because if our acting on an idea allows for a reconstructed experience, the noted consequences and connections that result from so acting are integrated into the habits that organize future primary experience. In other words, to deal with future contingencies, we integrate into our behavioral repertoire what is learned about the world from past problem solving. So primary experience is funded by what is learned through the process of thought, and future thought – when provoked by a new problematic situation – arises out of, and is guided by, a primary experience that incorporates past learning. So there is a temporally unfolding feedback cycle between experience and thought, which is what explains how they can be both homogeneous and independent of one another, and so how experience can be a tribunal for thought.[32]

---

[32] We examine this feedback cycle in more detail in Chapter 6.

The Unboundedness of the Situation

But we still, in fact, don't have a complete account of how experience can be a tribunal for thought. For while perhaps we have explained how *experience* can rationally bear on thought, we have not yet explained how experience enables, as McDowell puts it, "the layout of reality itself to exert a rational influence on what a subject thinks" (McDowell 1996a, 26). In other words, we still don't have an account of how for Dewey, or McDowell, experience allows the *world* to have a rational bearing on thought, and so for thought to be rationally constrained by it.

McDowell's account of how the layout of reality can rationally influence thought depends on his thesis that the conceptual is 'unbounded'. This language is meant to counteract a view of things offered by the coherentist in which the ability of one thing to stand as a reason for another is bounded or enclosed within our system of belief, and where the only transactions that can cross the line between mind and world are causal. If the world is to stand as reason for us to think that something is the case we must grasp how it is "not outside an outer boundary that encloses the conceptual sphere" (McDowell 1996a, 26).[33] But it is difficult to think this thought without falling into idealism, for it certainly seems, as Willaschek puts it, "that a world *essentially* within the reach of our thinking cannot be independent of our mental capacities" (Willaschek 1999, 35).

McDowell tries to counteract this conclusion by distinguishing between acts of thinking and the contents that can be thought by such acts – thinkable contents. The world, in both its existence and nature, is independent of our *acts* of thinking; it is not constituted by such acts. But while "constraint comes from outside *thinking*" it does not come "from outside what is *thinkable*" (McDowell 1996a, 28). Constraint by the world does not come from outside what is thinkable because the idea of what is thinkable is intelligible only when coupled with the idea of a fact. Here is how McDowell puts it:

> My claim is that we understand the idea of a thinkable and the idea of a fact – an element of the world, on the natural Tractarian conception – only together. It is not that we know anyway – independently of having the idea of a thought – what it would be for something to be the case, and work from there into a derivative understanding of what it would be for someone

---

[33] For a cashing out of the enclosure metaphor, see Wright 1996.

to think truly. Nor is it that we know anyway – independently of having the idea of a fact – what it is for someone to entertain a thought, and work from there, exploiting the idea of truth, into a derivative understanding of what it would be for something to be the case. Each of the two ideas is so much as intelligible only in the context of each other. (McDowell 2000a, 96)

Thought and worldly fact are 'sense-dependent', meaning that to think one it is necessary to think the other, and vice-versa. They are, in Hegelian terms, 'speculatively identical'. McDowell recognizes that this view is expressive of a kind of idealism. But it is not the kind of idealism that most of his critics have in mind, one in which the world "is a mere reflection of our self-standing subjectivity" (McDowell 2009b, 143). Rather, it is an idealism in which "thought and the world must be understood together. The form of thought is already just as such the form of the world. It is a form that is subjective and objective together" (McDowell 2009b, 143). The world cannot be a mere reflection of our self-standing subjectivity because, insofar as the most basic empirical content is a product of our receptivity in operation, a subject's mental states cannot have any content without the world *already* being in view. But because in this operation we are 'saddled' with thinkable content, what we experience of this open world is not, once we have moved our sense organs, under our control.

In his early work, Dewey, too, makes an unboundedness of the conceptual claim. There, Dewey is committed to the idea that there is no "duality between the object perceived and the thought conceived" (EW 3, 77). The claim is that because logical processes are involved in both perception and conception, nothing – a mere bit of the Given – can enter the logical world from the outside, untouched by these processes. "We do not have," therefore, "two things first given – one, the facts of observation, the other the mental concepts, and then, thirdly, a logical process, starting from this dualism, and attempting to make one side conform to the other" (EW 3, 80). Rather, we have a single world of knowledge that is everywhere logical:

> If there is no *pure* presentation, no fact of sense perception not already qualified by logical processes, how can it be said that logic has to do with a comparison of the concept with the datum of presentation? Logic seems somehow to be concerned with the observation itself. Instead of having a dual material supplied to it, it is present wherever there is any known material. There is but one world, the world of knowledge, not two, an inner and outer, a world of observation and a world of conception; and this world is everywhere logical. (EW 3, 81)

The perceived facts and our conception of these facts are speculatively identical: to think one is already to think the other and vice-versa. They can't be *strictly identical* for Dewey because even in his early work he saw them as involved in a temporal process involving both identity and difference. "There is a period ... in every science, and as to every subject matter in every science, when idea and fact are at one. But contradictions arise; the mind therefore holds idea and fact apart, regarding the idea as tentative and the fact as apparent." When a theory is developed that adequately explains the facts, "idea and fact again become one, to remain one until further contradictions are discovered when the process must again be gone through with" (EW 3, 88–89). The identity that is arrived at through this process between the facts perceived and facts conceived is a mediated identity, one that is enriched by what has been learned through past differentiation. But in no case does the achievement of this mediated identity require us to cross a boundary between the world of knowledge and another world that stands outside of it, the so-called external world. Both the identity of perception and conception and their difference are internal to the unbounded single world of knowledge.

In *Essays in Experimental Logic,* Dewey, in accord with his program to de-intellectualize his prior view, no longer speaks of the single world of knowledge but of a single 'situation'.[34] Like the single world of knowledge, a situation is antecedent to reflective thought and is an encompassing whole out of which functionally relevant parts emerge due to contradiction or indeterminacy. But unlike the world of knowledge, the situation is *lived* and not known. For in thinking of us primarily as agents whose thought emerges from the attempt to cope with conflicts in experience, rather than as subjects who represent the world, Dewey must situate agents and their thought-activity in an embodied action-oriented context. It is this context "in which we immediately live, that in which we strive, succeed, and are defeated" (LW 5, 243). This context Dewey calls the situation.

We can grasp the nature of a situation by contrasting it with objects. While an object is an "element in the complex whole that is defined in abstraction from the whole of which it is a distinction," the situation out of which the object is abstracted "is a complex existence that is held together in spite of its internal complexity by the fact that it is dominated and characterized throughout by a single quality" (LW 5, 246). While specific

---

[34] My discussion of the concept of a situation ranges beyond *Essays in Experimental Logic* and includes work from the later Dewey. However, I do not think that the development of the concept takes it in directions not already nascent in the *Essays*.

qualities like red, soft, loud, and hard are items that are discriminated *within* a situation, the situation is pervaded by a single 'tertiary' quality, for example, fear, anger, hopefulness, cheerfulness, etc. This quality unifies and individuates the situation, making it an anguished rather than an ecstatic, hopeful, or serene situation, an aesthetic situation rather than a mathematical or political one, or a determinate situation rather than an indeterminate or tensional one.[35]

We must be careful not to identify the pervasive quality of a situation with a feeling that a subject can have of this quality. For a feeling is a psychical state that is

> a product of a reflection which presupposes the direct presence of quality as such. "Feeling" and "felt" are names for a relation of *quality*. When, for example, fear exists, it is the pervading tone, color, and quality of persons, things, and circumstances, of a situation. When fearful we are not aware of fear but of these objects in their immediate and unique qualities. In another situation fear may appear as a distinct term, and analysis may then call it a feeling or emotion. (LW 5, 248)[36]

So feeling and what is felt are secondary modifications of a more primitive qualitative unity, a kind of qualitative attunement that underlies the possibility of our having a psychical state of feeling. Here, there is no dichotomy, for instance, between "the fearsome bear *and* my fright" (MW 7, 37). Rather, the bear is directly experienced as fearful. Fear *qualifies* the experience; it is not the object of experience. We can, in a separate and subsequent reflective experience, make the pervasive quality of fearfulness an object, distinguishing the feeling of fear from that which is feared. But this reflective experience can only take place because a new situation with a new pervading quality has come about, perhaps inquisitiveness as to one's state of being.

A situation, if it is to remain a situation, cannot therefore be an object of thought. This is not because it is "remote and transcendent, but because it is so engrossing and matter of course" (Dewey 2007, 38n). It is the immediate *background* against which every object stands forth:

> A background is implicit in some form and to some degree in all thinking, although as background it does not come into explicit purview; that is, does not form a portion of the subject-matter which is consciously attended to, thought of, examined, inspected, turned over ... Surrounding, bathing,

---

[35] For an excellent introduction to Dewey's account of quality, see the exchange between Bernstein 1961 and Kennedy 1961.
[36] I have changed Dewey's example from anger to fear.

saturating, the things of which we are explicitly aware is some inclusive situation which does not enter into the direct material of reflection. It does not come into question; it is taken for granted with respect to the particular question that is occupying the field of thinking. Since it does not come into question, it is stable, settled. (LW 6, 11–12)

Because the situation is always in the background, it can't be thought about or communicated about directly, for thought and communication are always about an object. Rather, one can only invite or remind others to note that each of their acts of thought or communication also takes place in a context. The "words 'experience', 'situation', etc., are" therefore "used to *remind* the thinker of the need of reversion to precisely something that never can be one of the terms of his reflection but that nevertheless furnishes the existential meaning and status of them all" (Dewey 2007, 37n).

As the background of thought, a situation's pervasive quality plays a crucial *logical* role in thought. Quality not only unifies and individuates the context of thought; it also "controls the terms of thought" (LW 5, 247) insofar as it regulates thought's continuity, pertinence, and direction.[37] It regulates the continuity of thought, and the pertinence of the items thought about to one another, insofar as it articulates the way that things in the situation *matter* to one another. It controls the direction of thought, on the other hand, because our getting out of an indeterminate situation depends on intuitively discerning the quality of the situation as a whole. In an indeterminate situation, the problem at issue "is had or experienced before it can be stated or set forth" (LW 5, 249). Because it is had before it is set forth, one is at a loss as to which objects in the situation are relevant to defining the problem and which are not. So if one's attention were *only* directed to objects by reflective thought, if in the indeterminate situation, reflection did not "spring from and make explicit a prior intuition" (LW 5, 249), then one would be at a loss as to which direction to take. To intelligently state the problem, and therefore set inquiry on a certain path, there must be, prior to discursive reasons and justifications, an intuitive discernment of the quality of the situation.[38]

---

[37] For a much more detailed account of the logical roles that quality plays in Dewey's thought, see Pappas 2016.

[38] Some interpreters – for instance Shusterman 1994, and Koopman 2009 and 2014 – have argued that Dewey's account of quality falls prey to the Myth of the Given. These authors pick up on the fact that the situation's pervasive quality is noncognitively felt and by Dewey's own admission immediately given. "The only thing that is unqualifiedly given is the total pervasive quality ... [T]he quality immediately exists, or is brutely there" (LW 5, 254). But for something to be Given in a mythical way, it is not enough that it be immediately given; it must also play a certain role in

What I want to claim is that the situation has a further logical feature: it is unbounded. It is not unbounded in the sense meant by Russell when he claimed that Dewey's concept of a situation involved a 'holism' that could embrace nothing "less than the whole universe" (Russell 1951, 139). For while a situation might extend to objects and events that are not contiguous in space and time, it only includes objects and events that are qualitatively relevant to one another in being unified by a single pervasive quality.[39] The situation is unbounded rather in the sense that whenever we think about something, we inescapably do so against the background of a particular situation in which there is no distinction between thought and what is thought about, subject and object, appearance and reality.[40] While we can, of course, distinguish between these by transferring our attention and making an element of the situation an object of reflective thought, this thought itself must take place *within* another qualitatively unified situation that stands as *its* background. So "this transfer never disturbs the whole contextual background: it does not all come into question at once. There is

---

knowledge. It is clear that for Dewey the undergoing of a situation's immediate quality does not count as knowledge or as evidence for knowledge. To think that it does is a deep mistake for Dewey. But as we just saw, he also says that a situation's pervasive quality plays a critical role in the regulation and guidance of thought. It is this point that Dewey's critics seize on. For although "immediate experience is invoked not to justify particular truth claims," it is meant "to ground the coherence of any thinking from which such claims emerge" (Shusterman 1994, 132). Because of this, Koopman argues that Dewey's account of "the regulatory and directive nature of the perceptual-but-nonconceptual arena of the qualitative just is an incipient form of empiricist givenism" (Koopman 2014, 151). But notice that this criticism thinks of qualitative immediacy as something like perceptual qualia. But for Dewey, the regulatory and directive role of the immediate quality of the situation is bound up with a subject's acts, habits, and whole 'subconscious'. As he puts it: the

> most highly intellectualized operations depend upon [immediate feeling-qualities] as a 'fringe' by which to guide our inferential movements. They give us our *sense* of rightness and wrongness, of what to select and emphasize and follow up, and what to drop, slur over, and ignore, among the multitude of inchoate meanings that are presenting themselves ... These qualities are the stuff of 'intuitions'. (LW 1, 227)

But intuitions for Dewey are not Given but the "the result of past experience funded into our direct outlook upon the scene of life" (LW 7, 266). Intuition is funded because the feeling-qualities that give one a sense of right and wrong are not qualia but *qualities of acts,* which themselves reflect "all the habits [one] has acquired; that is to say, all the organic modifications [one] has undergone" (LW 1, 227). Although experienced in an immediate fashion, the qualities of these intuitive acts are *mediated* by these acquired habits. Koopman considers this response but rejects it by pointing out that this mediation is not *conceptual* mediation. But this response begs the question as to whether the only kind of mediation that allows us to avoid the Given is conceptual. I take up this question in the next chapter.

[39] For decisive refutations of Russell's view, see Dewey LW 14, 29–33 and chapter 2 of Burke 1994.
[40] I agree with Burke 1997 that situations transcend the appearance/reality distinction, but I don't agree with him that Dewey meant the concept to play the role of an epistemological foundation. Its role is logical, not epistemological.

always that which continues to be taken for granted, which is tacit, being 'understood'" (LW 6, 12).

While any given feature of the situation can become questionable, it can't become questionable all at once, for if "everything were literally unsettled at once, there would be nothing to which to tie those factors that, being unsettled, are in process of discovery and determination" (LW 6, 12). In other words, if everything were questionable, if there were nothing in the situation that was taken for granted, we would not be able to so much as get inquiry off the ground.[41] But inquiry, as a matter of empirical fact, does manage to get off the ground. This is possible because while mind and world, subject and object, can come apart in any given instance, they can do so only because there is a qualitatively unified background situation in which they have not done so.[42] One can now understand the *logical reason* for Dewey's deep skepticism about epistemology, for this discipline depends on the idea that mind and world, subject and object, can come apart not just locally but globally.

But can this account of the unboundedness of the situation make sense of external constraint? To see that it can, we must grasp that while the situation is a logical structure, it is also a natural one. As we know, because there is no 'apart-thought' the unity of a primary experience is not the result of a 'transcendental synthesis' performed on a manifold of loose and separate sensory atoms. Rather, unity is the product of a passive or pre-predicative synthesis that takes place in our receptivity. It is because this passive synthesis is enacted by bodily habits interacting with the environment, rather than by concepts synthesizing a sensory manifold, that the unity of the situation is not discursive but qualitative. For the qualities that comprise a situation "*are precisely the* qualities that mark the deeper-seated adaptive reactions to the organism of its own environment" (MW 7, 36). In other words, the qualities of a situation are "the qualities *of* these reactions" (MW 7, 36), and the pervasive quality of the situation is the quality that characterizes the overall coordination of an organism's habits as they interact with the environment. Because this is so, qualities "never were 'in' the organism; they always were qualities of interactions in which

---

[41] Here we should be reminded of Peirce's claim that motivated doubt – unlike paper doubt – can only take place in a context where many if not most of the elements of the situation are not doubtful, and of Brandom's claim that justification has a default and challenge structure.

[42] Davidson's argument that belief is of its nature veridical is a communicative-theoretic version of this thought. See Davidson 1983.

both extra-organic things and organisms partake ... Hence they are as much qualities of the things engaged as of the organism" (LW 1, 198–199). While qualities could not be felt unless there were a living organism (a 'subject') to feel them, there would be no qualities to feel unless certain potentialities of the environment were activated through such interactions.

In light of this, we can understand Dewey's idea that a situation is an "environing experienced world" (LW 12, 72). An environment for Dewey is not equivalent to the natural world. "There is, of course, a natural world that exists independently of the organism, but this world is *environment* only as it enters directly and indirectly into life-functions" (LW 12, 40). An environment therefore depends both on the nature of a sector of the natural world and on how it is taken by an organism in light of its inbuilt and learned response capacities. In Dewey's terms, an environment intrinsically involves *selectivity*, the way that the organism selectively responds to the solicitations offered by the environment. Dewey talks of the environ*ing* experienced world because he wants to signal that the relationship of environment and organism is *dynamic:* the world solicits sensorimotor reactions by *acting on us*, while simultaneously these reactions *act on the world*, changing it in certain ways, hopefully favorable for our purposes and ends. "As a consequence" of these reactions, "the changes produced in the environment react upon the organism and its activities. The living creature undergoes, suffers, the consequences of its own behavior" (MW 12, 129). One's suffering of the changes produced in the environment by our acting upon it is registered in the creature by its qualitative feelings and emotions, some of which are tertiary. These tertiary qualities characterize and pervade the whole of the dynamic process by which self and world are coupled through time.

The point is that the situation in which one lives is not the product of a projection of our self-standing subjectivity but of these dynamic interactive processes. These processes involve both receptivity and spontaneity: the world acting on us triggers sensorimotor habits, and these habits, which are the products of past learning and experience, determine our modes of perception and reaction going forward. So while this process partly depends on us, on the selective modes of response that we have taken on through time, these modes are constrained within this process by the world and its solicitations. In this way, Dewey accounts for both unboundedness and constraint, for the fact that in a situation, we are not cut off from the world that nonetheless constrains what we can experience and therefore think about it.

Dewey, McDowell, and Embodied Coping

In this chapter I have used McDowell's minimal empiricism to motivate and explain Dewey's experimental empiricism. But why should we prefer Dewey's empiricism to McDowell's? If we only consider *Mind and World*, I think there is a fairly easy answer to this question: McDowell's minimal empiricism involves a kind of spectator theory in which experience is understood independently of our agency. For McDowell, experience involves doings, but only *mental* doings, and so is not constitutively intertwined with our embodied agency. In experiencing the world, we are open to it, have a view on it, but are not seen as within it or as necessarily interacting with it.

But in his exchange with Dreyfus, McDowell integrates embodied coping skills into his position, making this easy response difficult to make. Perception, he now admits, is openness to affordances, which are "necessarily bound up with embodied coping skills" (McDowell 2009d, 315). While McDowell still thinks that perception opens us up to experienced facts over and above affordances, to a 'world' and not just an 'environment', we could not be so open if perception were not intertwined with embodied coping skills. So McDowell now admits that our being open to the world depends on our embodied agency. Where McDowell and Dreyfus disagree concerns the question of whether such skills involve mindedness or rationality. For McDowell they do, while for Dreyfus they – once we have acquired them – don't. Here is how McDowell characterizes their disagreement:

> [O]n the view I am urging, the point is not, as Dreyfus has it, that our embodied coping skills are independent of any openness in which rationality figures – a ground floor level, supporting a distinct upper story at which openness involves rationality. If that were right, it would follow that our embodied coping skills cannot themselves be permeated with conceptual mindedness ... No doubt we acquire embodied coping skills before we acquire concepts, in the demanding sense that connects with rationality. But when our embodied coping skills come to constitute a background to our openness to the world, the openness to affordances that is an element in what it is for us to have embodied coping skills become *part* of our openness to the world. Openness to affordances draws on the rationality of subjects who are open to the world just as much as any other part of openness to the world does. (McDowell 2009d, 316)

The point is that when an agent who has embodied coping skills acquires, through a learning process, the ability to self-consciously respond to reasons, this ability transforms their skills such that they become informed by the conceptual mindedness that makes possible a larger worldview. In this way our openness to affordances becomes part of our openness to the world, which in the process transforms the affordance. "Affordances are no longer merely input to a human animal's natural motivational tendencies; now they are data for her rationality" (McDowell 2009d, 315). Or in language that McDowell uses elsewhere, affordances are now not only reasons to do something, for example, attack prey, but are reasons *as such* – inputs into a rational process that stands under the question of whether one *should* do what one is naturally motivated to do (see McDowell 2009b, 128).

Dewey agrees with McDowell, against Dreyfus, that embodied coping skills, once acquired, are not mindless. Mindedness is not only found in detached episodes of rationality but permeates the whole 'form of the rational animal', including actualizations of embodied coping skills in which we do not respond to reasons *as such*.[43] But Dewey thinks that McDowell is wrong in thinking that the only way that something, including coping skills, can involve mindedness is by involving actualizations of conceptual capacities. Dewey argues that a properly naturalistic account of the rational animal we are, and a satisfactory account of our answerability to the world, requires recognizing an intermediate layer of meaning that stands between physical processes and concepts. So the ultimate reason we have to prefer Dewey's empiricism to McDowell's concerns the naturalism it involves and the way that it supports an account of answerability. We take this up in the next chapter.

---

[43] Both McDowell and Dewey would say that Dreyfus has an 'added-on theory of rationality'. See Boyle 2016.

CHAPTER 6

Meaning, Habit, and the Myth of the Given

Introduction

In this final chapter, I want to look at the concept of experience at play in Dewey's later naturalistic empiricism.[1] This concept of experience goes beyond the one found in Dewey's experimental empiricism because it not only expands experience to include overt doings; it conceives of experience as continuous with nature. If we are to avoid a supernaturalism that thinks of the experiencing mind as something that stands outside of nature, then experience, Dewey argues, must be seen as a product of, and a participant in, nature.

The question of how experience and nature are related was in fact already at play in Dewey's experimental empiricism. If we remember, this view claims that experience can be a tribunal for thought because it is both independent of and homogeneous with thought. It is independent of thought because it is had rather than known, and what is had in it depends on its being organized by bodily habits and skills, not concepts. It is homogeneous with thought because these habits and skills incorporate, and are therefore funded by, what is learned through past inquiry and problem solving. For experience to meet both of these desiderata, it must therefore be able to be shaped by thought, yet must not be identical with it. How is this possible? Dewey's idea is that the habits that organize experience are neither rational in the way that thought is rational, nor merely natural if by nature we mean that which is subject to explanations that display natural-scientific intelligibility – disenchanted nature. Rather, habits and the experiences they inform are, through being part of a

---

[1] In this chapter, I look at the work Dewey did between *Human Nature and Conduct* (1922) and *Logic: Theory of Inquiry* (1938), focusing especially on *Experience and Nature* (1925).

feedback loop with thought, *second natural* – a product of a learning process that is proper to the type of creature that we are.[2]

I do three main things in this final chapter. First, I articulate the concept of experience at play in Dewey's later naturalistic empiricism. This concept is not merely methodological, as Dewey sometimes suggests, but substantive. Experience is *Erfahrung*, a developmental learning process that involves a feedback loop between the communicatively articulated meanings that comprise intelligence or mind and the bodily habits and skills that comprise our second nature. I show how this idea has its origin in Peirce's theory of meaning. Second, I argue that that Dewey's account of experience as second natural can, unlike McDowell's, support a realist construal of answerability.[3] According to what Dewey calls his 'natural realism' experience is not just developmental but also transactional; it, through interaction, incorporates elements of a world that stands mostly independent of it. Lastly, I examine Rorty's critique of this account of experience, namely that it falls prey to the Myth of the Given. I show that this critique does not hit its mark because it does not take the proper measure Dewey's account of linguistic communication. I end with Rorty's critique of Dewey because my goal in this book has been to show that a pragmatic account of experience can deliver a robust theory of objectivity while not falling prey to the Myth of the Given. In answering Rorty's critique, I meet last this explanatory goal.

Peirce, Meaning, and Habit

At the heart of Dewey's late account of experience (*Erfahrung*) is the idea that there is a feedback loop between meaning and habit.[4] In the pragmatic tradition, this idea did not originate with Dewey. For it is already found in the theory of meaning internal to Peirce's belief-doubt model of inquiry. It would be helpful to first go through this theory.

In his famous papers "The Fixation of Belief" and "How to Make Our Ideas Clear," Peirce outlines a dispositional theory of belief where the

---

[2] For Dewey use of the term 'second nature', see EW 4, 241, MW 5, 309, and LW 14, 259. See Testa 2017 for an excellent discussion of the concept of second nature in Dewey.
[3] Although a realist reading of Dewey is perhaps not the dominant reading, it has a distinguished lineage, including Boisvert 1982, Burke 1984, Sleeper 1986, and Godfrey-Smith 2013. Hildebrand 2003 argues that Dewey escapes the logic of the realist-antirealist controversy altogether.
[4] I agree with Kestenbaum 1977 that the connection between meaning and habit is central for Dewey. But I do not think that his phenomenological account properly grasps the pragmatic context in which the connection between meaning and habit is made.

meaning of a belief is cashed out by the habits it involves. "The essence of belief is the establishment of a habit, and different beliefs are distinguished by the different modes of action to which they give rise" (Peirce 1992, 129–130). He goes on: "To develop [a belief's] meaning, we have therefore simply to determine what habits it produces, for what a thing means is what habits it involves" (Peirce 1992, 131). What do these passages mean?

Belief, according to this dispositional account, "is not a momentary mode of consciousness; it is a habit of mind essentially enduring for some time, and mostly (at least) unconscious; and like other habits, it is (until it meets with some surprise that begins its dissolution) perfectly self-satisfied" (Peirce 1998, 336–337). Beliefs *can* be conscious states, for example, when we first settle into a new belief by overcoming doubt or surprise brought about by a recalcitrance to our thought or action. But in this process of arriving at a new belief, a process Peirce calls inquiry, we establish in our nature 'a rule of action', an enduring and mostly unconscious habit to act in certain ways in certain circumstances. This habit, which guides and shapes future routine coping, comprises the meaning of a belief.

Belief guides and shapes future routine coping because the habits it involves embeds within itself *expectations* about how the object of the belief will behave in certain conditions, expectations garnered from past learning. If I believe the proposition 'Fire is hot', then I expect that it will burn me if I get too near, that if put a pot of water on it then it will boil, etc. If I believe the proposition 'This fluid is red wine', then I expect that if I drink enough of it I will get drunk, that if I spill it on a white shirt the shirt will get stained, etc. These *habits of mind* in turn inform our *bodily* habits: to keep far enough away from flame, to take care not to spill the wine, etc. We should not think that mental habits, habits of inference that comprise one's *logica utens*, and bodily habits, habits that coordinate sensorimotor activity, are distinct. Rather they form a *circuit* in which habits of mind establish in our nature bodily habits, and in which the resistances that stand in the way of the smooth operation of our bodily habits provoke reflection and inquiry that result in modifications of our habits of mind, which then establishes in our natures new bodily habits, and so on.

One acquires both kinds of habit through interacting with the environment, through one's experience of an object's effects on oneself and on other objects, and through one's experience of the effects, or consequences, of acting on the object. Because of this, it is impossible "that we should have an idea in our minds which relates to anything but conceived sensible effects of things. Our idea of anything *is* our idea of its sensible effects" (Peirce 1992, 132). Through such experiences, we learn how the object of our experience behaves and its effects on us and on other objects, and this learning, which has its repository in our mental and bodily habits, prepares us to better deal with the object in the future. As such, these effects have what Peirce calls 'practical bearing'. The effects that have practical bearing comprise the meaning of the conceptions involved in the propositions that we believe. As Peirce famously puts it: "Consider what effects, that might conceivably have practical bearing, we conceive the object of our conception to have. Then, our conception of these effects is the whole of our conception of the object" (Peirce 1992, 132). In other words, if one makes explicit one's conception of the effects of the object due to our perceiving it and acting on it, and which in doing so have potential practical bearing, one will have made the content of the concept of that object as pragmatically clear as it can be.[5]

In "How to Make Our Ideas Clear," Peirce famously illustrates what it is to make one's conception of effects having practical bearing explicit by examining the meaning of the concept 'hard'. When we say 'this diamond is hard', what do we mean by hard? "Evidently that it will not be scratched by many other substances. The whole conception of this quality, as of every other, lies in its conceived effects" (Peirce 1992, 132). To make one's conception explicit here is to make explicit one's expectations about how hard things will behave in interacting with other things, including ourselves. But what if the diamond is not in fact scratched, if it is not brought to an experiential test? Is it hard in that case? Because in this early paper Peirce couches his answer in the indicative conditional (it *will not* be scratched *if* brought to the test), he has no basis to give an answer either way (see Misak 2004, 10). In his later discussions of the pragmatic maxim, Peirce adamantly rejects this conclusion, claiming that the diamond *would* resist being scratched by other substances, whether scratched or not. To mark this change in view, we must use the subjunctive conditional to articulate one's conception of effects rather than the indicative conditional.[6]

---

[5] This pragmatic elucidation of the meaning of a conception does not exhaust its meaning. For Peirce, there are three grades of meaning. The first grade involves the denotation of a concept, one's familiarity with the object of that term. The second grade involves connotation, or the abstract definition of the concept. It is only at the third grade of meaning that we get a pragmatic elucidation of meaning in terms of its practical effects.

[6] For more on the change, see Hookway 2012, 170.

Intellectual concepts ... convey more, not merely than any feeling, but more, too, than any existential fact, namely the *"would-acts"* of habitual behavior; and no agglomeration of actual happenings can ever completely fill up the meaning of a "would-be." But that the *total* meaning of the predication of an intellectual conception consists in affirming that, under all conceivable circumstances of a given kind, the subject of the predication would (or would not) behave in a certain way, – that is, that it either would, or would not, be true that under given experiential circumstances, (or under a given proportion of them, taken *as they would occur* in experience) – *that* proposition, I take to be the kernel of pragmatism (Peirce 1998, 401–402).

Why is this change important for us? It is important because if subjunctive conditionals are needed to make explicit our conception of an object's effects, and if this conception of effects is to have practical bearing, then the type of intelligibility involved in these conditionals must – even though it goes beyond all acts of actual habitual behavior – be able to *inform* the bodily habits that guide future sensory-motor coping with the object. Peirce therefore does not think of our bodily habits merely as rote connections between stimulus and response. Let's call such rote connections 'mere dispositions'. Using Ryle's terminology, we can say that mere dispositions are 'single-track', meaning that their actualization is uniform. The ascription of the mere disposition to bite one's nails to someone is the ascription of a likelihood of their biting one's nails in so-and-so conditions. There are no other actualizations for this susceptibility. The ascription of a habit is for Peirce, in contrast, the ascription of a susceptibility whose actualization is not single-track but 'heterogeneous'. It is heterogeneous because the total meaning of an intellectual concept is filled out by how the object of that concept would behave under *all* circumstances, given the laws of nature. Illustrating the point with Peirce's predicate 'hard', Ryle says: "When an object is described as hard, we do not mean only that it would resist deformation, we mean also that it would, for example, give out a sharp sound if struck, that it would cause us pain if we came into sharp contact with it, that resilient objects would bounce off it, and so indefinitely" (Ryle 1984, 44).[7] The point is that when our action, through past dealings with hard things, comes to be informed by a habit about hard

---

[7] My use of Ryle is not completely in keeping with his self-understanding. Ryle in his discussion of know-how makes a distinction between intelligent practices and habits. Intelligent practices involve a flexible form of know-how, while habits are blind and rote responses to stimuli. Both intelligent practices and habits are acquired and so second natural, but they are second natural in different ways. While "it is of the essence of merely habitual practices that one performance is a replica of its predecessors ... [i]t is of the essence of intelligent practices that one performance is modified by its predecessors" (Ryle 1984, 42). Ryle illustrates the difference by pointing to the difference between a

things, this habit does not lead to one single performance, one that simply repeats past performances. Rather, the habit could lead to an indefinite multiplicity of responses depending on the circumstances and the other habits that one has, and so the habit must involve a type of *varied* and *flexible* embodied practical understanding or know-how.

Dewey also makes a distinction between mere dispositions and habits, but in his terminology, the distinction is between 'routine' and 'intelligent' habits, which are on a continuum. For Dewey, "[h]abit is an ability, an art, formed through past experience" (MW 14, 48). Through past experience subjects inculcate "a mechanism of action, physiologically engrained, which operates 'spontaneously', automatically, whenever its cue is given" (MW 14, 50). Habits must be mostly automatic because if "each act has to be consciously searched for at the moment and intentionally performed execution is painful and the product is clumsy and halting" (MW 14, 51). This mechanism can harden and lead to the repetition of past acts. Think of the habits involved in performing a rudimentary task on an assembly line. But as one performs more and more complex actions to meet novel and variable circumstances, one's habits become infused with the thought and feeling necessary to deal with those circumstances, growing "more varied, more adaptable" (MW 14, 50–51) in the process. Through coping with novel situations we therefore develop intelligent and not just routine habits. Dewey illustrates by comparing the habits of an artist and a mere technician:

> How delicate, prompt, sure and varied are the movements of a violin player or engraver! How unerringly they phrase every shade of emotion and every turn of idea! . . . [T]he difference between the artist and the mere technician is unmistakable. The artist is a masterful technician. The technique or mechanism is fused with thought and feeling. The "mechanical" performer permits the mechanism to dictate the performance. It is absurd to say that the latter exhibits habits and the former not. We are confronted with two kinds of habit, intelligent and routine. (MW 14, 51)

For Peirce, the acquisition of heterogeneous or intelligent habits is not ultimately for the sake of instrumental efficiency but rather to institute – insofar as it 'is up to us' – what he calls 'concrete reasonableness', a state in which our dealings with things, theoretical and practical, are rationally

---

mountaineer moving across a field of ice-covered rocks and a normal person walking on pavement. But the pragmatist would say, I think rightly, that these two practices are on a continuum. Certainly one involves more skill than the other, but they are not so different as to be of different *kinds*. Both practices involve habits, but in the first case the habits are flexible while in the second they are rote. See Brett 1981 for an excellent critique of Ryle on this point.

self-controlled and for the sake of proper ends. Rational self-control does not stem from a faculty that is distinct from our practices, Reason with a capital R, but rather – because "every man exercises more or less control over himself by means of modifying his own habits" (Peirce 1998, 413) – from having the right mental and bodily habits. We reach a state of concrete reasonableness when, through a backward-facing type of self-criticism, we mold our future-facing intellectual and bodily habits so as to be for the sake of the proper ends – those ends of feeling, action, and thought prescribed by what Peirce calls the normative sciences. What I want to propose is that Dewey's account of experience (*Erfahrung*) as a learning process is fundamentally an account of a process that forwards concrete reasonableness. In this respect, there is a deep continuity between Peirce and Dewey. Let us see how.

Experience As a Learning Process

Although Dewey would distance himself from the mentalistic connotations of the terms 'belief' and 'doubt', his theory of inquiry follows Peirce's account of the belief-doubt cycle quite closely. As we saw in the previous chapter, this theory begins with an account of a situated agent coping pre-reflectively with a physical and social environment. But because the environment is precarious and unstable agents often find themselves in an indeterminate or disrupted situation, one in which absorbed modes of coping break down, giving rise to 'doubt'. To replace 'doubt' with 'belief' by overcoming indeterminacy, subjects must engage in a reflective process, inquiry, which involves a cycle of perception, inference, action, and perception. Here subjects, alone or with others, must both discern the facts of the case and creatively go beyond the facts by acting experimentally on an idea or hypothesis. If this action 'works' to unify the disrupted situation, to re-establish belief, then one is entitled to make a warranted judgment and be credited with knowledge.

While the ascertaining of a warranted or valid judgment through inquiry is still very important for Dewey, he, in his later theory of experience, comes to emphasize the distinction "between knowledge as the outcome of special inquiries (undertaken because of the presence of problems) and *intelligence* as the product and expression of cumulative funding of the meanings reached in these special cases" (LW 14, 6). In the latter case, when a unified situation is reestablished through reflective problem solving, the agent not only solves the problem at hand but also, however slightly, modifies their habits in light of what has been learned, making their habits – and therefore future primary experience – richer and more intelligent. Habits are therefore the repository of what is learned through past problem solving and the factor that prepares us for subsequently enriched experience. Here is how Dewey puts it:

> [T]he denotative reference of "mind" and 'intelligence' is to funding of meanings and significances, a funding which is both a product of past inquiries or knowings and the means of enriching and controlling the subject-matters of subsequent experience. The function of enrichment and control is exercised by incorporation of what was gained in past experience in attitudes and habits which, in their interaction with the environment, create the clearer, better ordered, "fuller" or richer materials of later experiences – a process capable of infinite extension. (LW 14, 6)

This process, capable of infinite extension, refers neither to primary experience nor to reflective or secondary experience. Rather, it is a developmental learning process that involves a feedback loop between primary and secondary experience – between immediately had experiences that incorporate what has been learned through past reflective experience, and reflective experiences that are more intelligent because they emerge from and draw upon such enriched experiences. This developmental learning process as a whole *is* experience, experience understood as *Erfahrung*.[8] Within this process, the meanings generated by reflective activity have a top-down influence on our bodily habits and skills, and our habits and skills have a bottom-up influence on meaning. When this process moves forward in a felicitous manner, there is *growth*, which is Dewey's naturalistic version of *Bildung*. Growth, we could say, is the unending process by which one takes on a second nature by making the concrete reasonable and the reasonable concrete.

Dewey's account of experience (*Erfahrung*) is complicated by two factors. First, his notion of meaning is connected not just to the world-directed habits of an individual subject, as it is on the Peirceian account discussed earlier, but also to an account of linguistic *communication*.[9] Indeed, he is committed to the thesis that meaning has its origin in communication. So if we are going to understand the relationship between meaning and habit that stands at the center of experience, we have to make

---

[8] Colin Koopman, in Koopman 2014, asks why 'experience' is the key term that characterizes Dewey's view rather than 'action' or 'conduct'. We can now see why: learning is more important for Dewey than action itself.

[9] Of course, Peirce also has a semiotics in which – because of the triangular nature of the sign – communication plays an essential role. One of the goals of Peirce's late pragmaticism is to integrate the pragmatic account of meaning found in his 1878 papers with this semiotics.

a detour to grasp Dewey's account of linguistic communication. This we shall do in the sections on 'Dewey on Linguistic Communication' and 'Meaning and Habit'. Second, habits for Dewey are natural and social functions that can only be specified by making mention of both organism and environment. Because this is so, the meanings that are incorporated in our habits somehow involve the environment. We shall see how this is so in the section on 'Dewey's Natural Realism'.

Dewey on Linguistic Communication

Language for Dewey is wider than oral or written speech. It includes all physical existents that operate as a medium of communication by having a representative capacity or meaning. So language includes, for example, gestures, rites, monuments, and the products of the industrial and fine arts (LW 12, 52). But oral and written speech, linguistic-behavior, is the heart of language for Dewey, and we shall focus on it.

We can grasp the distinctive nature of Dewey's account of speech by contrasting it with what we could call the Lockean or empiricist view. Both positions view speech functionally, as a *tool* to help us achieve our purposes and ends. For Dewey, famously, language is the 'tool of tools'. But the similarity ends there. On the Lockean view speech is a tool to helps one transmit one's private thoughts to other speakers. Meaning resides in these private thoughts, which in introspection are immediately present to our minds, words name or stand for these meanings, and speech is the means by which we get a hearer to understand them. As Dewey puts it, speech is a "mechanical go-between to convey observations and ideas that have prior and independent existence ... It consists of 'mere words', sounds, that happen to be associated with perceptions, sentiments and thoughts that are complete prior to language. Language thus 'expresses' thought as a pipe conducts water" (LW 1, 134). This view is profoundly Cartesian and individualist because it assumes that minds can possess meaningful perceptions, sentiment, and thoughts prior to social exchange and intercourse. While language helps a subject convey these states to others, something that is practically useful, it has no role in making meaning possible in the first place. It therefore has no "fundamental intellectual significance" (LW 1, 134).[10]

For Dewey, in contrast, the function of language is not to express thoughts that are intelligible in their own right, but to facilitate, through communication, social cooperation and mutual participation in joint

---

[10] For an excellent comparison of the Deweyian and Lockean views, see Black 1962.

activity. "The heart of language is not 'expression' of something antecedent, much less expression of antecedent thought. It is communication; the establishment of cooperation in an activity in which there are partners, and in which the activity of each is modified and regulated by partnership" (LW 1, 141). The Lockean view takes things the wrong way round. Communication does not express antecedently intelligible private thoughts; rather, such thoughts are made possible by communication. Here we find Dewey making an argument akin to Wittgenstein's private language argument:

> When the introspectionist thinks he has withdrawn into a wholly private realm of events disparate in kind from other events, made out of mental stuff, he is only turning his attention to his own soliloquy. And soliloquy is the product and reflex of converse with others; social communication is not an effect of soliloquy. If we had not talked with others and they with us, we should never talk to and with ourselves ... Through speech a person dramatically identifies himself with potential acts and deeds; he plays many roles, not in successive stages of life but in a contemporaneously enacted drama. Thus mind emerges. (LW 1, 135)

Because mind itself is a product of inner speech, and inner speech is a product of linguistic communication with others, "language makes the difference between brute and man" (LW 1, 134). Here Dewey agrees with Rorty. But Dewey, unlike Rorty, thinks that he has an obligation to explain *how* the mode of organized interaction that is linguistic communication *emerges* from modes of interaction that are not communicative. Unless one accepts a supernaturalism that posits "a breach of historic and natural continuity, cognitive experience must originate within that of a non-cognitive sort" (LW 1, 29–30).

Dewey attempts to meet this obligation by giving a naturalistic account of language as the medium of "social cooperation and mutual participation," in which "continuity is established between natural events (animal sounds, cries, etc.) and the origin and development of meaning" (LW 1, 6). While there is a significant distinction between minded creatures, those that can operate in the communicatively articulated space of meanings, and creatures that are not minded, this distinction is not an unbridgeable dualism because *communication* and so *meaning is itself natural*. Meaning is not found in nature independently of the development of language as the medium of our cooperative social practices, but nor is it projected onto nature by these practices. Rather, communication, and the meaning articulated through it, is an existential occurrence pertaining to a complex social association that brings out powers and potentialities *in us and in nature* that would not be there unless this association were instituted. Meaning is therefore "a genuine character of natural events when these attain the stage of widest and most complex interactions with one another" (LW 1, 7).[11]

Dewey's naturalist explanation of the origin of linguistic behavior attempts to explain how gestures and cries, which in nonhuman animals are merely organic behaviors that take part in stimulus-response chains, can develop into communicative signs that have meaning. They do so "not by intent and mind but by over-flow, by-products, in gestures and sound. The story of language is the story of *use* made of these occurrences" (LW 1, 139). In nonhuman animals gestures and cries can be signaling acts, acts that call out certain kinds of responses in other animals. Here one thinks of sexual displays or of cries that signal the presence of predators. But the responses to such an act by the animal that performs it and the animal that witnesses it are not responses to a meaningful sign, but merely reactions to stimuli. How does it come about that these responses to stimuli become responses to meaningful signs? It comes about when the response to the gestures or cries of another individual is undertaken

> from a standpoint that is not strictly personal but is common to them as participants or "parties" in a conjoint undertaking. It may be directed by and toward some physical existence. But it first has reference to some other person or persons with whom it institutes *communication* – the making of something common. Hence, to that extent its reference becomes general and "objective." (LW 12, 52)

To illustrate, Dewey compares the behavior of hens being fed by a farmer with the behavior of a developing infant. When the farmer raises his hand to throw grain, the hens scatter. "They act as if alarmed, his movement is thus not a sign of food; it is a stimulus to flight" (LW 1, 140). In other words, they do not understand the significance of his arm movement, that it *means* something beyond its movement. An infant, on the other hand, begins to treat such events "as signs of an ulterior event so that his response is to their meaning. He treats them as means to consequences. The hen's activity is egocentric; that of the human being participative" (LW 1, 140). The infant breaks out of the egocentric predicament by learning to see things from the other's point of view, to grasp their intentions given the situation.[12] In Mead's terms, they can 'take the

---

[11] For much more on this, see Dewey's paper 'The Inclusive Philosophical Idea', in LW 3.
[12] Dewey's concept of intention is not the one found in the Gricean program. Because meaning involves taking the standpoint of the other, understanding things from their perspective, "meaning

standpoint of the other', and in so doing can attribute meaning to the other's gestures. When this ability is transferred to physical existences, sounds or marks, whose meaning is 'conventional', the child is able to take part in coordinated linguistic behavior, to communicate.

Here we should be reminded of Davidson's account of triangulation. For the essential difference between human and nonhuman animals on that account is that human animals, unlike nonhuman animals, can enter a communicative triangle in which "[s]omething is literally made common in at least two different centers of behavior" (LW 1, 141). Meaning emerges in this triangle insofar as one's "response to another's act involves contemporaneous response to a thing as entering into the other's behavior, and this upon both sides" (LW 1, 141). It would be difficult to find a better paraphrase for Davidson's idea.

How does this account of the origin of linguistic behavior bear on Dewey's account of linguistic meaning?[13] The meaning of the physical items that are used as signs in linguistic behavior, sounds or marks, is conventional. But "the convention or common consent which sets it apart as a means of recording and communicating meaning is that of agreement in *action*: of shared modes of responsive behavior and participation in their consequences. The physical sound or mark gets its meaning in and by conjoint community of functional use, not by any explicit convening in a 'convention'" (LW 12, 52). In being, a shared mode of response, meaning is not anything psychic. It is primarily a functional property of behavior; it exists, as it were, in between cooperating agents and the world. For this reason meanings are objective. "Meanings are objective because they are modes of natural interaction; such an interaction, although primarily between organic beings ... includes things and energies external to living creatures" (LW 1, 149).[14]

Dewey illustrates the point by discussing a traffic policeman who directs traffic by hand gesture and whistle. Like sounds and marks, these physical existences have a conventional meaning. The whistle does not merely stimulate a reliable response disposition but is a sign that means something

---

is intent." But it is not intent in any "private and exclusive sense" (LW 1, 142) since intent only comes about within the cooperative behavioral situation. The Griceian program is a version of the empiricist or Lockean program. See chapter 4 of Tiles 1988.

[13] This account of the origin of communication is promissory insofar as it names the capacity that must be acquired to communicate linguistically, taking the role of the other, rather than explaining how it comes about. I take it Dewey thought Mead provided this explanation. See Mead 1962.

[14] Dewey's response to the charge of psychologism is found here. While meanings, including logical meanings, do not reside in a Platonic third realm, they are not subjective or reducible to psychic processes. Meanings are rather objective functional properties of conjoint behavior.

because it "embodies a rule of social action" (LW 1, 149) that both policeman and driver understand.[15] Grasp of this rule allows them to reciprocally take up the 'role of the other', to grasp the expectations and attitudes of the other toward the conjoint situation. But these expectations and attitudes are expressive of "the rule, comprehensive and persisting, the standardized habit, of social interaction, and for the sake of which the whistle is used" (LW 1, 149). The meaning of the whistle is thereby specified by articulating the rule, embodied in habits acquired from past experience, that determines how in a given situation we are to coordinate our action with others.[16] But we cannot specify the rule embodied in our habits without reference to objective features of the world – i.e., to the "orderly arrangement of the movement of persons and vehicles established by social agreement as its consequence" (LW 1, 150). So the meaning of the whistle, while dependent upon agreements in use, refers to the coordination of physical things and ultimately to the "total consequent system of social behavior" (LW 1, 150).

But meaning is, secondarily, also a property of the objects that play a role in this cooperative behavior. In playing a role in cooperative behavior, an object "ceases to be just what it brutely is at the moment, and is responded to in its potentiality, as a means to remoter consequences" (LW1, 142). When an "event has meaning, its potential consequences become its integral and funded feature" (LW 1, 143). For instance, some of the consequences of the way in which fire interacts with other things concern us insofar as we use fire in our conjoint activities. In light of this concern, fire is no longer just an existential occurrence, it rather means, potentially, heat for warmth or cooking, the ability to sow a field or to smelt ore, etc. Accordingly, the "meaning, or essence, denominated fire, is

---

[15] We could, of course, make exactly the same point if we were talking about an order that the officer might make in speech: the order for one to stop is not merely a stimulus to behave in a certain way, because it involves a rule of action that both the officer and the one ordered to stop understand.

[16] As Max Black points out, there seems to be a slide here between the language of rules and the language of habits. While a rule has normative force such that when an officer whistles, one *ought* to stop, a habit is a regularity such that when one hears the whistle, one stops. While one can break or go against a rule, one can't go against a habit; it either exercises itself in response to stimuli or it doesn't. But Dewey does not accept this dichotomy between the 'ought-ness' of rules and 'is-ness' of habits. For him, the rules that govern a practice are instituted by the expectations that participants in the practice reciprocally have due to their taking up of the role of the other. But these expectations, which are mostly implicit, are grounded in their ongoing learned habits of response. So rules are ultimately grounded in habits, but habits, as we know, are not mere responses to stimuli but 'concrete forms of reasonableness'. Our ability to go against a rule is not the product of a disembodied act of 'stepping back' from the rule and deciding to do otherwise, but the product of an embodied situation in which two habits conflict, requiring conscious deliberation to put one's finger on the scale of decision.

the consequences of certain natural events within the scheme of human activities, in the experience of social intercourse, the hearth and domestic alter, shared comfort, working of metals, rapid transit, and other such affairs" (LW 1, 150). These consequences are, through experience, embodied in our habits, which supply the rules for our subsequent dealings with fire. Meanings and the signs which through agreements in use denote these meanings, are therefore elements in human experience that are both social and world directed, involved in our cooperative activity with each other and in our joint attempt to cope with a changing and insecure environment.

Meaning and Habit

I said earlier that the communicatively articulated meanings that are utilized by intelligence in reflective experience have a downward influence on the habits and bodily skills that organize primary experience, and that these habits have an upward influence on meanings. I can now cash this thought out.

Habits have an upward influence on the use of reflective intelligence because the "'stuff' from which thinking draws its material in satisfying need by establishing a new relation to the surroundings is found in what, with some extension of the usual sense of the word, may be termed habits: namely the changes wrought in our ways of acting and undergoing by prior experience" (LW 2, 106). Dewey extends the usual sense of the term because while habits are organic modifications, they nonetheless, in mediating the coordination of our sensorimotor system, have what we would normally consider to be cognitive effects. The first effect is negative: habits fix the boundaries of reflective thought, keeping it focused and on track. "Outside the scope of habits, thought works gropingly, fumbling in confused uncertainty" (MW 14, 121). Reflective thought is not fumbling in inquiry because "old habit supplies content, filling, definite, recognizable subject-matter. It begins as vague presentiment of what we are going towards" (MW 14, 126). The second effect is positive insofar as habits positively enable our ability to attend, perceive, and think. "[H]abit ... signifies a building up and solidifying of certain desires; and increasing sensitiveness and responsiveness to certain stimuli, a confirmed or an impaired capacity to attend to and think about certain things" (LW 7, 171). Because habits have this enabling role, the "more numerous our habits the wider the field of possible observation and foretelling. The more flexible they are, more refined is perception in its discrimination and the more delicate the presentation evoked in imagination. The sailor is intellectually at home on the sea, the hunter in the forest, the painter in the studio, the man of science in the laboratory" (MW 14, 123). What an experienced sailor is able to notice and attend to, and is therefore able to think about, is quite distinct from the non-sailor, and the same goes for the hunter, the painter, the man of science, etc. For Dewey, therefore, there "is no immaculate conception of meanings or purposes. Reason pure of all influence from prior habit is a fiction" (MW 14, 25).

But meaning also has a downward influence on the habits and organic feelings that organize primary experience. "Meanings acquired in connection with the use of tools and of language exercise a profound influence on organic feelings. In the reckoning of this account, are included the changes effected by all the consequences of attitude and habit due to *all* the consequences of tools and language – in short, civilization" (LW1, 227–228). Indeed, Dewey thinks that this – the extent to which our organic feelings and habits are "saturated with the results of social intercourse and communication" – is the feature of "everyday experience which has been most systematically ignored by philosophers" (LW 1, 6). This saturation has both substantive and formal effects.

We can grasp both of these effects by considering three strands of linguistic meaning hinted at but not explicitly discussed earlier, what Dewey calls 'referential', 'immanent', and 'symbolic' meaning.[17] Referential meaning is at play when "something means something else in the sense of signifying it, being a sign of it. This is equivalent to taking one thing as evidence for something else, a ground for inference to the other thing, as when we say smoke means fire" (LW 3, 87). Here smoke as an event in space and time means – is a natural index of – another event in space and time, fire. Immanent meanings are parasitic on referential meanings insofar as they "exist in consequence of the repeated successful outcome of referential or evidential meanings." In this case, they become "the directly taken-for-granted-meaning, of subsequent situations" (LW 3, 87).[18] To

---

[17] For a very good account of referential and immanent meaning, see Pratt 1997. Dewey talks about symbols and their meaning, but not 'symbolic meaning' strictly speaking (see LW 12, 57). But I think the concept is implicit in Dewey's discussion.

[18] In *Experience and Nature*, Dewey calls immanent meaning 'sense' and referential meaning 'significance'.

> Sense is distinct from feeling, for it has recognized reference, it is the qualitative characteristic of something, not just a submerged unidentified quality or tone. Sense is also different from signification. The latter involves use of a quality as a sign or index of something else, as when the red of a light signifies danger ... The sense of a thing, on the other hand, is an immediate and immanent meaning; it is meaning which is itself felt or directly had. (LW 1, 200)

illustrate, Dewey, following Everett Hall, gives the example of a sailor hearing the sound of a sail blowing out of its bolt ropes. For an inexperienced sailor, the sound would only have referential meaning. They would hear the sound and have to do something, make an observation or inference, to find out what it meant.

> If, however, the sailor is experienced, the consequences of his prior-tested and verified inferences enter directly into the object of perception; the noise will *be*, to him, a sail blown out of its bolt ropes. This sort of thing is what is intended by the phrase "immanent meaning" ... In such cases there is no distinction of something as a sign and something else as a thing signified; there is a total situation "had", having its direct meaning-content. (LW 3, 89)

Of course, this immanent meaning may be the basis for a future referential meaning – for instance, when the experienced sailor wants to know not only that, but why, the sail blew out of its bolt ropes. To ascertain this, they must go beyond the immanent meaning of the situation.

The immanent meaning of this experience, the 'total situation had', can have this character because habits "enter into the *constitution* of the situation; they are in and of it, not, so far as it is concerned, something outside of it" (Dewey 2007, 141). In other words, it is the sailor's habits, the repository of what they have learned though past experience and the shaper of their capacity to attend, perceive, and think about certain things, that carry the immanent meaning of the situation they are in. This, we could say, is the *substance* of the situation. But they can only have these habits due to 'past tests and verified inferences', which depend on the referential meanings that they have gleaned. So the experience is both immediate and mediated. "[S]ituations are *immediate* in their direct occurrence, and mediating and mediated in the temporal continuum constituting life-experience" (LW 14, 30). The sail blowing out is directly and non-inferentially heard by the sailor. But the condition of possibility for their directly hearing the sound as the sail blowing out is their already having undergone a learning process. In Sellars' classic rendering, the experience is non-inferential but *not* presuppositionless. The experience, while immediate, is therefore not Given.[19]

Referential meanings not only become immanent meanings, however, but also come to be denoted by the artificial signs or symbols that enter into linguistic discourse. In so being, these meanings are significantly transformed. For example, when the symbol 'smoke' is developed, the meaning smoke "is *liberated* with respect to its representative function. It is

---

[19] For Sellars, one of the chief causes of the Myth of the Given is the belief that the relation of presupposition *must* be an inferential relation. See Sellars 1997, 69.

no longer tied down. It can be related to other meanings in the language system; not only to that of fire but to such apparently unrelated meanings as friction, change of temperature, oxygen, molecular constitution, and, by intervening meaning-symbols, the laws of thermodynamics" (LW 14, 58). The symbol 'smoke', unlike the referential meaning smoke, is not *evidence* for, or a natural sign of, something else, fire; rather, it refers, *through the agreements in use made possible by communication,* to an object, to an event with meaning. Because symbols can refer to objects when they are not present, or even when they do not exist, they make thought and reasoning possible:

> When communication occurs, all natural events are subject to reconsideration and revision ... Events turn into objects, things with meaning. They may be referred to when they do not exist, and thus be operative among things distant in space and time ... Events when once they are named lead an independent and double life. In addition to their original existence, they are subject to ideal experimentation, their meanings may be infinitely combined and re-arranged in imagination, and the outcome of this inner experimentation – which is thought – may issue forth in interaction with crude and raw events. (LW 1, 132)

We now have our three forms of meaning on the table: the referential meanings by which one thing is a natural index or sign of another thing, the learned immanent meanings that immediately fund a situation, and the liberated symbolic meanings that are the object of discourse and thought. This last form of meaning is critical for understanding the formal effects of the saturation of our habits by the results of social intercourse and communication, for symbolic meaning allows, in an unprecedented way, the "consequences of the experience of one form of life" to be "integrated in the behavior of others" (LW 1, 213). In other words, symbolic meaning allows for new kinds of intersubjective learning processes insofar as such processes can now be detached from what is immediately present in a situation of instruction. While referential and immanent meanings are critical for such learning processes – for without them what is learned would be disembodied and not able to be integrated into a conspecific's routine behavioral repertoire – symbolic meanings allow for the transmission not only of present consequences of experience, but also of past and envisaged future consequences. Now,

> [n]ot merely its own distant world of space-time is involved in its conduct but the world of its fellows. When consequences which are unexperienced and future to one agent are experienced and past to another creature with which it is in communication, organic prudence becomes conscious

expectation, and future affairs living present realities. Human learning and habit-formation present thereby an integration of organic-environmental connections so vastly superior to those of animals without language that its experience appears to be super-organic. (LW 1, 213–214)[20]

For animals that do not engage in linguistic communication, "habit-forming wears grooves; behavior is confined to channels established by prior behavior ... The very operation of learning sets a limit to itself, and makes subsequent learning more difficult" (LW 1, 214). The habits of the animal have a routine rather than intelligent form. But the sheer complexity of the meanings at play in the intergenerational learning processes made possible by communication removes this limit, making it possible for our habits to take on an intelligent form:

> Communication not only increases the number and variety of habits, but tends to link them subtly together, and eventually to subject habit-forming in a particular case to the habit of recognizing that new modes of association with exact a new use of it. Thus habit is formed in view of possible future changes and does not harden so readily ... Each habit demands appropriate conditions for exercise and when habits are numerous and complex, as with the human organism, to find these conditions involves search and exploration; the organism is compelled to make variations, and exposed to error and disappointment ... Hence instability, novelty, emergence of unexpected and unpredictable combinations. The more an organism learns – the more that is, the former terms of a historic process are retained and integrated in the present phase – the more it has to learn, in order to keep itself going. (LW 1, 214–215)

Dewey's Natural Realism

We now understand how Dewey's account of experience (*Erfahrung*) involves a feedback loop between meaning and habit. But we must also see that this loop is nothing 'subjective', something that pertains merely to the meaning of *our* representations of how things are. The meanings at play in this learning process are transactional; they *incorporate* the world. This is the basis of what Dewey calls his natural realism (see LW 1, 260).

To grasp what this means we must see how Dewey situates his account of experience within a wider biological or ecological account of

---

[20] For a deeply worked out account of cultural learning consistent in the main with Dewey's, see Tomasello 1999.

organism-environment relations.[21] The organic structure of a living thing is not self-standing because it can only maintain its unity in the face of entropic forces through interacting with the environment. "Whatever else organic life is or is not, it is a process of activity that involves the environment. It is a transaction extending beyond the spatial limits of the organism. An organism does not live *in* an environment: it lives by means of an environment" (LW 12, 32). Dewey mentions breathing and the intake of food, but we could also mention locomotion and the activation of one's sensory system as capacities that require literal interaction with the environment. Unlike inanimate things, which are merely subject to physical forces, living organisms are "self-maintaining," they perpetuate their form through maintaining "a fairly uniform integration with the environment" (LW 12, 33).[22]

Different organisms maintain relative balance with the environment differently depending upon their distinct capacities, which means that the environment is not a uniform concept. The environmental affordances that stand out to a creature, that are taken by a creature, depend not just on the intrinsic nature of an environment but also on the organization and capacities of the creature's body, its creaturely interests and ends, etc. An environment, unlike nature generally, is therefore the result of an organism/world coupling in which what is passively given and what is actively taken are mutually determining. This stands in contrast to the standard view that supposes

> that organism and environment are "given" as independent things and interaction is a third independent thing which finally intervenes. In fact, the distinction is a practical and temporal one, arising out of the state of tension in which the organism at a given time, in a given phase of life activity, is set over the environment as it then and there exists. There is, of course, a natural world that exists independently of the organism, but this world is *environment* only as it enters directly and indirectly into life-functions. The organism is itself a part of the larger natural world and exists as organism only in active connections with the environment. (LW 12, 40)

Because living creatures try to maintain homeostatic unity through continual interaction with the environment, there is 'good' and 'evil' for

---

[21] The origin of this account can be found in Dewey's reading of Hegel's philosophy of Subjective Spirit. See Dewey 2010, Pearce 2014, Levine 2015c, and Testa 2017.
[22] See Thompson 2007 for an enactive account of the self-maintenance of the organism that is consistent with Dewey's view.

living creatures: good being that which advances continued unity through difference (survival), evil being that which disperses it (death). As Dewey puts it, "natural energies sometimes carry the organic functions prosperously forward, and sometimes act counter to their continuance. Growth and decay, health and disease, are alike continuous with activities of the natural surroundings. The difference lies in the bearing of what happens upon future life activity" (MW 10, 7). To forward 'good', a creature must continually, in the face of the need that arises with disequilibrium, recover equilibrium with the environment through search and exploration. If it achieves recovery, there is fulfillment or satisfaction. In higher organisms especially, this cycle of disturbance and recovery is not a "*restoration* of the previous *state* of the *organism*" but rather "the institution of an integrated *relation* . . . compatible with definite change in both the organism and the environment" (LW 12, 35). There is change in the environment because to recover equilibrium requires that one modify the environment rather than just adapt *to* it – it requires that one "change the environmental changes going on around it" (MW 10, 7). And there is change in the organism because to successfully sustain equilibrium, advantageous changes in behavior must be learned and stored by the organism. This is achieved "through change in the organic structures that conditions further behavior. This modification constitutes what is termed habit" (LW 12, 38).

Habit is an organization of organic life, and so, like life, involves the environment. In this habits can be "profitably compared to physiological functions like breathing, digesting" (MW 14, 15). Unlike these functions, however, habits are acquired. But, like them, habits require "the cooperation of organism and environment" (MW 14, 15) and cannot be specified without making mention of both. Both "functions and habits are" therefore "ways of using and incorporating the environment in which the latter has its say as surely as the former" (MW 14, 15). But while physiological functions institute integrated relations with the physical environment, human habits institute integrated relations with both the physical *and* the social/cultural environment. Indeed, the social environment has a type of primacy because to "a very large extent the ways in which human beings respond to even physical conditions are influenced by their cultural environment. Light and fire are physical facts. But the occasions in which humans respond to things as merely physical in purely physical ways are comparatively rare" (LW 12, 48).

The main difference between the physical and social environments concerns the fact that the structures that comprise the social environment – customs, social practices, and institutions – are transmitted historically through learning processes rather than physical heredity:

> Man, as Aristotle has remarked, is a *social* animal. This fact introduces him into situations and originates problems and ways of solving them that have no precedent upon the organic biological level. For man is social in another sense than the bee and ant, since his activities are encompassed in an environment that is culturally transmitted, so that what man does and how he acts, is determined not by organic structure and physical heredity alone but by the influence of cultural heredity, embedded in traditions, institutions, customs and the purposes and beliefs they both carry and inspire. (LW 12, 49)

As mentioned earlier, language plays a central role here because it "is itself a cultural institution ... among many such institutions" and "it is (1) the agency by which other institutions and acquired habits are *transmitted*, and (2) it *permeates* both the forms and the contents of all other cultural activities" (LW 12, 51). Because linguistic communication allows for cultural transmission and permeates what is transmitted, there can be cumulative intersubjective learning processes through time. This allows us to develop complex means of coping with the environment – customs, traditions, and institutions – that seem to have no precedent in nature.

But the *substance* of these transmitted customs, practices, and institutions depends not just on their permeation by language but also on their incorporation into our habits:

> [T]he neuro-muscular structures of individuals are modified through the influence of the cultural environment upon the activities performed. The acquisition and understanding of language with proficiency in the arts (that are foreign to other animals than men) represent an incorporation within the physical structure of human beings of the effects of cultural conditions, an interpenetration so profound that resulting activities are as direct and seemingly "natural" as are the first reactions of the infant. To speak, to read, to exercise any art, industrial, fine, or political, are instances of modifications wrought *within* the biological organism by cultural environment. (LW 12, 49)

Insofar as habits are the result of the modifications wrought within the human organism *by* the social environment, we can understand what Dewey means when he says that habits "are things done *by* the environment" (MW 14, 15) to the organism. Habits are accordingly natural and social functions insofar as their acquisition institutes integrated relations between us and the customs, practices, and institutions that make up the social environment.

In light of this, we can see that when Dewey says that habits "involve" both "skills of sensory and motor organs ... and objective materials," that they "assimilate objective energies and eventuate in command of the environment" (MW 14, 15–16), he therefore means that they assimilate physical *and* social materials and energies. With respect to the latter, think about what it takes to engage in complex social practices like playing the piano, stone masonry, or going to a dinner party. "We should laugh at any one who said that he was master of stone working, but the art was cooped up within him and no wise dependent upon support from objects and assistance from tools" (MW 14, 16). We would laugh because it is obvious that to successfully take part in these practices requires not only interacting with 'objective materials' – piano, stone, the sentiments and emotions of other people[23] – but also incorporating their energies into oneself by conforming one's activity *to* their properties, connections, and typical behaviors. The habits that sustain fluid and expert practice are the result of this incorporation. But, of course, the differing ways that we assimilate objective energies into our practice depends not just on the object of the practice, its properties, relations, and typical behaviors, but also on the culturally transmitted history of the practice itself. Both the stonemason and the sculptor have stone as their object, but they integrate its objective energies into their habits and skills in quite different ways due to the demands of their historically reproduced practices.

We are now in a position to understand how experience as a learning process incorporates the world. As we know, what is learned through inquiry is incorporated into our habits. Habits, as stated earlier, are the repository of what is learned through past experience, and they prepare the way for subsequent experience. But habits are also physical and social functions that cannot be specified without making mention of both organism and environment, physical and social. So when the stonemason changes their habits through solving a problem in their practice, they do not just change *their* habits and skills; they change their integrated

---

[23] Concerning the interaction with the emotions and sentiments of other people, Dewey says this about anger specifically:

> In short, the meaning of native activities is not native; it is acquired. It depends upon interaction with a matured social medium. In the case of a tiger or eagle, anger may be identified with a serviceable life-activity, with attack and defense. With a human being it is as meaningless as a gust of wind on a mudpuddle apart from a direction given it by the presence of other persons, apart from the responses they make to it ... They and all similar human displays ... are not pure impulses; they are habits formed under the influence of association with others who have habits already. (MW 14, 65–66)

relations with the environment. In acting on stone and being acted on by it in a new way they institute a new relationship with the environment generally. Because an environment is constituted by interaction, a change in the nature of this interaction, on either side, *changes the environment*. But there is no commitment to idealism here, to the idea that this change *constructs* the environment or its objects. In instituting a new integrated relationship with stone through action, the stonemason does not construct it as an object but *reconstructs* it:

> To call action of thought in constituting objects direct is the same as to say that it is miraculous. For it is not thought as idealism defines thought which exercises the reconstructive function. Only action, interaction, can change or remake objects. The analogy of the skilled artist still holds. His intelligence is a factor in forming new objects which mark a fulfillment. But this is because intelligence is incarnate in overt action, using things as means to affect other things. (LW 1, 126)

The reconstructed object "is the same object" upon which the stonemason was working before, "but the same object with a difference, as a man who has been through conditions which try the temper of his being comes out the same man and a different man" (LW 4, 236). The question is whether this account, very plausible in the case of a practice like stonemasonry, can be transferred to theoretical practices that have more disinterested forms of knowledge as their goal.

Realist critics of Dewey answer this question negatively.[24] While they might admit that Dewey denies that thought brings objects into existence, they nevertheless find the idea that thought 'reconstructs' the object of knowledge, and *not just our view of the object*, to be expressive of a kind of idealism. Here is how Misak recently put it: "For Dewey, the object of knowledge is not something that exists before we inquire. Inquiry creates the object of knowledge. Things emerge out of our inquiries. We construct them, rather than discover them" (Misak 2013, 122). Since Misak here equates 'objects of knowledge' with 'things', it is clear that she thinks that Dewey is committed to an idealism in which the things that populate the world are constructed by inquiry rather than discovered. It is also clear that she agrees with Dewey's realist opponents when they argue that he denies the "core realist tenet" that "there is an external world and we can have knowledge of it" (Misak 2013, 122).

---

[24] For a representative sample of such critics, see McGilvary 1908, Cohen 1940, Murphy 1951, Russell 1951, Santayana 1951, and Misak 2013. For Dewey's engagement with early twentieth-century realists and idealists, see Shook 1995 and Hildebrand 2003.

Meaning, Habit, and the Myth of the Given

Let us consider an example discussed by Dewey, the discovery of America.[25] America as an existence obviously existed before its discovery. As Dewey says, "existence antecedent to search and discovery is of course admitted" (LW 1, 124), and existence "certainly does not ask leave from thought to exist" (LW 4, 236). But was America an *object of knowledge* before search and discovery, before real changes were brought about through our interaction with it? Dewey's answer is no. The "object of knowledge is eventual; that is, it is an outcome of directed experimental operations, instead of something in sufficient existence before the act of knowing" (LW 4, 136–137).

To grasp what Dewey means here, we must realize that he has a much narrower conception of knowledge and of an object of knowledge than contemporary philosophers. According to Dewey, one can be credited with knowledge, and so with grasping an object of knowledge, only when one achieves what contemporary philosophers call *understanding*. Here one discerns with insight not so much that something is the case, but *why*, to some degree or other, it is the case.[26] But this latter discernment can't be achieved through our being a spectator on the world or through our mere contemplation of it; rather, it is achieved through our experimentally intervening into the world so as to bring out "the *connection* between something done and something undergone in consequence of the doing" (LW 4, 142).[27] As I put it in the previous chapter, to gain understanding, we must push the world to see how it pushes back. One can be credited with *knowledge*, and so with grasping an object of knowledge, only *after* this experimental process has produced genuine understanding. Before this process, we had primary experiences whose meaning was funded by prior reflective inquiries, and after it we have another more mindful or intelligent primary experience, but not knowledge *per se*. It is only when understanding something with insight is the focus of an inquiring experience that we can say that knowledge and an object of knowledge in Dewey's technical sense are present. But saying that an object of

---

[25] Dewey is here talking about the European discovery of America, seemingly ignoring that native peoples had already discovered it.
[25] Dewey often uses knowledge and understanding interchangeably, for example at LW 4, 138. See Grimm 2006 for a contemporary account of understanding.
[27] The grasp that something is the case can be achieved through perceiving an object's primary and secondary properties. But to understand why something is the case, one must grasp an object in its connections and relations, causal and otherwise, to other things. For this reason, knowledge for Dewey is primarily a knowledge of *relations*.

knowledge in this technical sense only appears after inquiry is *not* the same as saying that the *existence* that is now seen with insight did not exist previously to our gaining this insight.[28]

> I deny the identity of things had in direct experience with the object of knowledge *qua* object of knowledge. Things that are *had* in experience exist prior to reflection and its eventuation in an *object* of knowledge; but the latter, as such, is a deliberately effected re-arrangement or re-disposition, by means of overt operations, of such antecedent existences. (LW 5, 211–212)

Antecedent existences exist, just as a man who has had a trying experience is the same man that existed before the experience, even if he is altered.

But this consideration would not appease the realist critic, for Dewey is still committed to the idea that when an existence becomes an object of knowledge through our gaining insight into it, something about *the existence* is reconstructed over and above our view of it. Is this not idealist? Lets come back to America as an object of knowledge. For Dewey, it is an object of knowledge not merely because it is found or come across, but because what is found has led us to modify our beliefs:

> [U]nless the newly found and seen object was used to modify old beliefs, to change the sense of the old map of the earth, there was no discovery in any pregnant intellectual sense ... Discovery of America involved insertion of the newly touched land in a map of the globe. This insertion, moreover, was not merely additive, but transformative of a prior picture of the world. (LW 1, 125)

So it is important that the object of knowledge changes one's beliefs and so one's worldview to one degree or another. But – and this is the crucial point – this change in belief *is also an existential change in the world* because, as we have seen, the content of a belief, its meaning, is *conferred by the habits of physical and social interaction that its use involves*. So to change our beliefs due to our experimental interaction with an object is to change the habits that regulate our interaction with the object and with other subjects about this object, and to change these habits is to change our beliefs. This gives Dewey a clear way to respond to the realist who says that the discovery of America only changes our view of the world but not the world itself:

> It was not simply states of consciousness or ideas inside the heads of men that were altered when America was actually discovered; the modification

---

[28] For non-idealist readings that reject the equation of the object of knowledge with existences generally, see Dicker 1972, Boisvert 1982, and Godfrey-Smith 2013.

Meaning, Habit, and the Myth of the Given 217

was one in the public meaning of the world in which men publicly act. To cut off this meaning from the world is to leave us in a situation where it makes no difference what change takes place in the world, one wave more or less in a puddle is of no account. Changing the meaning of the world effected an existential change. The map of the world is something more than a piece of linen hung on the wall. A new world does not appear without profound transformation in the old one; a discovered America was a factor interacting with Europe and Asia to produce consequences previously impossible. A potential object of further exploration and discoveries not existed in Europe itself; a source of gold; an opportunity for adventure; an outlet for crowded and depressed populations ... [I]n short an agency of new events and fruitions, at home as well as abroad. In some degree, every genuine discovery creates some such transformation of both the meanings and the existences of nature. (LW 1, 125)

The realist could respond that "it was not the world which was changed" by the discovery of America, "but only the map". But, of course, the map itself "is part of the world, not something outside of it, and that its meaning and bearings are so important that a change in the map involves other and still more important objective changes" (LW 1, 125). In changing the map we change our present and future causal interactions with the world, and so change that portion of the world. This thought stands at the basis of Dewey's natural realism, which "accepts the causal connection of ideas with events and their potential reference to subsequent events" (LW 1, 260). A change in the map of the world 'reconstructs' the world because through these new interactions the world "thereby gains new potencies, new capacities" (MW 14, 206). In other words, through these new patterns of interaction, which are existential and meaningful, real and intentional, certain of the world's "qualities and relations previously potential become actualized" (LW 5, 208).

It is not clear, however, how this account can work with respect to existences upon which our actions can have no causal effect – for example, the stars. If we are not to posit a miraculous action at a distance, how can we say that our interaction with the stars reconstructs them and not just our beliefs about them? Here is Dewey's answer: "Perception of things as they are is but a stage in the process of making them different. They have already begun to be different by being known, for by that fact they enter into a different context, a context of foresight and judgment of better and worse" (MW 14, 206). In perceiving and coming to know the stars, we do not make them different in the sense of changing their intrinsic properties, the properties that they have irrespective of their relation to anything else. But in perceiving and coming to know them, we do change certain of their relational properties.²⁹ For example, when we learn to navigate by using the stars, new conjoint activities become possible. The stars now play a new role in our cooperative communicative behavior, and in doing so take on a new meaning. But this meaning is not just 'in our heads', having just to do with representations or even the inferential patterns internal to a system of concepts; rather, it is embodied in the world-directed habits that underlie the context in which we act. When these habits change the context of action, the *situation* in which we act changes. In this situation, the objects that make it up, including the stars, have come to have different intentional and real relations and so different meanings. They have been reconstructed.

McDowell, Second Nature, and Answerability

At the end of Chapter 5 and in the introduction to this chapter, I claimed that Dewey's account of experience as second natural can support a realist theory of answerability while McDowell's can't. I will now justify this claim.

McDowell, like Dewey, has a rich account of second nature.³⁰ He arrives at his account as part of a diagnosis of why his take on experience is difficult for philosophers to keep in view. It is difficult to keep in view because of a theoretical pressure characteristic of Modernity. This theoretical pressure is generated by the modern conception of nature as disenchanted, a conception that thinks of nature as what is subject to explanations that display a natural-scientific form of intelligibility.³¹

---

[29] I realize that the relation of intrinsic and relational properties is a difficult one in Dewey. See Godfrey-Smith 2013 for an excellent discussion of the point. Dewey on the one hand, argues that "every natural existence, in its own unique and brutal particularity of existence ... *has* immediacy." But, he says, to "*have* traits ... is not to *be* them," and the characteristic traits that any particular thing has "are to be accounted for as 'intersections' or 'interpenetration' ... of the immediate and the nexional or mediatory" (LW 3, 77). I take this to mean that a particular thing is the particular thing it is through both its immediate properties and how those properties are mediated through interaction with the other properties that they are associated with, "since in interaction alone are potentialities released and actualized" (LW 3, 41). Things have traits immediately, but these traits only actualize what the something truly *is* through interaction. In light of this distinction, we could say that the star's immediate properties do not change, but they are interpenetrated by new relational properties which further bring out what they are when they enter into the context of foresight and judgment (amongst other contexts).
[30] See Welchman 2008 and Godfrey-Smith 2010 for a comparison of their accounts of second nature.
[31] In *Mind and World*, McDowell puts the point by saying that this conception thinks of nature as that which is in the logical space of natural law. But McDowell has given up that way of speaking, and I follow him in that here.

If one thinks that this conception is the only one there can be of natural things, then one has no means of understanding how the responsiveness to reasons that the actualization of conceptual capacities involves might be operative in sensory consciousness – a natural sentient capacity that we share with animals.

We have landed in this predicament, McDowell argues, because we have become "forgetful of the very idea of second nature" (McDowell 1996a, 85), forgetful of the fact that responsiveness to reasons is itself natural, not when nature is parsed in terms of the modern disenchanted conception, but in terms of our initiation, in the normal course of our coming to maturity, into the space of reasons. Nature includes more than what is subject to natural-scientific explanations – i.e., it includes our acquisition of a second nature through a process of *Bildung* – and it is the forgetting of this fact that makes it seem as if responsiveness to reasons must be explained either in reductive naturalistic terms or be seen as something outside of nature – something supernatural. But if conceptual capacities "belong to our mode of living," and "our mode of living is our way of actualizing ourselves as animals" (McDowell 1996a, 78), then we have removed "any need to try to see ourselves as peculiarly bifurcated: with a foothold in the animal kingdom and a mysterious separate involvement in an extra-natural world of rational connections" (McDowell 1996a, 78). In other words, if the acquisition and actualization of conceptual capacities are natural to the kind of animal we are, then we are no longer faced with the mystery of how the realm of reason is related to the realm of nature, and so the mystery of how, in experience, we can be responsive to reasons in sensory consciousness.[32]

But while conceptual capacities are natural to the kind of animal we are, the space of reasons into which we are initiated through their acquisition is nonetheless *sui generis*. This means two things for McDowell. First, it means that the patterns that result from the exercise of these capacities, inferential and behavioral, cannot be captured by explanations that display natural-scientific intelligibility. For patterns in the space of reasons to so much as make sense, our explanation of them must be controlled by what Davidson calls the 'constitutive ideal of rationality'. Here, we discern "patterns in a way of living" (McDowell 1996a, 78) that are different from

---

[32] It is important to see that McDowell's account of reason is not just meant to mark the capacity to be responsive to epistemic reasons but, more fundamentally, to mark "our capacity to recognize and bring into being the kind of intelligibility that is proper to meaning" (McDowell 1996a, 71).

the exceptionless patterns that one finds in inanimate nature.[33] Second, McDowell accepts a 'naturalized Platonism' in which the rational connections that comprise these patterns, which we work our way into seeing through the process of *Bildung*, are there whether we have developed the capacity to see them or not. While these rational connections can only be seen from within the space of reasons and not from sideways-on, they "are there in any case, whether or not we are responsive to them" (McDowell 1996a, 82).

McDowell thinks that advancing the explanatory goals of *Mind and World* does not require that he explain how our second nature emerges from, or is related to, our first nature. This follows from his Wittgensteinian conception of philosophy as a therapeutic practice in which "illusions of problems are unmasked by reminders of the obvious" (McDowell 2008, 223). The concept of second nature is offered not as part of a constructive theory, but simply as a reminder that what is second natural is natural.[34] This, he thinks, is enough to quell the philosophical anxiety that stems from our inability to understand how things that are rational can also be natural (see McDowell 2008, 221). By relieving this anxiety we are able to grasp that the theoretical pressure we took ourselves to be under to *answer* the question of how mind is answerable to world – a pressure that generates the oscillation between coherentism and the Myth of the Given – is in fact illusory (see McDowell 1996a, xi). Once we have been reminded that what is second natural is natural we are able to see that there is *no problem of mind and world that a constructive philosophical account must solve*. As McDowell puts it, "The naturalism of second nature that I have been describing is precisely a shape for our thinking that would leave even

---

[33] Of course, natural-scientific explanations of inanimate nature are also governed by rational principles. So what distinguishes these explanations from those that fall under the constitutive ideal of rationality? The difference, as Davidson came to realize in his later work, is that natural-scientific explanations do not posit that the behavior of *their object* is constituted by rational principles, whereas explanations informed by the constitutive ideal of rationality do. See Davidson 1991, 215.

[34] In *Mind and World*, McDowell seems to do more than merely give reminders – for example, when he says: "Second nature could not float free of potentialities that belong to a normal human organism. This gives human reason enough of a foothold in the realm of law to satisfy any proper respect for modern natural law" (McDowell 1996a, 84). This passage is cited by critics who urge McDowell to develop a constructive and not merely therapeutic conception of second nature (see Gubeljic et al. 2000). But McDowell came to "regret the 'foothold' remark." He goes on: That remark seems to promise more, in the way of a continuity between the naturalness of human responsiveness to reasons and the naturalness of phenomena subsumable under natural law, than my purposes require" (McDowell 2000b, 99). His view aims to be, we could say, resolutely therapeutic.

the last dualism [of mind and world, norm and nature] not seeming to call for constructive philosophy" (McDowell 1996a, 94–95).

Dewey agrees with McDowell that philosophy has a therapeutic moment in which philosophical problems are unmasked as illusory. As he says, the value of a philosophical theory "is bound up with the genuineness of the problem which it purports to be a solution. If the basic concept is a fiction, there is no call for a solution" (MW 10, 19). But he does not think that reminders of the obvious are usually enough to quell anxiety. There are two reasons for this. First, what is obvious or evident is not itself obvious – for what is obvious, according to Dewey, is determined by an agent's value-laden background understanding of the world, which itself depends on the historical state of culture. Consider those who have developed, in late Modernity, what James calls a 'tough-minded' temperament. They think that intellectual integrity requires them to courageously face up to the disenchanted world that has been detailed for us by the natural sciences. It's not that they have forgotten the concept of second nature; it's rather that – because their temperament includes 'thick concepts' having factual and evaluative components – they actively reject the concept, given their background understanding of how things are and must be. Given their value-laden background understanding, a reminder that second nature is natural is simply not a reminder about something that is *obvious*. Second, Dewey thinks that to not address the mystery of *how* second nature is related to first nature leaves open an explanatory gap that has been, and will continue to be, filled in by the natural-scientific explanatory schema that gave rise to the overlooking of second nature in the first place. Intellectual life, like nature, abhors a vacuum, and to not fill this gap correctly opens the door for it to be filled incorrectly.

To fill the gap correctly, Dewey thinks, requires recognizing that there is a form of natural-scientific explanation that does not lead to a disenchanted conception of nature, one that has no room for responsiveness to reasons or, more widely, to value. Here, of course, he has post-Darwinian biological explanation in mind.[35] The tough-minded would argue that this form of intelligibility is simply the natural-scientific form of intelligibility that delivers to us a disenchanted conception of nature. But Dewey argues that this result is not entailed by Darwinian biology itself

---

[35] McDowell recognizes that biological explanations are distinct from physical or mechanistic explanations, but he makes no use of this point.

but by a philosophical interpretation *of* biology that we have no reason to accept.[36] If we separate this form of intelligibility from this distorting interpretation we can use its three main explanatory ideals to generate non-reductive, yet naturalist, accounts of reason and meaning.[37]

Dewey takes it that biological explanation is functional, developmental, and governed by what he calls the 'principle of continuity'. For an object to display a biological pattern of intelligibility an interpretation of it must see it as a purposive and self-maintaining item whose state of being is dependent not just on its structure but also on the process of historical development that it has undergone. According to the principle of continuity, it must also be seen as something continuous with the rest of nature. The principle "excludes complete rupture on the one side and mere repetition of identities on the other; it precludes reduction of 'higher' to the 'lower' just as it precludes complete breaks and gaps" (LW 12, 30). While there is genuine change in nature, such change must be seen as coming about because of the actualization of potentialities and forces that already exist in nature.[38]

---

[36] One way to look at Dewey's overall theoretical strategy (and James's as well) is as an attempt to argue that biology does not lead to a picture of the world in which it is meaningless and valueless, one in which reason and freedom are not possible, but rather one in which subjects act to achieve ends in a precarious value-laden space of genuine possibilities. These possibilities, depending on the developmental process that acting agents have undergone, can be engaged intelligently so as to harness contingency and to achieve one's ends, or not. So the modern post-Darwinian conception of nature does not lead to nihilism, as the tough-minded think, but to a melioristic view of the world in which human action can, if we act intelligently, bring about conditions in which our flourishing is possible. For an interpretation of Dewey along these lines, see Joas 1996.

[37] See chapter 1 of Brandom 2011a for an excellent discussion of how biology provided the pragmatists with a model to develop new fundamental concepts.

[38] In light of this principle, Dewey in *Experience and Nature* outlines a complex ontological picture in which matter, life, and mind are three distinct yet continuous 'plateaus of existence'. On the one hand, each plateau is distinct because they have different properties and qualities depending on the level of "complexity and intimacy of interaction among natural events" (LW 1, 200) that obtains at each plateau. On the other hand, the plateaus are continuous because while more complex plateaus have properties that the less complex one's don't have, they are not the properties of different substances or modes of being. The difference between matter and life, for instance, concerns the different "*way* in which physico-chemical energies are interconnected and operate" (LW 1, 195) in material and living things. Life "does not denote an abrogation of the physico-chemical"; rather it involves a more complex organization of the physico-chemical, which brings about "certain qualities and efficacies not displayed by the inanimate" (LW 1, 196). As Arvi Särkelä pointed out to me, we should not equate the concept of the plateaus with the concepts of first and second nature. The concept of the plateaus is an ontological concept while the concepts of first and second nature come from genetic psychology, anthropology, and social theory broadly speaking. The concepts of first and second nature, however, draw upon the concept of the plateaus for their sense. Second nature, while primarily a phenomenon of life and mind, involves the development of first nature, of the material plateau strictly speaking, and conversely, first nature, while primarily a material phenomenon, in fact gives rise to that which is second natural and is therefore continuous with life and mind.

We saw in the last chapter how the first and second explanatory ideals apply to experience. But how does the principle of continuity apply to experience (*Erfahrung*)? It entails that experience is not identical with, nor reducible to, physical nature (understood as that which is subject to natural-scientific explanation), and that its emergence as second natural (through its involving a feedback loop between meaning and habit) does not entail a fundamental break or gap with nature so understood. The concepts and meanings that comprise the thoughts and judgments that circulate in the space of reasons are continuous with the embodied meanings found in the habits and skills that organize primary experience, which are continuous with the feeling-qualities that pertain to living things generally, which in turn are continuous with inorganic nature.

We can now clearly see the interrelation between Dewey's naturalism and his account of answerability: subjects are answerable to a world that mostly stands independent of them because the relations that one comes to have with the world through interacting with the social and natural environment in experience *are themselves natural* – not when nature is parsed in terms of the disenchanted conception, but in terms of Dewey's conception of second nature. Through this ongoing interaction, we develop both *real relations* to the environment through habits and *intentional relations* to it in thought. In calling the relations that we have with the environment through habits 'real', I do not mean to suggest that they are merely causal, for as we know, the integrated relations that learned habits set up with the environment involve a kind of rational intelligibility.[39] What I mean to suggest is that habits, though rationally intelligible, are *also* concrete, and therefore that the relations that they establish with the real are *within* the order of the real. Thoughts, on the other hand, do not have the magical property of intentionally being about things. Rather, thoughts are of or about things that can be absent or nonexistent because they involve meanings that are based in 'agreements in use'. In being grounded in agreements in use, meaning is nothing psychic. Rather, it, as we saw earlier, is a natural and objective feature of world-directed cooperative behavior grounded in our shared habits.

For McDowell, the acquisition of a second nature is the acquisition of conceptual capacities through an intersubjective learning process. When 'light dawns over the whole' – i.e., when one acquires the ability make moves in the space of reasons, one becomes able to relate to the order of the real. Unlike Sellars or Rorty, McDowell has a relational theory of

---

[39] In this way, these relations are not like Sellars' picturing relations.

meaning. If all goes well, the actualization of conceptual capacities in receptivity puts us into relation with the real and not into relation with a highest-common representation that we can have independently of that relation. But this relation to the real is for McDowell always intentional, meaning that it is a conceptual relation that is established from within the *sui generis* space of reasons. But this means that McDowell has no account of how our relationship to the real is itself real – when real is understood in the above fashion. McDowell, despite his attempt to integrate embodied coping skills into his picture, remains in some fundamental sense a cognitivist: concerned with how *mental states* are intentionally related to the world rather than with how an embodied subject as a whole is related to it. In this respect, he is still committed to a kind of spectator theory of thought.

While McDowell is willing to cross the line between the intentional and the real in holding that conceptual capacities are actualized in sensory consciousness, he is not willing to similarly cross this line when our relation to the real is at issue. Why not? I think it is because of a meta-theoretical commitment that McDowell has to not examine rationality or meaning from the 'sideways-on'.[40] While he sees it as necessary to naturalize the rational connections that comprise the space of reasons (by seeing them as second natural), he thinks that to naturalize the relations that those connections have with the order of the real requires stepping outside of these connections and viewing them from the sideways-on. This would be to reject the *sui generis* nature of the space of reasons. Since for McDowell to take the sideways-on view *just is* to take the perspective of the explanatory schema that delivers a disenchanted conception of nature, this move cannot help us see that what is rational can be natural – rather, it is what blocks this from our view.

But Dewey would question the dichotomy that McDowell sets up between the point of view taken by self-conscious subjects and the sideways-on view, and his assumption that positing a sideways-on view must deliver a disenchanted conception of nature that occludes reason and meaning. For Dewey, we must distinguish between sideways-on views that are completely detached from the point of view of self-conscious subjects, for instance chemistry and physics, and those that are not, for instance biology, anthropology, and developmental psychology. While the latter views are not directly based on the everyday experience of individual subjects, their insights are still based *in* experience, in a collective learning

---

[40] Here I follow an argument made by Godfrey-Smith (Godfrey-Smith 2010, 315).

process that has our form of life as its object. Unlike chemistry or physics, we are both the subject and object of these sciences, and their goal is to help us become *self-conscious* about the kind of natural yet rational creature we are. They can do so because their results can intelligibly feed back into our self-understanding, informing experience going forward.[41] To trace the natural origin of rationality and meaning with the help of these views, as Dewey does in his account of linguistic communication, is not to give a reductive account of them or to eliminate them, but to show how their emergence as second natural in experience is related to nature more widely. This project does not disenchant nature but shows that nature already includes the potentialities for reason and meaning that are in fact actualized in human life.

Rorty's Critique

I would like to finish with Rorty's critique of Dewey's concept of experience because it takes direct aim at Dewey's attempt to establish continuity between us and the rest of nature. Rorty's critique is this: in trying to secure continuity, Dewey's account of experience falls prey to the Myth of the Given and leads to a kind of panpsychism.[42] Here is how he puts the first argument, about the Myth of the Given:

> Darwinism requires that we think of what we do and are as continuous with what amoebas, spiders, and squirrels do and are. One way to expound this continuity is ... we may think of these members of other species and of ourselves as sharing something called "experience" – something not the same as consciousness or thought, but something of which consciousness or thought is a more complex and developed form. One way of obtaining continuity is illustrated by Locke's attempt to tell a story about how we get from the baby's mind to the adult's – by adding in more simple ideas and then joining them to produce complex ideas. This way of procuring continuity blurs the distinction Peirce draws between cognitive and

---

[41] The results of the special sciences are considerably transformed when integrated into a philosophical picture because philosophy for Dewey is descriptive or denotative, not explanatory. See the Introduction of LW 1.
[42] Rorty first made this argument in his paper "Dewey's Metaphysics" (Rorty 1982), which he first presented in 1975. He expanded the argument considerably in "Dewey Between Hegel and Darwin" (Rorty 1998e). Both papers are entries in Rorty's project to distinguish between the 'good' and the 'bad' Dewey by portraying him as a Hegelian historicist and a 'positivistic' Darwinian naturalist rather than a radical empiricist and panpsychist. I do not here take up and evaluate the overall contours of this reading. Rather, I am just interested in the two specific criticisms of Dewey's concept of experience found in these papers. See Hildebrand Forthcoming for a detailed account of Rorty's reading and the relationship between Rorty and Dewey generally.

noncognitive mental states — between, for example, sensations and beliefs. As I have argued in my *Philosophy and the Mirror of Nature*, it also blurs the distinction between the question "what causes our beliefs?" and the question "what justifies our beliefs?" — a blurring that is essential for any representationalist theory of knowledge. (Rorty 1998e, 295–296)

On the face of it Rorty's argument is strange, as it calls on Locke to illustrate the insufficiency of Dewey's account. But of course Lockeian atomism is one of Dewey's main critical targets. But Rorty's point in making the comparison is this: for Locke there is no fundamental difference between sensations and beliefs, sentient states that we causally undergo and rational states that we justify in the space of reasons. Beliefs, complex ideas, are not different in kind from sensations or simple ideas, they are just an aggregate of simple ideas. But if this is so, then there is continuity between the brutes and us insofar as they, too, entertain simple ideas. While both share the capacity to undergo sensations, we just have the extra capacity to associate them into complex ideas, which is thought. But this extra capacity is nothing unprecedented in nature; it is just an augmentation of the more primitive associative capacities had by nonhuman animals.

If we translate this picture into functionalist terms, we can see that Dewey's view is similar. As we saw last chapter, consciousness and thought, sensations and ideas, are not original existences, but instruments that are forged and used by reflection to reunify disrupted experiences. Experience is more primitive than sensory consciousness or thought; it is an unanalyzed totality that contains both within itself. We share the ability to experience with nonhuman animals, and we also share the ability to go beyond it by dichotomizing the situation by using instruments that represent features that are both present (sensations) and absent (ideas). After all, nonhuman animals, like human animals, engage in instrumental action that attempts to bring about ends that are presently absent or nonexistent. This basic pattern of behavior "definitely foreshadows the general pattern of inquiry. For inquiry grows out of an earlier state of settled adjustment, which, because of disturbance, is indeterminate or problematic (corresponding to the first phase of tensional activity), and then passes into inquiry proper, (corresponding to the searching and exploring activities of an organism)" (LW 12, 40). So both human and nonhuman animals have integrated experiences that become disturbed and then become integrated again if search and exploration are successful. What distinguishes human from nonhuman animals is the enhanced ability to create, imagine, and act on hypotheses or ideas. But this ability

Meaning, Habit, and the Myth of the Given 227

is nothing unprecedented in nature; it's just an augmentation of capacities already found in nonhuman animals.

But this account – in which sensations and ideas are continuous because emergent from a more basic kind of state had by human and nonhuman animals, i.e., experience – is a disaster for Rorty. What is driving Rorty's thinking here is this: in positing continuity Dewey makes, in Sellars' terms, "a radical mistake – a mistake of a piece with the so-called 'naturalistic fallacy' in ethics" (Sellars 1997, 19). The mistake is to think that epistemic facts about ideas or beliefs can be 'analyzed without remainder' into non-epistemic facts about consciousness.[43] This is a mistake because the content and epistemic status of belief is a *normative* affair, an affair "of justifying and being able to justify what one says" (Sellars 1997, 76) in the space of reasons, while consciousness is merely a *causal* affair in which one's sense organs are stimulated. Instead of positing two types of fundamental state or episode, beliefs and conscious states that merely cause beliefs, the partisan of the Given posits a prior single state, experience, that is both conceptual and sensory, normative and causal. In this way, Dewey blurs the line between states whose propositional content is conferred in the normatively governed space of reasons and states that lack propositional content.

So in positing experience, Dewey's view falls prey to the Myth of the Given. But what does this have to do with panpsychism? Rorty argues that Dewey's strategy to ensure continuity does not just blur the line between cognitive and noncognitive mental states but also the line "between properties of the agent and properties of her environment" (Rorty 1998e, 295). Here is how he puts it:

> The problem with [Dewey's] way of obtaining continuity between us and the brutes is that it seems to shove the philosophically embarrassing discontinuity back down to the gap between say, viruses and amoebas. But why stop there? Only giving something like experience to protein molecules, and perhaps eventually to quarks – only a full-fledged panpsychism – will eliminate such embarrassments. (Rorty 1998e, 296)

We could call this argument the 'where does it stop?' argument. The argument is based on our inability to answer this question: if we obtain continuity between human and nonhuman animals by thinking that both have experience, where can we place the gap between experiential and non-experiential being? If we accept Dewey's principle of continuity that says

---

[43] To be clear, by 'consciousness', here Rorty means something like noncognitive conscious states, sensations, impressions, or 'raw feels'.

that there are no gaps in nature, that nothing emerges from something wholly unlike itself, then nothing experiential can emerge from something completely non-experiential.[44] In that case, we have no basis to place that gap between experiential and non-experiential beings at the gap between amoebas and viruses or even at the boundary between molecules and quarks. If experience exists, and there are no jumps in nature, then experiential properties must go all the way down the ladder of life and nature. Here we have a view that is clearly panpsychic.

In my view, neither of Rorty's two charges sticks. Let's begin with the charge of Givenness. Rorty is of course right that Dewey does not accept a hard line between cognitive and noncognitive states. For as we have seen, the primary experiences that result from experience understood as a learning process are – insofar as they are had rather than known – not in the space of reasons, yet they are informed by the downward influence of communicatively articulated meanings on the bodily habits and skills that organize them. It is clear that primary experiences are normative and causal, meaningful and natural. How is this not a clear case of Givenness?

In my view, something is Given in a mythical way if it said to have *authority* with respect to our thought or action without its *being able* to be mediated by reasons proffered by the subject who thinks or acts.[45] I emphasize that thought or action must only *be able* to be mediated by reasons because one should not deny that thought or action can be justified and have authority without reasons, in fact, being offered. For Sellars, for example, perceptual experience is immediate, not in the sense that it presupposes no language learning or concept formation, but in the sense that it is not the product of an act of inference. While reasons can be given for why a perceptual experience is justified – i.e., that it was undertaken in standard conditions, etc., – such reasons do not need to be marshaled for it to have this status. Similarly, we correctly undertake many actions by responding directly to circumstances without prior deliberation. While reasons can be proffered after the fact for these actions, their justification does not depend on reasons having been given.

It is clear that Dewey's view does not posit Givens that have authority with respect to our thought or action that do not admit of potential

---

[44] Panpsychism is based partly on the denial of emergence. See Nagel 1979 and Strawson 2017. Of course, Dewey has an "'emergent' theory of mind" (LW 1, 207), which should already make us question whether he could be a panpsychist in any standard sense.

[45] To put it in the language of the German Idealists, in trying to avoid the Myth of the Given, one is trying to avoid dogmatism. See McDowell 2009a for an account that correctly puts the Myth of the Given in this context.

mediation. On the one hand, all experiences admit of potential reason giving in becoming tensional or indeterminate. Any experience can go from being had to being reflected upon, though this transformation must be motivated rather than merely the product of disembodied choice. On the other hand, all experiences that are had are themselves mediated by prior operations of reflective problem solving and reason giving. Through this process, experiences incorporate funded meanings. While experiences can be immediate, they nonetheless *presuppose* such meanings. Because experience (*Erfahrung*) is a *temporal process* in which any given experience is already mediated and always potentially in question, Dewey is easily able to avoid the Myth of the Given.

It seems to me that Rorty's view depends on an unargued premise, namely, that mediation can only ever be *conceptual* mediation. While Dewey does not deny that mediation is often conceptual, he thinks that this misses the main way that experience is mediated – i.e., by meanings that are embodied 'in the workings of organic life' in habit. Rorty cannot accept this view, because, as we saw in Chapter 1, he accepts the Kantian idea that there is a hard line between reason and nature, which for him is the line between the linguistically articulated space of reasons and the space of causes.[46] But then one has the problem that Dewey's instrumentalism tried originally to solve, namely the question of how experience can both be independent of and homogeneous with thought such that it can provoke thought, guide its direction, and stand as its tribunal. If we accept a hard line between reason and nature and tailor our concept of experience accordingly, then we can only think of it as the causal antecedent of thought, as the work of epistemically neutralized sense impressions. But then we would again face the Kantian problem of understanding how merely Given sense-impressions can so much as 'speak to' thought. Of course, Rorty thinks that we can opt out of answering this question by understanding objectivity in terms of solidarity. But Dewey, like McDowell, rejects this as a sham solution.

Dewey's question is: how can we avoid Kantian dualism, idealism, and the Myth of the Given? In the last chapter, we saw how he avoided dualism and idealism. We can now see how he avoids the Myth of the Given, not by positing a difference in kind between cognitive and noncognitive states, but by extending the realm of reason all the way out to bodily habits and

---

[46] Rorty takes language use and rationality to be synonymous: "all that rationality amounts to – all that marks human beings off from other species of animals – is the ability to use language and thus to have beliefs and desires" (Rorty 2000, 14).

skills. In acquiring such habits and skills, one enters a space of embodied meanings and senses, those embodied in the cooperative social practices and customs of the community made possible by communication. The meanings and senses involved in these practices and customs are not Given because they are linguistically mediated and historically transmitted. Linguistic reason giving is surrounded by, and imbricated by, this horizon of embodied meanings. The holism that pertains to the space of reasons is therefore not just articulated by the concepts that enter into propositionally structured judgments, thoughts, and beliefs, but also by this more inchoate horizon. The space of reasons is not one that has a clear boundary, with linguistic practices on the one side and physical processes on the other. Rather, the space of reasons is a space of linguistic *and* embodied practices, the latter being anchored in and incorporating the world through our habits and bodily skills.

But if the space of reasons involves both linguistic and embodied practices – practices that, vis-à-vis our bodily habits and skills, incorporate the world – is this not to blur the line between properties of agents and properties of nature, to re-enchant nature by accepting a metaphysically implausible panpsychism? I don't think so. The first thing to say is that Rorty's account of panpsychism is not stable. Sometimes he characterizes panpsychism as the view that the basic constituents of physical reality have *qualitative experiential* states. The most basic constituents of reality have mental properties in the specific sense that they exist *experientially*. But sometimes he means by panpsychism the more general idea that nature can embody mental properties. While Dewey accepts the second idea, he rejects the first. While experience is nothing unprecedented in physical nature, for it *in fact* emerged in nature, we know that physical nature existed before qualitative experience came on the scene and continues to exist in a way that transcends the environments set up through the coupling of organism and nature.[47] To say that habits invest a portion of

---

[47] As I mentioned in note 39, the ontology given in *Experience and Nature* posits three plateaus or levels of being that characterize the increasingly complex fields of relation that determine the nature of something (see LW 1, 208). The first field is physical, the second biological or psychophysical, the last mental. At the first plateau, in which things have properties distinctive of the mathematical-mechanical systems discovered by physics, qualitative properties, much less experience of those properties, are not on the scene. Qualitative properties, and beings that can have qualitative experiences, only emerge at the second plateau. There is, of course, the difficulty of how, on Dewey's account, qualitative properties emerge from a world that is not qualitative. The panpsychist would press this question. I do not claim that Dewey's exact account of emergence would satisfy the contemporary philosopher. But it is important to see that Dewey and the panpsychist approach answering this question in entirely different ways. For the panpsychist, the question is how qualitative *states* can come about in a world in which there are no such states. Since

nature with mental properties is simply to say either that when we acquire habits and bodily skills through learning a practice, we must integrate the objective energies of nature into our practice, or that when we change our habits in response to an exercise of intelligent problem solving, we alter, to however small a degree, certain of the real relations that comprise a situation, namely the patterns of discernment and interaction that we have with a portion of nature. Through acting on the world and being acted on by it, i.e., through 'experiment', we see whether a portion of nature can become part of a transactional learning process. There is no guarantee that it can. This mundane position is clearly not panpsychic, which says that we know *in advance* that *nature as a whole* contains mental properties, whether experiential or not.

As we saw earlier, Rorty's main argument for why the pragmatic concept of experience leads to panpsychism is what we called the 'where does it stop?' argument. If there are no jumps in nature, then we have no principled way of marking the gap between experiential and non-experiential beings. This leads to the conclusion that all of nature is experiential. We can avoid this conclusion, Rorty argues, by dropping the concept of experience and recognizing that there *is* a principled way of marking the gap between human and nonhuman animals, i.e., language. To avoid panpsychism, Dewey, Rorty argues, should have "agreed with Peirce that a great gulf divides sensation and cognition, decided that cognition was possible only for language users, and then said that the only relevant break in continuity was between non-language users (amoebas, squirrels, babies) and language users" (Rorty 1998e, 297).

But, as Rorty himself recognizes, there is a difficulty with this position, one that underlies Dewey's call for continuity. The problem is that the position seems to recapitulate the intellectualism and rationalism of the Platonic tradition that Rorty so vehemently rejects. It seem to be, in Sellars' words, the last stand of 'Special Creation', the idea that "the

---

it does not make sense to say that there can be a jump from a state of affairs in which there are no states to one in which there are, the panpsychist concludes that such states must already be baked into the basic physical features of the world. But Dewey thinks this is the wrong question because quality is not a state but an emergent characteristic of an 'organized pattern of activity' that aims to perpetuate that self-same activity – i.e., a *living* body. Qualities are emergent features of organized patterns of activity interacting with an environment as they evolve through time. Because sensitivity to qualities is characteristic of bodies that have a certain level of organization, rather than a state had by a consciousness distinct from a body, he thinks that we have no need to say that qualitative state are original features of the basic elements of nature.

transition from pre-conceptual patterns of behavior to conceptual thinking was a holistic one, a jump to a level of awareness which is irreducibly new, a jump which was the coming into being of man" (Sellars 1991, 6).

Rorty is here in the same position as his hero Sellars. On the one hand, both take their start from the naturalistic fallacy, thinking that items in the normatively governed space of reasons are not reducible to items that are not. This institutes a divide between the causal and normative domains, between physical nature narrowly understood and mind broadly understood. But both are naturalists, so both are also committed to saying that this divide is nothing nonnatural. Sellars holds onto both of these thoughts by saying that while the divide between the normative and nonnormative is conceptually irreducible (in the manifest image), it is nonetheless causally reducible (in the scientific image).[48] What this means is that finished science will be able to give a causal explanation of the antecedents and effects of normative behavior, including linguistic behavior, without that explanation itself making normative assertions, assertions that say how things ought to be. So the explanation, although comprised of descriptive statements, will nonetheless capture normative behavior in its net.

Rorty agrees with Sellars that there is both continuity and discontinuity between normative behavior and nonnormative behavior, between linguistic behavior and nonlinguistic behavior. But unlike Sellars he cannot fill out the claim about continuity in terms of what finished science will say. For once one drops, as Rorty does, the representationalist idea that certain vocabularies correspond to reality better than others, and accepts a pragmatic view in which "all our idioms are tools for coping with the world" (Rorty 1999a, 576), then "there can be no philosophical interest in reducing one idiom to another, nor in asking whether and how a non-extensional language might be replaced with an extensional one" (Rorty 1999a, 576).[49] Rorty, in fact, fills out the continuity claim in the same way that Dewey does, by gesturing toward a naturalistic account of the development of linguistic behavior:

> [T]he development of linguistic behavior – of social practices that use increasingly flexible vocal cords and thumbs to produce longer and more complex strings of noises and marks – is readily explicable in naturalistic,

---

[48] For Sellars' attempt to articulate a 'Naturalism with a Normative Turn', see O' Shea 2007 and Levine in press a.
[49] This is also because Rorty rejects Sellars' concept of picturing. See Rorty 1991e.

Darwinian terms. We can tell as good stories about the success of species that gradually developed such practices as we can about the success of species that developed practices of migrating or hibernating. How meaning becomes a property of certain strings of marks and noises is as unmysterious as how tableness becomes a property of batches of molecules. It differs in this respect from experience or consciousness. (Rorty 1998e, 297–298)

Linguistic behavior is explicable in Darwinian terms because if we explicate meaning in terms of the use to which we can put strings of marks and noises rather than in terms of mysterious semantic relations, then language becomes just another tool or instrument that allows us to cope with the world given our interests and projects. Language as the 'tool of tools' is nothing unprecedented in nature, but merely an augmentation of prior coping strategies.

But if this is so, then the 'where does it stop?' argument seems to apply to Rorty's position. For certainly the coping strategies that language makes possible are continuous with coping strategies that go all the way down the ladder of life. We cope, gazelles cope, and so do amoebas. Rorty thinks that because the continuity between language users and non-language users is merely causal, we can avoid positing "a sort of protolanguage in amoebas" (Rorty 1998e, 298). But if amoebas causally cope with their environment in a way continuous with the way that language as an instrument allows us to cope with ours, we still have no principled way of drawing a line between prelinguistic and linguistic coping. Rorty is convinced that the explanation of meaning differs from that of experience because the explanation of meaning is 'unmysterious' while that of experience is mysterious. But if linguistic meaning is based on the coping relation, and if we have no principled way of distinguishing between the coping strategies pursued by language using and non-language using creatures, then it seems that the explanation of the emergence of linguistic meaning is just as mysterious as that of experience. It is unclear to me why, by his own lights, we ought not accuse Rorty of panpsychism.

Rorty is in a bind. On the one hand, to avoid Special Creation, he must give an account of the continuity between linguistic and nonlinguistic creatures. But this claim about continuity is subject to the 'where does it stop?' argument. To avoid this, Rorty always retreats back to a position that posits discontinuity, one where there is a 'great gulf' dividing cognitive and noncognitive states, a gulf created by the acquisition of a language. In my view, Rorty's position is unstable, oscillating back and forth between a position that posits continuity and a position that posits discontinuity. This oscillation cannot come to a rest because Rorty has no way of bringing continuity and discontinuity together, but nor has he a way to disown either thought. Here is precisely the type of breakdown in our thinking that makes the type of philosophical reconstruction undertaken by Dewey so necessary. What we must do is think continuity and discontinuity together by describing how linguistic communication calls upon and yet transforms prior capacities. And this is precisely what Dewey has done.

Conclusion

Pragmatism and Antirealism

Davidson once said that antirealism, in all of its forms, is a "manifestation of that irrepressible urge in Western philosophy to insure that whatever is real can be known: antirealism attempts to achieve this by reading out of existence whatever it decrees lies beyond the scope of human knowledge" (Davidson 1997a, 69). Does the pragmatic account of objectivity that I have outlined in this book manifest this urge by reducing reality to what can be known, or more generally, to what can be thought about?

My account of objectivity has two parts: an account of the grasp of the concept of objectivity and an account of how thought can in fact be answerable to the way things are. Let me take these in order. My account of the grasp of the concept of objectivity is an account of how subjects could grasp that all things can exist unperceived. It is meant, therefore, to explain how, based on experience, we can conceive of realities that are, and can remain, unknown and unthought. So the *object* of this explanation is realist: how subjects, from their point of view, can grasp that reality extends beyond, and does not depend on, their point of view. But while the object of this explanation is realist, one could argue that its *form* manifests the antirealist urge insofar as it seems to make that which lies beyond human knowledge depend on *our coming to have a concept* that there is something beyond human knowledge. However, my claim is not that the *existence* of things that lie beyond human knowledge and thought depends on our coming to have a concept that there are such things, but rather that our coming to have the concept that there are such things depends on our *experience* that there are such things. My argument does not reduce reality to what can be known or thought about because it simply does not make claims that go beyond our subjectivity.

But is not this just a more virulent expression of the antirealist urge? To answer this question, it is important to see that while for James the concept of things that lie beyond human knowledge and thought does not transcend what is grasped by our subjectivity, experience itself does. As I pointed out, James does not mean by experience what the classical empiricists meant by it. James rejects the idea that conscious experiences are to be accounted for by the association of loose and separate sensory atoms, and he thinks that we must see experience as active and not just passive – though we should not think of this activity in Kantian terms. Experience is active rather in the sense that we must select from the much-at-once-ness present in the environment by actualizing our natural capacity to intend the same through attention and discrimination. The content of the concept of objectivity, of existence unperceived, is based in the fact that as we move through spatial fields, the vividly present and the marginal more are co-given, and that we can recapture at will what was perceived by reversing our attention and, if the spatial field is absent, moving back to it. In tracking the exercise of these capacities in memory, we come to have a sense that objects lying 'beyond the margin' not just of our current spatial field but also of fields not currently present are available to be made present by our attending and moving to them.

While this account is phenomenological, it is *also* naturalistic, for our sense that objects exist unperceived is based in the exercise of capacities – perception, movement, memory, attention, and discrimination – that James thinks we share with nonrational animals. Although in *The Principles* James endorses a methodological dualism, it is clear that here sense making is already seen as something that requires the interaction of these capacities with the environment. To grasp this, however, we must discern the rootedness of conceptual representations in meanings that are pre-predicatively developed in experience through the world-bound exercise of these capacities.[1] Part of the purpose of James's phenomenology is to help us in this task. This account does not reduce reality to what can be known or thought about but rather says that the concept of objectivity is based in an experiential encounter with reality that lies *below* human knowledge and thought.

Dewey's account of primary and secondary experience, the interaction of which forms the basis of his realist account of answerability, develops this feature of James's view. In light of this, let us move to the second part of my account of objectivity. We can call Dewey's realism a *participatory* or

---

[1] Here we can see a deep affinity between James and Merleau-Ponty. He argues, like James, that atomism and neo-Kantianism must be seen as internally connected positions, and that conceptual intentionality is founded in a kind of more basic intentionality (motor-intentionality) that cannot be specified without making mention of both creature and world. For more on this, see Levine 2018.

interactive realism: through interacting with reality (through acting on and being acted upon by it), rather than merely representing it (or knowing it), we are able to develop thoughts that are answerable to it.[2] This answerability, while fallible, is objective because experience (*Erfharung*) is a learning process involving a feedback loop between habits and reflective thought in which we continually adjust to what antecedently exists in light of our experimental ideas and actions. But if Dewey's account of objectivity is correctly characterized as interactive, then it seems to focus not on reality as it is independently of us, but precisely on the point of our interaction with it. Has our account of his position really answered the suspicion, expressed by Santayana and Cohen, that Dewey's view is 'anthropomorphic', concerned with what is within the scope of human experience – with the foreground of nature as Santayana says – rather than what is beyond that scope – the background of nature?[3] Is not Dewey's position the *paradigmatic expression* of the antirealist urge?

Dewey responds to the charge of anthropomorphism in two ways. First, he asks just what it is to have an account of the background of nature. Dewey rejects out of hand accounts that claim that our access to the background of nature depends on the exercise of nonnatural capacities, mystical intuition for example. But he takes seriously accounts that take recourse to the natural scientific conception of nature. Philosophers who think that natural science provides us with an account of the background of nature – nature as it is, independently of its relation to us – typically say this: while the method through which we arrive at a conception of nature in inquiry makes reference to the human endowments and abilities that relate to nature, the content of this conception makes no mention of them. In rejecting the idea that we can have a conception of the background of nature that is not accessed through the foreground, they go on, the pragmatist commits a genetic fallacy: they confuse the endowments and abilities necessary for us to relate to nature, and thereby arrive at a conception of nature, with the content of the conception arrived at. The content of this conception makes no mention of these endowments and abilities; it is a conception of what is 'there anyway'.

While Dewey accepts the idea that it is instrumental to the grasping of natural scientific objects that we abstract from certain ways that their

---

[2] I call Dewey's realism 'participatory' as well as 'interactive' because the term interactive can be misleading insofar as it suggests that there are two distinct things that come to interact. But for Dewey, as we know, we are not separate from the environment with which we interact, but in and of it.
[3] See Santayana 1951 and Cohen 1940.

interaction with us manifests itself to us, for instance as colored, he rejects the idea that the content of such conceptions can be understood in *complete* abstraction from human endowments and abilities. Dewey rejects this idea because, as we saw in Chapter 6, he accepts Peirce's idea that the content of a conception is filled out not by representations but by habits. Our conception of something is cashed out by the habits of interaction that we have with that thing, habits acquired through our past interactions with it. It's not that the *existence* of physical nature depends on inquiry into it or our conception of it. Dewey is serious when he says that existence 'does not ask leave from thought to exist'. Nor does the fact that a conception is developed in this way, and so is in that sense 'ours', mean that it can't get things right. Indeed, we have argued that Dewey aims to provide us with an account of how we can be answerable to the way things are. It just means that our conception of how nature is, independently of our interaction with it – of how things associate with other things independently of us – is dependent on our developing that conception through interacting with nature. Reality has its own way of being, it is just that for us to grasp this way of being requires our participation in, and interaction with, reality. This claim should not be transformed into the claim that reality *is* what reality is for-us.

Dewey responds to the charge of anthropomorphism in a second way. He argues that the foreground of nature – i.e., which is given through our interaction with nature – is not "a screen which conceals the background" but rather that it "conducts our thought to the background" (LW 3, 76). We are justified in thinking this because, as we saw in Chapter 6, *our interaction with nature in experience and inquiry is nothing outside of nature*. Realist positions that wish for a more direct way of getting in touch with the background of nature than through the foreground cannot accept this naturalistic thesis. Here is how Dewey puts it:

> [T]he existence of experience is a fact, and it is a fact that the organs of experience, the body, the nervous system, hands and eyes, muscles and sense, are means by which we have access to the non-human world. It would seem then as if the philosophy which denies that it is possible for experienced things and processes to form a road into the natural world must be controlled by an underlying postulate that there is a breach of continuity between nature and man and hence between nature and human experience. (LW 14, 144)

In other words, such positions are controlled by a conception in which there is a fundamental break between human experience and nature because on their view access to the background of nature requires *getting around* the foreground, which means getting around the finite human endowments and abilities through which we interact with nature. But why would we need to get around finite human endowments and abilities if it were not assumed that they were a block to our understanding of nature through being fundamentally discontinuous with it?

As we saw in Chapter 6, Dewey thinks that an account of answerability depends on more than what can be ascertained from within the perspective of a self-conscious subject. He accordingly rejects the idea that an individual subject could develop a freestanding transcendental argument to establish answerability. His account of answerability is rather based on what we find out about our relationship to nature through the developmental learning processes that experience involves. In this sense, the account is circular; we develop a justification of answerability by calling on the results of first-order learning processes that are already taken to be answerable to the way things are. This circular argument is not problematic, however, for two reasons. First, as we saw in Chapter 5, these first-order learning processes are self-correcting in the sense that their development is based on coping with surprising recalcitrances, which signal that mind and world have 'slipped out of phase'. This slipping out of phase, however, does not imply that the mind is *globally* distant from the world. This is because, at the level of these first-order processes, the question is not how mind can be answerable to the world *in general*, but how a surprising recalcitrance in this *specific situation* can be overcome through reflective inquiry. Since in a situation a recalcitrance only shows up *as* a recalcitrance against the background of factors that are settled and taken for granted, we have no reason to infer that our being out of phase with reality in this instance signals that we our of phase with it generally. This inference, which supports skepticism and so the epistemology industry, is only rationally compelling if one overlooks our embeddedness in the situation.

Second, this circular argument involves an account of its own origins. By giving an account of the origin of the ability to communicate, and hence of the ability to marshal meanings in thought, we find that the space of reasons, the space in which we can have thoughts that are answerable to the world, is itself natural – second natural. We find this out by forming a philosophical picture that utilizes the results of the special sciences, biology, anthropology, developmental psychology, etc. In doing so, we grasp that we as communicating beings are also experiencing and living beings, and that such beings must literally interact with the environment to live and advance their well-being. While Dewey, of course, does not reduce our cognitive accomplishments to this interaction, giving us a rich account of communication and thought, these accomplishments are nonetheless developments of potentialities already *internal to life*. This is the ultimate justification for thinking that the foreground of nature, which is given through these accomplishments, can lead us to the background of nature – for now we are able to grasp that nature, though mostly existing independently of us, is nothing foreign to us.

Control and Objectivity

Dewey once said that the goal of his philosophy is to 'intellectualize practice' rather than to 'practicalize intelligence'.[4] Practice is intellectualized by being funded by meanings, meanings that are generated through the cooperative, developmental, and interactive learning process that experience involves. Through this process, we, alone and as part of the community of inquirers, come to discover and actualize qualities, connections, and relations of objects that were previously potential. Through linguistic communication, these features of objects become meanings and are recorded, stored, and reproduced through time, and through integration of these meanings into our habits and customs, we are better able to cope, in our subsequent interactions, with objects that have these features. Through these means we gain

> control of the *ways* in which [we] the organism participates in the course of events. In the case of simple needs and simple environments, existing organic structure practically enforces correct participation; the result is so-called instinctive action. Within this range, modifications undergone by the organism form in the main effective habits. But organic preparation for varied situations having many factors and wide-reaching consequences is not so easily attained. Effective participation here depends on the use of extra-organic conditions, which supplement structural agencies; namely, tools and other persons, by means of language spoken and recorded. Thus the ultimate buttress of the soundness of all but the simplest ideas consists in the cumulative objective appliances and arts of the community, not in anything found in the "consciousness" itself or within the organism. (LW 1, 261)

But is control of objects and events the same thing as being answerable to them? For Dewey, the ultimate aim of the "active control of objects ... is the securer, freer and more widely shared embodiment of values in

---

[4] See Eldridge 1998, 5.

experience" (LW 4, 30). So control is ultimately for the sake of enriching the *goods* of experience. If one interprets Dewey as thinking that the goods of experience are practical in a narrow sense, *and* that answerability to the world is solely a theoretical aim, then it would follow that answerability could only be of secondary importance for him. In this case, the view of Dewey's realist critics would be partly vindicated. But this common interpretation of Dewey is wrong, on two fronts.

First, in rejecting the primacy of contemplation and the spectator theory of knowledge, Dewey does not simply turn things upside down and make practice in a narrow sense preeminent.[5] As Dewey puts it: "Constant and effective interaction of knowledge and practice is something quite different from an exaltation of activity for its own sake" (LW 4, 30). For Dewey, the intertwined use of "*both* knowledge and practice" is a "means of making goods – excellences of all kinds – secure in experienced existence" (LW 4, 30n). So his goal is to help us secure goods of all kinds, not just narrow practical or instrumental goods. Indeed, the most important goods are secured communicatively and not instrumentally, for example, the goods of fixing belief in scientific inquiry or the goods of ethical and political conduct. Second, answerability for Dewey is not just an aim that we have in our theoretical practice, for to secure goods of all kinds requires that one be answerable to the object of our experience by engaging in a feedback-governed process involving knowledge and practice, reflective thought and experiment. For instance, moral action, which depends on moral perception, imaginative rehearsal, and experiential learning, requires our being answerable to the world (the social world) just as much as theoretical practice. Control of objects and events and answerability to them are, for Dewey, intertwined ideals.

In *Experience and Nature*, the account of control is part of a larger discussion in which Dewey distinguishes between two kinds of action: action that works for "objective transformation" and "action that is fanciful, 'wish-fulfilling,' romantic, myth making" (LW 1, 260). Both kinds of action are grounded in the same organic mechanisms insofar as fanciful action, too, is based in meanings generated by the interaction of organism and environment, both physical and social. Past consummations of experience that are pleasing are retained in habit and condition subsequent behavior, while consummations that are displeasing are ignored as far as possible. In trying to reproduce pleasing consummations, "a bias in organic modification is set up; it acts to perpetuate, wherever possible,

---

[5] For an excellent dismantling of this misinterpretation of Dewey, see Bernstein 1960.

awareness of fruitions, and to avert perception of frustrations and inconvenient interruption" (LW 1, 259). Because they have the same organic basis, we cannot, collectively and individually, move from fanciful to objective action – the facilitation of which we could say is the aim of Dewey's philosophy as a whole – through extra-organic means, through acts of a disembodied Will or Ego. We cannot will ourselves as individuals to not be wish fulfilling, or reason our way out of the propensity to engage in motivated reasoning. Rather, communities and individuals must develop techniques to mold the organic mechanisms that ground both kinds of action by integrating the intelligent practices made possible by the use of tools and language into their habits, and they must set these funded practices free. It is only in this way that individuals within a community can develop thoughts that are sound and not wish fulfilling, thoughts that are able, in a clear-sighted way, to confront objects of whatever kind. This commitment to clear-sightedness is a commitment to objectivity.

References

Alexander, T. M. (1987), *John Dewey's Theory of Art, Experience, and Nature: The Horizons of Feeling*. Albany, NY: State University of New York Press.
Avramides, A. (2001), "Davidson, Grice, and the Social Aspects of Language," in G. Cosenza (ed.) *Paul Grice's Heritage*. Turnhout: Brepols.
Bernstein, R. J. (1960), "Introduction," in R. J. Bernstein (ed.) *On Experience, Nature, and Freedom*. Indianapolis, IN: The Bobbs-Merrill Company.
  (1961), "John Dewey's Metaphysics of Experience," *Journal of Philosophy*, 58: 5–14.
  (1964), "Peirce's Theory of Perception," in E. C. Moore and R. S. Robin (eds.) *Studies in the Philosophy of Charles S. Peirce*. Amherst, MA: University of Massachusetts Press.
  (1971), "The Challenge of Scientific Materialism," in D. Rosenthal (ed.) *Materialism and the Mind-Body Problem*. Upper Saddle River, NJ: Prentice-Hall.
  (1992), "The Resurgence of Pragmatism," *Social Research*, 59: 813–840.
  (1995), "American Pragmatism: The Conflict of Narratives," in H. J. Saatkamp, Jr. (ed.) *Rorty and Pragmatism: The Philosopher Responds to His Critics*. Nashville, TN: Vanderbilt University Press.
  (2007), "The New Pragmatists," *Graduate Faculty Philosophy Review*, 28: 3–38.
  (2010), *The Pragmatic Turn*. Cambridge: Polity Press.
Black, M. (1962), "Dewey's Philosophy of Language," *Journal of Philosophy*, 59: 505–523.
Blattner, W. (2008), "What Heidegger and Dewey Could Learn from Each Other," *Philosophical Topics*, 36: 57–78.
Boisvert, R. (1982), "Dewey, Subjective Idealism, and Metaphysics," *Transactions of the Charles S. Peirce Society*, 18: 232–243.
Bourdieu, P. (1990), *The Logic of Practice*, trans. R. Nice. Cambridge: Polity Press.
Boyle, M. (2016), "Additive Theories of Rationality: A Critique," *European Journal of Philosophy*, 24: 527–555.
Brandom, R. (1994), *Making It Explicit*. Cambridge, MA: Harvard University Press.
  (1995), "Knowledge and the Social Articulation of the Space of Reasons," *Philosophy and Phenomenological Research*, 55: 895–908.

(1996), "Perception and Rational Constraint: McDowell's *Mind and World*," *Philosophical Issues*, 7: 241–259.
(1997), "Replies," *Philosophy and Phenomenological Research*, 57: 189–202.
(2000a), *Articulating Reasons*. Cambridge, MA: Harvard University Press.
(2000b), *Rorty and His Critics*. Malden, MA: Blackwell Press.
(2000c), "Vocabularies of Pragmatism," in Brandom 2000b.
(2000d), "Facts, Norms, and Normative Facts: A Reply to Habermas," *European Journal of Philosophy*, 8: 356–374.
(2002a), "The Centrality of Sellars' Two-Ply Account of Observation to the Arguments of 'Empiricism and the Philosophy of Mind'," in *Tales of the Mighty Dead*. Cambridge, MA: Harvard University Press.
(2002b), "Non-Inferential Knowledge, Perceptual Experience, and Secondary Qualities: Placing McDowell's Empiricism," in N. H. Smith (ed.) *Reading McDowell: On Mind and World*. London: Routledge Press.
(2002c), "No Experience Necessary: Empiricism, Non-Inferential Knowledge, and Secondary Qualities," unpublished manuscript.
(2005), "Responses," *Pragmatics and Cognition*, 13: 227–249.
(2008a), *Between Saying and Doing*. Oxford: Oxford University Press.
(2008b), "Response to Rödl," *Philosophical Topics*, 36: 152–155.
(2010a), "Reply to Stout," in B. Weiss and J. Wanderer (eds.) *Reading Brandom: On* Making It Explicit. London: Routledge Press.
(2010b), "Reply to McDowell," in B. Weiss and J. Wanderer (eds.) *Reading Brandom: On* Making It Explicit. London: Routledge Press.
(2011a), *Perspectives on Pragmatism: Classical, Recent, and Contemporary*. Cambridge, MA: Harvard University Press.
(2011b), "Linguistic Pragmatism and Pragmatism about Norms: An Arc of Thought from Rorty's Eliminative Materialism to His Pragmatism," in Brandom 2011a.
Brett, N. (1981), "Human Habits," *Canadian Journal of Philosophy*, 11: 357–376.
Bridges, J. (2006), "Davidson's Transcendental Externalism," *Philosophy and Phenomenological Research*, 73: 290–315.
Brodsky, G. (1969), "Absolute Idealism and Dewey's Instrumentalism," *Transactions of the Charles S. Peirce Society*, 5: 44–62.
Brown, M. (2012), "John Dewey's Philosophy of Science," *HOPOS: The Journal of the International Society for the History of Philosophy of Science*, 2: 258–306.
Burge, T. (2009), "Perceptual Objectivity," *Philosophical Review*, 118: 285–324.
Burke, T. (1991), *Ecological Psychology and Dewey's Theory of Perception*, Report No. CSLI-91–151, Stanford, CA: CSLI Publications.
(1994), *Dewey's New Logic: A Reply to Russell*. Chicago, IL: University of Chicago Press.
(2000), "What Is a Situation?," *History and Philosophy of Logic*, 2: 95–113.
Campbell, J. (1985), "Possession of Concepts," *Proceedings of the Aristotelian Society*, 85: 149–170.
(1986), "Conceptual Structure," in Charles Travis (ed.) *Meaning and Interpretation*. Oxford: Blackwell Press.

(1993), "A Simple View of Color," in John J. Haldane and C. Wright (eds.) *Reality, Representation, and Projection*. Oxford: Oxford University Press.
(1994), *Past, Space, and Self*. Cambridge, MA: MIT Press.
Campbell, J. and Cassam, Q. (2014), *Berkeley's Puzzle: What Does Experience Teach Us?* Oxford: Oxford University Press.
Carr, D. (2014), *Experience and History*. Oxford: Oxford University Press.
Cassam, Q. (2005), "Space and Objective Experience," in J. L. Bermúdez (ed.) *Thought, Reference, and Experience: Themes from the Philosophy of Gareth Evans*. Oxford: Oxford University Press.
Church, J. (2013), *The Possibilities of Perception*. Oxford: Oxford University Press.
Cobb-Stevens, R. (1974), *James and Husserl: The Foundations of Meaning*. The Hague: Martinus Nijhoff.
Cohen, M. R. (1940), "Some Difficulties in Dewey's Anthropomorphic Naturalism," *Philosophical Review*, 49: 196–228.
Cooke, E. (2011), "Phenomenology of Error and Surprise: Peirce, Davidson, and McDowell," *Transactions of the Charles S. Peirce Society*, 47: 62–86.
Crowther, T. (2006), "Two Conceptions of Conceptualism and Nonconceptualism," *Erkenntnis*, 65: 245–276.
Davidson, D. (1982), "Rational Animals," in Davidson 2001a.
(1983), "A Coherence Theory of Truth and Knowledge," in Davidson 2001a.
(1988), "The Myth of the Subjective," in Davidson 2001a.
(1990), "Epistemology Externalized," in Davidson 2001a.
(1991), "Three Varieties of Knowledge," in Davidson 2001a.
(1992), "The Second Person," in Davidson 2001a.
(1994), "The Social Aspect of Language," in Davidson 2005.
(1995), "The Problem of Objectivity," in Davidson 2004.
(1997a) "Indeterminism and Anti-Realism," in Davidson 2001a.
(1997b), "The Emergence of Thought," in Davidson 2001a.
(1997c), "Seeing through Language," in Davidson 2005.
(1999), "Reply to Føllesdal," in L. E. Hahn (ed.) *The Philosophy of Donald Davidson*. Chicago, IL: Open Court.
(2001a), *Subjective, Intersubjective, Objective*. Oxford: Oxford University Press.
(2001b), "Externalisms," in P. Kotatko and S. Kotatko (eds.) *Interpreting Davidson*. Stanford, CA: CSLI Press.
(2004), *Problems of Rationality*. Oxford: Oxford University Press.
(2005), *Truth, Language, and History*. Oxford: Oxford University Press.
DeVries, B. and Triplett, T. (2002), *Knowledge, Mind, and the Given: Reading Wilfrid Sellars' "Empiricism and the Philosophy of Mind."* Indianapolis, IN: Hackett Publishing.
Dewey, J. (1969–1990), *The Collected Works of John Dewey 1882–1953 (Early Works, Middle Works, and Late Works)*. Carbondale, IL: Southern Illinois University Press.
(2007), *Essays in Experimental Logic*. Carbondale, IL: Southern Illinois University Press.

(2010), "1897 Lecture on Hegel," in J. R. Shook and J. A. Good (eds.) *John Dewey's Philosophy of Spirit*. New York, NY: Fordham University Press.

Dicker, G. (1972), "John Dewey on the Object of Knowledge," *Transactions of the Charles S. Peirce Society*, 8: 152–166.

Dreyfus, H. (2000), "A Merleau-Pontyian Critique of Husserl's and Searle's Representationalist Accounts of Action," *Proceedings of the Aristotelian Society*, 100: 287–302.

(2013), "The Myth of the Pervasiveness of the Mental," in J. K. Schear (ed.) *Mind, Reason, and Being-in-the-World: The McDowell-Dreyfus Debate*. London: Routledge Press.

Eilan, N. (1997), "Objectivity and the Perspective of Consciousness," *European Journal of Philosophy*, 5: 235–250.

(2007), "Consciousness, Self-consciousness and Communication," in T. Baldwin (ed.) *Reading Merleau-Ponty: On Phenomenology of Perception*. London: Routledge.

Eldridge, M. (1998), *Transforming Experience: John Dewey's Cultural Instrumentalism*. Nashville, TN: Vanderbilt University Press.

Evans G. (1982), *The Varieties of Reference*. Oxford: Oxford University Press.

(1985), "Things without the Mind," in *Collected Papers*. Oxford: Oxford University Press.

Friedman, M. (1999), *Reconsidering Logical Positivism*. Cambridge: Cambridge University Press.

Gibson, J. J. (1986), *The Ecological Approach to Visual Perception*. London: Lawrence Erlbaum Associates, Publishers.

Girel, M. (2003), "The Metaphysics and Logic of Psychology: Peirce's Reading of James's Principles," *Transactions of the Charles S. Peirce Society*, 39: 163–203.

Godfrey-Smith, P. (2010), "Dewey, Continuity, and McDowell," in M. De Caro and D. Macarthur (eds.) *Naturalism and Normativity*. New York, NY: Columbia University Press.

(2013), "Dewey and the Question of Realism," *Nous*, 50: 73–89.

Good, J. A. (2006), *A Search for Unity in Diversity: The "Permanent Hegelian Deposit" in the Philosophy of John Dewey*. Lanham, MD: Lexington Books.

Grimm, S. (2006), "Is Understanding a Species of Knowledge?," *British Journal for the Philosophy of Science*, 57: 515–535.

Gubeljic, M., Link, S., Müller, P., and Osburg, G. (2000), "Nature and Second Nature in McDowell's *Mind and World*," in M. Willaschek (ed.) *John McDowell: Reason and Nature*. Münster: Lit Verlag.

Gurwitsch, A. (1966a), "On the Object of Thought," in *Studies in Phenomenology and Psychology*. Evanston, IL: Northwestern University Press.

(1966b), "William James's Theory of the 'Transitive Parts' of the Stream of Consciousness," in *Studies in Phenomenology and Psychology*. Evanston, IL: Northwestern University Press.

(1985), *Marginal Consciousness*. Athens, OH: Ohio University Press.

Habermas, J. (2000), "Richard Rorty's Pragmatic Turn," in Brandom 2000b.

(2003), *Truth and Justification*. Cambridge, MA: MIT Press.

Haugeland, J. (1998), "Objective Perception," in *Having Thought*. Cambridge, MA: Harvard University Press.
High, R. P. (1981), "Shadworth Hodgson and William James's Formulation of Space Perception: Phenomenology and Perceptual Realism," *Journal of the History of the Behavioral Sciences*, 17: 466–485.
Hildebrand, D. (2003), *Beyond Realism and Anti-Realism: John Dewey and the Neo-Pragmatists*. Nashville, TN: Vanderbilt University Press.
  (ed.) (2014), Symposium: Language or Experience: Charting Pragmatism's Course for the 21st Century. *European Journal of Pragmatism and American Philosophy*, 6. http://journals.openedition.org/ejpap/275.
  (in press), "Dewey," in A. Malachowski (ed.) *The Wiley-Blackwell Companion to Rorty*. Malden. MA: Wiley Blackwell.
Hookway, C. (2012), "The Principle of Pragmatism: Peirce's Formulations and Examples," in *The Pragmatic Maxim: Essays on Peirce and Pragmatism*. Oxford: Oxford University Press.
Husserl, E. (1950), *Cartesian Meditations*, trans. D. Cairnes. Dortrecht: Kluwer Academic Publishers.
  (2001), *Analyses Concerning Passive and Active Synthesis*, A. J. Steinbock (ed.) Dortrecht: Kluwer Academic Publishers.
Jackman, H. (1998), "James' Pragmatic Account of Intentionality and Truth," *Transactions of the Charles S. Peirce Society*, 34: 155–181.
James, W. (1975a), *Pragmatism*, Cambridge, MA: Harvard University Press.
  (1975b), *The Meaning of Truth*. Cambridge, MA: Harvard University Press.
  (1976), *Essays in Radical Empiricism*. Cambridge, MA: Harvard University Press.
  (1978), *Essays in Philosophy*. Cambridge, MA: Harvard University Press.
  (1979), *The Will to Believe*. Cambridge, MA: Harvard University Press.
  (1981), *Principles of Psychology*. Cambridge, MA: Harvard University Press.
  (1983), *Essays in Psychology*. Cambridge, MA: Harvard University Press.
  (1988a), *Manuscript Essays and Notes*. Cambridge, MA: Harvard University Press.
  (1988b), *Manuscript Lectures*. Cambridge, MA: Harvard University Press.
Jay, M. (2005), *Songs of Experience*. Berkeley, CA: University of California Press.
Joas, H. (1996), *The Creativity of Action*. Chicago, IL: University of Chicago Press.
Kennedy, G. (1961), "Comment on Professor Bernstein's Paper, 'John Dewey's Metaphysics of Experience'," *The Journal of Philosophy*, 58: 14–21.
Kestenbaum, V. (1977), *The Phenomenological Sense of John Dewey: Habit and Meaning*. Atlantic Highlands, NJ: Humanities Press.
Kitcher, P. (2012), "Pragmatism and Realism: A Modest Proposal," in *Preludes to Pragmatism*. Oxford: Oxford University Press.
Klein, A. (2009), "On Hume on Space: Green's Attack, James's Empirical Response," *Journal of the History of Philosophy*, 47: 415–449.
Kloppenberg, J. T. (1986), *Uncertain Victory: Social Democracy and Progressivism in European and American Thought, 1870–1920*. Oxford: Oxford University Press.
  (1996), "Pragmatism: An Old Name for Some New Ways of Thinking?" *Journal of American History*, 83: 100–138.

Koopman, C. (2009), *Pragmatism as Transition: Historicity and Hope in James, Dewey, and Rorty*. New York: Columbia University Press.
  (2014), "Conduct Pragmatism: Beyond Experientialism and Lingualism," in Hildebrand 2014.
Lafont, C. (2002), "Is Objectivity Perspectival: Reflexions on Brandom's and Habermas' Pragmatist Conceptions of Objectivity," in M. Aboulafia, M. O. Bookman, and C. Kemp (eds.) *Habermas and Pragmatism*. London: Routledge Press.
Laurier, D. (2005a), "Pragmatics: Pittsburgh Style," *Pragmatics and Cognition*, 13: 141–160.
  (2005b), "Between Phenomenalism and Objectivism: An Examination of R. Brandom's Account of the Objectivity of Discursive Deontic Status," *Journal of Philosophical Research*, 30: 189–214.
Levine, S. (2010), "Rorty, Davidson, and the New Pragmatists," *Philosophical Topics*, 36: 167–192.
  (2012), "Brandom's Pragmatism," *Transactions of the Charles S. Peirce Society*, 48: 125–140.
  (2013) "Does James Have a Place for Objectivity?: A Response to Misak," Symposium on Cheryl Misak's *The American Pragmatists*, in the *European Journal of Pragmatism and American Philosophy*, 5. http://journals.openedition.org/ejpap/551
  (2015a), "Norms and Habits: Brandom on the Sociality of Action," *European Journal of Philosophy*, 23: 248–272.
  (2015b), "McDowell, Hegel, and Habits," *Hegel Bulletin*, 36: 184–201.
  (2015c), "Hegel, Dewey, and Habits," *British Journal for the History of Philosophy*, 23: 632–656.
  (2016), "Sellars and Nonconceptual Content," *European Journal of Philosophy*, 24: 855–878.
  (2017), "Comment on Axtell's *Objectivity*," in S. F. Aikin (ed.) "Symposium on Guy Axtell's *Objectivity*," *Syndicate*, https://syndicate.network/symposia/philosophy/objectivity/
  (2018), "James and Phenomenology," in A. Klein (ed.) *The Oxford Handbook of William James*. Oxford: Oxford University Press. www.oxfordhandbooks.com/view/10.1093/oxfordhb/9780199395699.001.0001/oxfordhb-9780199395699-e-24
  (in press a), "Rethinking Sellars' Naturalism," in P. Giladi (ed.) *Responses to Naturalism: Critical Perspectives from Idealism and Pragmatism*. New York, NY: Routledge Press.
  (in press b), "Rorty, Davidson, and Representation," in A. Malachowski (ed.) *The Wiley-Blackwell Companion to Rorty*. Malden, MA: Wiley-Blackwell Press.
Linschoten, H. (1968), *On the Way toward a Phenomenological Psychology: The Psychology of William James*. Pittsburgh, PA: Duquesne University Press.

Loeffler, R. (2005), "Normative Phenomenalism: On Robert Brandom's Practice-Based Explanation of Meaning," *European Journal of Philosophy*, 13: 32–69.
Lotze, H. (1887), *Logic*, trans. B. Bosanquet. Oxford: Clarendon Press.
Ludwig, K. (2011), "Triangulation Triangulated," in C. Amoretti & G. Preyer (eds.) *Triangulation: From and Epistemological Point of View*. Frankfurt: Ontos Verlag.
Malachowski, A. (2014), *The New Pragmatism*. New York, NY: Routledge Press.
McDowell, J. (1996a), *Mind and World*. Cambridge, MA: Harvard University Press.
  (1996b), "Response to Perception and Rational Constraint," *Philosophical Issues*, 7: 290–300.
  (1998a), "Reply to Brandom," *Philosophy and Phenomenological Research*, 58: 403–409.
  (1998b), "Reply to Peacocke," *Philosophy and Phenomenological Research*, 58: 414–419.
  (2000a), "Towards Rehabilitating Objectivity," in Brandom 2000b.
  (2000b) "Response to Willaschek," in M. Willaschek (ed.) *John McDowell: Reason and Nature*. Münster: Lit Verlag.
  (2000c) "Response to Gubeljic, Link, Müller, and Osburg," in M. Willaschek (ed.) *John McDowell: Reason and Nature*. Münster: Lit Verlag.
  (2008), "Response to Halbig," in J. Lingaard (ed.) *Experience, Norm, and Nature*. Malden, MA: Blackwell Publishing.
  (2009a), "Self-Determining Subjectivity and External Constraint," in *Having the World in View*. Cambridge, MA: Harvard University Press.
  (2009b), "Conceptual Capacities in Perception," in *Having the World in View*. Cambridge, MA: Harvard University Press.
  (2009c), "Avoiding the Myth of the Given," in *Having the World in View*. Cambridge, MA: Harvard University Press.
  (2009d), "What Myth?" in *The Engaged Intellect*. Cambridge, MA: Harvard University Press.
McGilvary, E. B. (1908), "The Chicago 'Idea' and Idealism," *The Journal of Philosophy*, 5: 589–597.
Mead, G. H. (1962). *Mind, Self, and Society: From the Standpoint of a Social Behaviorist*. Chicago, IL: University of Chicago Press.
Merleau-Ponty, M. (2013), *Phenomenology of Perception*, trans. D. Landes. New York, NY: Routledge Press.
Misak, C. (2000), *Truth, Politics, Morality*. New York, NY: Routledge Press.
  (2004), *Truth and the End of Inquiry*. Oxford: Oxford University Press.
  (2007), *New Pragmatists*. Oxford: Oxford University Press.
  (2013), *The American Pragmatists*. Oxford: Oxford University Press.
  (2014), "Language and Experience for Pragmatism," in Hildebrand 2014.
Mounce, H. (1997), *The Two Pragmatisms: From Peirce to Rorty*. New York, NY: Routledge Press.
Murphy, A. E. (1951), "Dewey's Epistemology and Metaphysics," in P. A. Schilpp (ed.) *The Philosophy of John Dewey*. New York, NY: Tudor Publishing Company.

Myers, G. (1986), *William James: His Life and Thought*. New Haven, CT: Yale University Press.
Nagel, T. (1979), "Panpsychism," in *Mortal Questions*. Cambridge: Cambridge University Press.
Noë, A. (2004), *Action in Perception*. Cambridge, MA: MIT Press.
O'Shea, J. (2007), *Wilfrid Sellars: Naturalism with a Normative Turn*. Cambridge: Polity Press.
Pappas, G. (2016), "John Dewey's Radical Logic: The Function of the Qualitative in Thinking," *Transactions of the Charles S. Peirce Society*, 52: 435–468.
Peacocke, C. (1998), "Nonconceptual Content Defended," *Philosophy and Phenomenological Research*, 58: 381–388.
  (2001), "Does Perception Have a Nonconceptual Content?" *Journal of Philosophy*, 98: 239–264.
Pearce, T. (2014), "The Dialectical Biologist, circa 1890: John Dewey and the Oxford Hegelians," *Journal of the History of Philosophy*, 52: 747–777.
Peirce, C. S. (1992), *The Essential Peirce, Volume 1: Selected Philosophical Writings, (1867–1893)*, N. Houser and J. K. Kloesel (eds.). Bloomington, IN: Indiana University Press.
  (1998), *The Essential Peirce, Volume 2: Selected Philosophical Writings, (1893–1913)*. The Peirce Edition Project (ed.). Bloomington, IN: Indiana University Press.
Pollard, B. (2006), "Explaining Action with Habits," *American Philosophical Quarterly*, 43: 57–68.
Price, H. (2003), "Truth as Convenient Friction," *Journal of Philosophy*, 100: 167–190.
  (2013), *Expressivism, Pragmatism, and Representationalism*. Cambridge: Cambridge University Press.
Prien, B. (2010), "Robert Brandom on Communication, Reference, and Objectivity," *International Journal of Philosophical Studies*, 18: 433–458.
Pratt, S. (1997), "'A Sailor in a Storm': Dewey on the Meaning of Language," *Transactions of the Charles S. Peirce Society*, 33: 839–862.
Putnam, H. (1987), *The Many Faces of Realism*. Chicago, IL: Open Court.
  (1990a), "Realism with a Human Face," in *Realism with a Human Face*. Cambridge, MA: Harvard University Press.
  (1990b), "James' Theory of Perception," in *Realism with a Human Face*. Cambridge, MA: Harvard University Press.
  (1997), "James' Theory of Truth," in R. A. Putnam (ed.) *The Cambridge Companion to William James*. Cambridge: Cambridge University Press.
  (1998), "Pragmatism and Realism," in M. Dickstein (ed.) *The Revival of Pragmatism*. Durham, NC: Duke University Press.
  (1999), *The Threefold Cord: Mind, Body, and World*. New York, NY: Columbia University Press.
Ramberg, B. (2000), "Post-Ontological Philosophy of Mind: Rorty versus Davidson," in Brandom 2000b.

Rorty, R. (1965), "Mind-Body Identity, Privacy, and Categories," in D. Rosenthal (ed.) *Materialism and the Mind-Body Problem*. Upper Saddle River, NJ: Prentice-Hall.
  (1970), "Incorrigibility as the Mark of the Mental," *Journal of Philosophy*, 67: 399–424.
  (1971), "In Defense of Eliminative Materialism," in D. Rosenthal (ed.) *Materialism and the Mind-Body Problem*. Upper Saddle River, NJ: Prentice-Hall.
  (1979), *Philosophy and the Mirror of Nature*. Princeton, NJ: Princeton University Press.
  (1982), "Dewey's Metaphysics," in *The Consequences of Pragmatism*. Minneapolis, MN: University of Minnesota Press.
  (1985), "Comments on Sleeper and Edel," *Transactions of the Charles S. Peirce Society*, 21: 39–48.
  (1991a), *Objectivity, Relativism, and Truth*. Cambridge: Cambridge University Press.
  (1991b), "Solidarity or Objectivity," in Rorty 1991a.
  (1991c), "Texts and Lumps," in Rorty 1991a.
  (1991d), "Inquiry as Recontextualization," in Rorty 1991a.
  (1991e), "Representation, Social Practice, and Truth," in Rorty 1991a.
  (1998a), *Truth and Progress*. Cambridge: Cambridge University Press.
  (1998b), "Charles Taylor on Truth," in Rorty 1998a.
  (1998c), "Robert Brandom on Social Practices and Representations," in Rorty 1998a.
  (1998d), "The Very Idea of Human Answerability to the World: John McDowell's Version of Empiricism," in Rorty 1998a.
  (1998e), "Dewey between Hegel and Darwin," in Rorty 1998a.
  (1999a), "Davidson's Mental-Physical Distinction," in L. E. Hahn (ed.) *Donald Davidson (Library of Living Philosophers)*. Peru, IL: Open Court Press.
  (1999b), "Pragmatism As Anti-Authoritarianism," in *Revue Internationale de Philosophie*, 53: 7–20.
  (2000), "Universality and Truth," in Brandom 2000b.
  (2000a), "Reply to Ramberg," in Brandom 2000b.
  (2000b), "Reply to Davidson," in Brandom 2000b.
  (2007), "Pragmatism and Romanticism," in *Philosophy as Cultural Politics*. Cambridge: Cambridge University Press.
Rock, I. (1990), "A Look Back at William James's Theory of Perception," in M. G. Johnson and T. B. Henley (eds.) Reflections on *The Principles of Psychology*: William James after a Century. Mahwah, NJ: Lawrence Erlbaum Associates.
Rödl, S. (2008), "Infinite Explanation," *Philosophical Topics*, 36: 123–134.
Rouse, J. (2015), *Articulating the World*. Chicago, IL: Chicago University Press.
Russell, B. (1951), "Dewey's New *Logic*," in P. A. Schilpp (ed.) *The Philosophy of John Dewey*. New York, NY: Tudor Publishing Company.
  (1996), "Warranted Assertibility," in *An Inquiry into Meaning and Truth*, 2nd edn. New York, NY: Routledge Press.

Ryle, G. (1984), *The Concept of Mind*. Chicago, IL: Chicago University Press.
Sachs, C. (2009), "Natural Agents: A Transcendental Argument for Pragmatic Naturalism," *Contemporary Pragmatism*, 6: 15–37.
  (2014), *Intentionality and Myths of the Given*. New York, NY: Routledge Press.
Sacks, M. (2000), *Objectivity and Insight*. Oxford: Oxford University Press.
Santayana, G. (1951), "Dewey's Naturalistic Metaphysics," in P. A. Schilpp (ed.) *The Philosophy of John Dewey*. New York, NY: Tudor Publishing Company.
Sellars, W. (1968), *Science and Metaphysics*. London: Routledge and Kegan Paul.
  (1975), "Autobiographical Reflections," in Hector-Neri Castañeda (ed.) *Action, Knowledge, and Reality: Critical Studies in Honor of Wilfrid Sellars*. Indianapolis, IN: Bobbs-Merrill.
  (1981), "Foundations for a Metaphysics of Pure Process (The Carus Lectures)," *The Monist*, 64: 3–90.
  (1991), *Science, Perception and Reality*. Atascadero, CA: Ridgeview Publishing.
  (1997), *Empiricism and the Philosophy of Mind*. Cambridge, MA: Harvard University Press.
Shook, J. (1995), "John Dewey's Struggle with American Realism, 1904–1910," *Transactions of the Charles S. Peirce Society*, 31: 542–566.
Shusterman, R. (1994), "Dewey on Experience: Foundation or Reconstruction?" *The Philosophical Forum*, 26: 127–148.
Siewert, C. (2005), "Attention and Sensorimotor Intentionality," in D. W. Smith and A. L. Thomasson *Phenomenology and the Philosophy of Mind*. Oxford: Oxford University Press.
Skrupskelis, I. L. (1989), "James and Kant's Second Analogy," *Kant-Studien*, 80: 173–179.
Siegfried, C. H. (1978), *Chaos and Context: A Study in William James*. Athens, OH: Ohio University Press.
Sleeper, R. (1986), *The Necessity of Pragmatism: John Dewey's Conception of Philosophy*. Urbana, IL: University of Illinois Press.
Speaks, J. (2005), "Is There a Problem about Nonconceptual Content?" *The Philosophical Review*, 114: 359–398.
Stern, R. (2000), *Transcendental Arguments and Skepticism: Answering the Question of Justification*. Oxford: Oxford University Press.
Strawson, G. (2017), "Physicalist Panpsychism," in S. Schneider and M. Velmans (eds.) *The Blackwell Companion to Consciousness*, 2nd edn. Malden, MA: Wiley-Blackwell.
Strawson, P. (1959), *Individuals*. London: Routledge Press.
  (1966), *The Bounds of Sense*. London: Methuen and Co.
Stout, J. (2007), "On Our Interest in Getting Things Right: Pragmatism without Narcissism," in C. Misak (ed.) *New Pragmatists*. Oxford: Oxford University Press.
Stout, R. (2010), "Being Subject to the Rule to Do What the Rules Tell You to Do," in B. Weiss and J. Wanderer (eds.) *Reading Brandom: On Making It Explicit*. London: Routledge Press.

Testa, I. (2017), "Dewey, Second Nature, Social Criticism, and the Hegelian Heritage," *European Journal of Pragmatism and American Philosophy* 9. http://journals.openedition.org/ejpap/990

Tiles, J. E. (1988), *Dewey (Arguments of the Philosophers)*. London: Routledge Press.

(2010), "The Primacy of Practice in Dewey's Experimental Empiricism," in M. Cochran (ed.) *The Cambridge Companion to Dewey*. Cambridge: Cambridge University Press.

Thompson, E. (2007), *Mind in Life*. Cambridge, MA: Harvard University Press.

Tomasello, M. (1999), *The Cultural Origins of Human Cognition*. Cambridge, MA: Harvard University Press.

Wanderer, J. (2008), *Robert Brandom*. Montreal and Kingston: McGill-Queens University Press.

Welchman, J. (2008), "Dewey and McDowell on Naturalism, Values, and Second Nature," *Journal of Speculative Philosophy*, 22: 50–58.

Willaschek M. (1999), "On 'The Unboundedness of the Conceptual'," in M. Willaschek (ed.) *John McDowell: Reason and Nature*. Münster: Lit Verlag.

Williams, M. (2000) 'Epistemology and the Mirror of Nature', in Brandom 2000b (ed.) *Rorty and His Critics*. Malden, MA: Blackwell Press.

Wilshire, B. (1968), *William James and Phenomenology: A Study of the "Principles of Psychology."* Bloomington, IN: Indiana University Press.

Wright, C. (1992), *Truth and Objectivity*. Cambridge, MA: Harvard University Press.

(1996), "Human Nature?" *European Journal of Philosophy*, 4: 235–254.

Index

a priori, relative, 162
absence. *See* presence and absence
abstractionist theory, of concept formation, 30–32
action, 48, 57–61
  bodily, in egocentric space, 114–115
  Brandom on, 48–54, 59
  Dewey on, 179–180, 241–242
  fanciful and objective, 241–242
affordances, 80, 190–191
answerability, 5, 9, 99–100
  Brandom on, 43, 72, 83, 85–86
  classical pragmatists on, 5–6
  Dewey on, 157–159, 162–163, 165–166, 191, 193, 218, 223, 236–241
  empiricism and, 10
  Erlebnis, Erfahrung and, 16–17
  James on, 157
  new pragmatists on, 21
  of perception, 80–81
  realism on, 18, 193
  Rorty on, 1–3, 39
anthropomorphism, 237–238
antirealism, 235–240
  Davidson on, 235
  Dewey and, 237
  of Rorty, 39
association, 132, 144, 146, 226
atomism
  of Brandom, 44, 55–57, 61–62
  Dewey's critique, 62–63, 226
  intellectualism and, 44, 57, 127
  James on, 125–131, 141, 144, 146–147, 153, 235–236
  of Locke, 129–130, 225–226
  of the TOTE cycle, 55, 61–63, 81
attention
  Dewey on, 6, 79, 205
  James on, 13, 17, 124–125, 130, 136, 144–147, 149–151, 155–156, 235–236
  reversing, in time, 151

belief
  Peirce on, 193–195
  as veridical, 188
Berkeley, George, 111, 146
Bernstein, Richard J., 1–3, 10, 32, 185, 241
Bildung, 14–15, 18, 199, 219–220
biology, 209–210, 221–222. *See also* Darwinism
Black, Max, 200, 204
Bourdieu, Pierre, 59
Boyle, M., 53, 191
Brandom, Robert, 10, 87–94. *See also* commitments; scorekeeping; TOTE cycle
  on action, 48–54, 59
  on answerability, 43, 72, 83, 85–86
  atomism of, 44, 55–57, 61–62
  on Cartesian mind, 26
  communicative-theoretic account of objectivity of, 15–16, 82–100, 118–119
  on *de re* ascriptions, 88–91
  default and challenge structure of, 75–77, 188
  on *Erlebnis* and *Erfahrung*, 11–13, 15, 43–44, 66–67, 69–75, 79, 81, 83
  McDowell and, 70–74
  mind-body distinction of, 44, 61
  Myth of the Given and, 40–42, 50, 52, 56, 60, 70–71, 75, 166–167
  objectivity rehabilitated by, 28–29, 40–42
  on perception, two-ply theory of, 51–53, 61–62, 70–71
  phenomenalism and, 94–96
  on practical Myth of the Given, 49–53, 60
  on rational constraint, 67–75, 78
  rationalist pragmatism of, 15, 43–47, 66–67
  on regulism, 44–45
  reliabilism of, 71–72
  on representation, 28, 45–46

254

Index

Rorty and, 15, 21–23, 26–29, 33, 37, 39–44, 69
  social externalism of, 70–71
  Stout, R., on, 49
  Wanderer on, 85–86
Bridges, J., 102–103, 107
Burge, Tyler, 125, 148
Burke, T., 5, 80, 159, 187, 193

Campbell, John, 109–111, 115–116
Cartesian. *See* Descartes
Cassam, Q., 111
cognitive map, 115–117
Cohen, M. R., 237
coherentism, 78, 81, 167
  Dewey and, 164–166, 168, 179–180
  McDowell and, 182, 220
commitments, 47–51, 53
  communication and, 87–92, 94, 96–98
  substitutional-inferential, 90–91
  TOTE cycle and, 53–57, 66–69, 75–78, 81, 86
communication, 3, 15–16
  Brandom on, 87–94
  Bridges on, 102
  commitments and, 87–92, 94, 96–98
  Grice on, 105–106
  intention in, Davidson on, 105–106
  interpretation and, 88
  linguistic, Dewey on, 199–209, 212, 240
  linguistic, environment and, 212
  linguistic, Lockean account of, 200
  linguistic, Rorty on, 232–234
  Myth of the Given and, 229–230
  scorekeeping and, 87–92
  triangulation and, 105–108
communicative-theoretic account of objectivity, 3, 15
  of Brandom, 15–16, 82–100, 118–119
  Campbell and, 109–110
  of Davidson, 15–16, 82–83, 101–110, 117–118, 123, 188
  perceptual-theoretic account and, 83, 109–110, 117–118
conception
  James on, 149–150
  Peirce on, 194–196
  perception and, Dewey on, 168–169, 183–184
consciousness
  attention and, Dewey on, 79
  control, optimality and, 59–60
  Dewey on mind and, 79
  James on, 123–125, 145
  objective, 145

control, 41
  conscious, optimality and, 59–60
  Dewey on, 240–242
correspondence theory, of truth, 8–9, 165

Darwinism, 221–222, 225–226, 232–233
Davidson, Donald, 167
  on antirealism, 235
  on communication, intention in, 105–106
  communicative-theoretic account of objectivity and, 15–16, 82, 101–110, 117–118, 123, 188
  egocentric, objective space and, 117–118
  experience eschewed by, 10
  Myth of the Given and, 166–167
  objectivity as public-ness for, 108–109
  perceptual-theoretic account and, 109–110, 117–118
  on surprise, 102–103
  triangulation of, 37, 101–108, 117–118, 203
  on truth and error, 101–103
  Wittgenstein and, 103–104, 108
de re and *de dicto* ascriptions, 93–94
  Brandom on, 88–91
  distinction between, 88–90
  in scorekeeping terms, 89–90, 97, 99
  in substitutional-inferential commitments, 90–91
default and challenge structure, 75–77, 188
Descartes
  Brandom on, 26
  epistemology and, 34–36
  incorrigibility of, 23–24
Dewey, John, 3, 10, 13–15, 225. *See also* environment
  on action, 179–180, 241–242
  on answerability, 157–159, 162–163, 165–166, 191, 193, 218, 223, 236–241
  anthropomorphism and, 237–238
  atomism critiqued by, 62–63, 226
  on attention, 6, 79, 205
  Bildung and, 14–15, 18, 199
  biology and, 209–210, 221–222
  coherentism and, 164–166, 168, 179–180
  on conflicted situation, 176–178
  on control, 240–242
  on correspondence theory, 165
  empiricism of, 17–18, 158–159, 190, 192–193
  epistemology and, 6–8, 188, 239
  Erfahrung and, 14–15, 17–18, 44, 79, 193, 197–200, 209, 223, 228
  Erlebnis and, 11, 80
  on existence, plateaus of, 222, 230–231

Dewey, John (cont.)
  on experiment, 13, 17–18, 173–174, 179–180, 198, 215–217, 230–231, 237
  on facts, 178–179, 184
  fringe or marginal consciousness and, 173, 175
  habit and, 14–15, 17–18, 172–175, 181, 189, 192–193, 197–200, 204–207, 209, 211–214, 223, 229–231, 237–238, 240–242
  Hegel and, 158, 161–162, 170–171, 210, 225
  inquiry and, 6–7, 179, 188, 198–199, 213–214, 226
  on intention, 202–203
  on intrinsic and relational properties, 217–218
  James and, 3, 62–63, 162, 221, 236
  on Kant, 160–173, 181, 229–230
  on know-how, 59
  on knowledge, 214–217
  on linguistic communication, 199–209, 212, 240
  logic of, 158–162, 168–169, 183, 188, 229
  McDowell and, 17–18, 164–166, 168–170, 173–175, 190–191, 193, 221, 229
  on meaning, 14–15, 18, 66, 79, 164–165, 180, 191, 193, 202–209
  on mind and consciousness, 79
  Myth of the Given and, 9–10, 18, 79–80, 164–168, 180, 186–187, 193, 225–230
  natural realism of, 209–218
  naturalism of, 58, 192–193, 201–203, 238
  panpsychism and, 228, 230–231
  Peirce and, 3, 160, 193, 198, 238
  on perception, 79–81, 168–174, 179, 183–184, 217–218
  on philosopher's fallacy, 171
  on primary experience, 170–176, 178, 181, 188, 215–216, 228
  on quality, 184–189, 206, 230–231
  realism and, 193, 209–218, 236–241
  on reason, 224–225
  on receptivity, spontaneity and, 168–170, 172–173, 181, 189
  on reflex arc, 62–63, 65–66, 170
  Rorty and, 18, 193, 201, 225–234
  Russell on, 177, 187
  on science, logic of, 160–161
  on science, spirit of, 161–163
  second nature and, 192–193, 199, 218, 221–223, 239–240
  on situations, 184–189
  on stimulus and response, 62–66
  on surprise, 177
  on thought, 163–169, 179, 185–186, 214
  TOTE cycle and, 55–56, 62–63, 65–66
  on tribunal, experience as, 17–18, 158–159, 166, 168, 175–176, 180–182, 192–193
  on truth, 7, 179
  in two-pragmatist reading, 4–6, 9
  on unboundedness, 183–184, 187–189
  Wittgenstein and, 201
Dilthey, Wilhelm, 12
disposition. *See* habit
Dogmatism, 228
  Erlebnis and, 77
  TOTE cycle and, 77–78
doubt
  Dewey on, 177, 198
  Peirce on, 177, 188
Dreyfus, H., 190–191

Eilan, N., 112
eliminative materialism
  abstractionist theory and, 31–32
  of Rorty, 22–23, 27, 29–32, 34, 38, 40
embodied coping skills, 190–191
emergence, panpsychism and, 228, 230–231
empiricism, 16, 123, 160–161, 202–203
  association in, 132, 144, 226
  on content, abstractionist theory of, 30–31
  of Dewey, 17–18
  of Dewey, experimental, 158–159, 190, 192–193
  of Dewey, naturalistic, 192–193
  James and, 132, 134–136, 144
  minimal, 10–11, 17–18, 158–159, 166, 190
  Myth of the Given and, 30, 158–159
Enlightenment. *See* second Enlightenment
environment, 209–211
  habit in, 211–214
  language and, 212
  situation as, 189
  social, 211–213
epistemic neutralization, of sensation, 33–34, 36–37
epistemic objectivity
  Dewey on, 6–8
  inquiry in, 7–9
  Misak on, 7–9
epistemology
  Descartes and, 34–36
  Dewey and, 188, 239
  Erlebnis in, 12
  as first philosophy, 1
  Locke and, 34–38
  Plato and, 36–37
  Rorty on, 34–38
Erfahrung, 11–12, 79–81, 237. *See also* Hegel, G. W. F.
  answerability and, 16–17
  Brandom on, 11–12, 15, 43–44, 66–67, 69–70, 75, 79, 81, 83

Dewey and, 11, 14–15, 17–18, 44, 79, 193, 197–200, 209, 223, 228
James and, 11, 13, 139
as temporal, 228–229
TOTE cycle and, 66–67, 75–76, 78
Erlebnis, 85–86
answerability and, 16–17
Brandom on, 11–13, 15, 43–44, 66, 69–75, 83
Dewey and, 11, 80
Dilthey on, 12
double-checking and, 77
in epistemology, 12
in experiential-theoretic account of objectivity, 15, 123
James on, 11–13, 17, 123, 139
perception and, 81
rational constraint and, 72–75, 78–79
TOTE cycle and, 77–78
Evans, Gareth, 110–111, 125
experiential-theoretic account and, 125
James and, 126, 149
perceptual-theoretic account of, 82–83, 110–117, 123
on spatial concepts, egocentric and absolute, 113–117
on spatial consciousness, 16, 110–111, 113–115
existence, plateaus of, 222, 230–231
experience. *See* specific topics
experiential-theoretic account of objectivity, 3, 16–18, 123, 125–126
Dewey and, 176–181, 187–189, 209–218, 223
James and, 123, 125–126, 139–143, 151–156
experiment, 180
Dewey on, 13, 17–18, 173–174, 179–181, 198, 215–217, 230–231, 237
Erfahrung and, 237
in inquiry, 179, 198
primary experience and, 173–174
spontaneity and, 181
experimental empiricism. *See* empiricism
externalism, 70–71

facts
Brandom on, 85
Dewey on, 178–179, 184
foundationalism, 5, 35–36, 41–42, 75–76
fringe or marginal consciousness, 136, 150–151, 173, 175

German Idealism, 163, 228
Gibson, J. J., 80
Grice, Paul, 105–106, 202–203

Habermas, Jürgen, 2–3, 85–86
habit, 61. *See also* know-how
Dewey and, 14–15, 17–18, 172–175, 181, 189, 192–193, 197–200, 204–207, 209, 211–214, 223, 229–231, 237–238, 240–242
disposition and, 193–197
in environment, 211–214
in *Erfahrung*, 14–15, 199
intelligent practices and, Ryle on, 196–197
intentional action and, 57–61
meaning and, 14–15, 18, 66, 205–209
Myth of the Given and, 60–61, 229–230
Peirce on, 193–198
Hall, Everett, 206–207
Haugeland, J., 77
Hegel, G. W. F., 11–12
Dewey and, 158, 161–162, 170–171, 210, 225
neo-Kantian tradition and, 161
Hildebrand, D., 1, 17, 193, 214, 225
Husserl, Edmund, 142–143

incorrigibility
Brandom on, 27–28, 40
in Cartesian tradition, 23–24
Rorty and, 15, 22–28, 40
Ryleans and, 23–25, 35
inquiry, 5–6
Dewey and, 6–7, 179, 188, 198–199, 213–214, 226
epistemic objectivity and, 7–9
experiment in, 179, 198
Peirce on, 7, 193–194
instrumental logic. *See* logic
intellectualism
atomism and, 44, 57, 127
Brandom and, 44–47, 55–57
rationalist pragmatism and, 44–47

James, William, 3
on answerability, 157
on atomism, 125–131, 141, 144, 146–147, 153, 235–236
on attention, 13, 17, 124–125, 130, 136, 144–147, 149–151, 155–156, 235–236
on conceptions, 149–150
Condillac and, 140
on consciousness, objective, 142–143
on consciousness, sensory and cognitive, 123–124
on consciousness as selecting agency, 124–125
Dewey and, 3, 62–63, 162, 221, 236
empiricism and, 132, 134–136, 144
Erfahrung and, 11, 13, 139
on *Erlebnis*, 11–13, 17, 123, 139

James, William (cont.)
    on experience, 3–5, 11–13, 124–125, 143, 157, 162, 235–236
    field of view and, 149–156
    Husserl and, 142–143
    on identification, synthesis of, 142
    on intending the Same, 125, 138–139, 142–143, 148
    on interest, 148–149
    introspection and, 141
    Kant and, 12–13, 131–132, 149, 235–236
    Kierkegaard and, 151–152
    on marginal more, 154–156, 236
    Merleau-Ponty and, 236
    Myth of the Given and, 9–10
    naturalism of, 236
    on objectivity, experience of, 151–156
    phenomenology of, 236
    on presence and absence, 153–156
    on psychologist's fallacy, 127–129, 171
    on quality, 130, 140–142, 145, 147
    on self-transcendence, 139–141
    on sensation, definitions of, 144–145
    on spatial consciousness, 144–156, 235–236
    Strawson, Evans and, 126, 149
    on succession, in spatial consciousness, 150–151
    on thought, characteristics of, 128–139, 153
    on thought, stream of, 134–135, 138–139, 142, 151–152
    triangulation and, 142–143
    in two-pragmatist reading, 4–5, 9
    on unity and objectivity, 139–143
    on voluminousness, 145

Kant, Immanuel
    Dewey on, 160–162, 173, 181
    dualism of, Dewey on, 161, 163–172, 229–230
    James and, 12–13, 131–132, 149, 235–236
    logic of, 160–161
    on objectivity, Davidson and, 101
    Rorty and, 26, 35, 229
    on space, Evans and, 111
Kestenbaum, V., 193
Kierkegaard, Søren, 151–152
know-how, 59, 196–197
knowledge
    Dewey on, 214–217
    experiment and, 215
    non-idealist readings of, 216
Koopman, Colin, 186–187, 199

language. *See* communication
Lewis, C. I., 9
linguistic communication. *See* communication
linguistic turn, 1–3, 21–22, 26
Locke, John, 35–36, 202–203
    atomism of, 129–130, 225–226
    James on, 129–130, 144
    Myth of the Given and, 35–36
    Rorty on, 34–38, 225–226
    simple ideas of, 129–130, 144, 225–226
    on speech, 200
logic
    Dewey and, 159–162, 168–169, 183, 188
    empiricist, 160–161
    instrumental, of Dewey, 158, 229
    Kantian, 160–161
    life-function and, 160
    Peirce on, Dewey and, 160
    post-Fregian, 159–160
Lotze, H., 163–172

McDowell, John, 38, 221
    on *Bildung*, 18, 219–220
    Brandom and, 70–74
    coherentism and, 182, 220
    Dewey and, 17–18, 164–166, 168–170, 173–175, 190–191, 193, 221, 229
    Dreyfus and, 190–191
    on intuitional content, 174–175
    on judgment, 10, 167–168
    minimal empiricism of, 10–11, 17–18, 158–159, 166, 190
    on Myth of the Given, 70, 164–165, 167–168, 220, 229
    naturalized platonism of, 220
    on perception, 190–191
    on rational constraint, 73–74, 182
    on reason, 219–221, 224
    on second nature, 218–221, 223–224
    on tribunal, experience as, 10–11, 17–18, 158–159, 167–168, 176, 182
    on unboundedness, 182–183
    Wittgenstein and, 220
Mead, G. H., 202–203
meaning
    Dewey on, 14–15, 18, 66, 79, 164–165, 180, 191, 193, 202–209
    habit and, 14–15, 18, 66, 205–209
    McDowell on, 223–224
    Peirce on, 10, 193–195, 199–200
    referential and immanent, 206–209
    symbolic, 206–209
Merleau-Ponty, Maurice, 58–59, 148, 236

Index

Mill, John Stuart, 160–161
mind-body distinction, 44, 61–62
Misak, Cheryl, 2–3
  on answerability, 9
  on Dewey, 214
  on epistemic objectivity, 7–9
  on new pragmatists, 2–3, 9–10
  on truth, 6–7
  two-pragmatist reading of, 4–5, 9–10
Myth of Jones. *See* Ryleans
Myth of the Given, 2, 17–18, 60–61
  authority and, 228–229
  Brandom and, 40–42, 50, 52, 56, 60, 70–71, 75, 166–167
  communication and, 229–230
  Dewey and, 9–10, 18, 79–80, 164–168, 180, 186–187, 193, 225–230
  Dogmatism and, 228
  empiricism and, 30, 158–159
  experiential-theoretic account and, 18
  James and, 9–10
  Locke and, 35–36
  McDowell on, 70, 164–165, 167–168, 220, 229
  Peirce and, 10
  practical, Brandom on, 49–53, 60
  Rorty and, 18, 30, 32–38, 166–167, 193, 225–229
  Sellars on, 1, 9, 34, 50–51, 207

naturalism
  of Dewey, 58, 192–193, 201–203, 209–218, 223, 238
  fallacy of, 232
  of James, 236
  platonist, of McDowell, 220
  of Rorty, 232–233
neo-Hegelianism, 161, 170–171
neo-Kantianism
  on answerability, 157
  atomism and, 236
  neo-Hegelianism as, Dewey on, 161
  perceptual-theoretic account in, 110, 123
  on spatial consciousness, 146
neo-pragmatism, of Rorty, 1–2, 21
new pragmatists, 23
  Misak on, 2–3, 9–10
  on objective correctness, 21–22
Noë, A., 80
nominalism, psychological
  of Rorty, 33–34, 38–39
  Ryleans and, 33–34
  of Sellars, 32–33
norm, of optimality, 58–60

object-as-it-is-intended, 128–129, 133–134, 136–139
objectivity. *See* specific topics
objectivity of content, 5–6, 8–10
object-which-is-intended, 137–139

panpsychism, 225–228
  Dewey and, 228, 230–231
  Rorty on, 230–231, 233
Peirce, C. S., 9–10
  on belief, 193–195
  on conceptions, 194–196
  on concrete reasonableness, 197–198
  Dewey and, 3, 160, 193, 198, 238
  on doubt, 177, 188
  on habit, 193–198
  on inquiry, 7, 193–194
  on meaning, 10, 193–195, 199–200
  Myth of the Given and, 10
  Rorty on, 225–226, 231
  semiotics of, 199
  subjunctive conditional of, 195–196
  on truth, 7
  in two-pragmatist reading, 4–6, 9
perception
  affordances and, 80, 190–191
  answerability of, 80–81
  conception and, 168–169, 183–184
  Dewey on, 79–81, 168–174, 179, 183–184, 217–218
  in *Erfahrung*, 80–81
  Erlebnis and, 81
  James on, 146–147
  McDowell on, 190–191
  photograph model of, 80
  Sellars on, 228
  spatial conditions of, 16, 112–113, 123
  temporal conditions of, 112
  in TOTE cycle, 79–81
  two-ply theory of, Brandom on, 51–53, 61–62, 70–71
  veridical, 16, 109–110, 113
perceptual-theoretic account, 82
  Campbell and, 109–110
  communicative-theoretic account and, 83, 109–110, 117–118
  Davidson and, 109–110, 117–118
  of Evans, 82–83, 110–117, 123
  as neo-Kantian, 110, 123
  scorekeeping and, 118–119
  of Strawson, 82–83, 110, 123
phenomenology, 137, 193, 236
Plato
  dualism of, 62
  epistemology and, 36–37

Plato (cont.)
    McDowell and, 220
    Rorty and, 231–232
pragmatism. *See* specific topics
Price, H., 21, 23, 167
primary experience. *See* Dewey, John
private language argument, 201
psychologist's fallacy, 127–129, 171
public-ness, objectivity as, 108–109
Putnam, Hilary, 2–3, 21

quale, spatial, 145
quality
    Dewey on, 184–189, 206, 230–231
    James on, 130, 140–142, 145, 147
    of situation, 188–189

rational constraint, 182
    answerability and, 72
    Brandom on, 67–75, 78
    Erfahrung and, 75
    Erlebnis and, 72–75, 78–79
    Myth of the Given and, 166–167
    reliabilism and, 72
rationalist pragmatism, 15, 43–47, 66–67
realism. *See also* antirealism
    and answerability, 18, 193
    Dewey and, 193, 209–218, 236–241
    and objectivity, two questions of, 17
    of Dewey, 223
    of Peirce, 197–198
receptivity, spontaneity and, 168–170, 172–173, 181, 189
reflex arc, 62–63, 65–66, 170
reliabilism, 71–72
    rational constraint and, 72
    scorekeeping and, 71–74
representation
    Brandom on, 28, 45–46, 87–91
    communication and, 28, 87–91
    Locke on, Rorty and, 35–36
Rorty, Richard, 5, 223–224
    on answerability, 1–3, 39
    antirealism of, 39
    Brandom and, 15, 21–23, 26–29, 37, 39–44, 69
    on causal and rational constraint, 36–38, 41
    coherentism of, 167
    on Darwinism, 225–226, 232–233
    Dewey and, 18, 193, 201, 225–234
    dualism of, McDowell on, 38
    eliminative materialism of, 22–23, 27, 29–32, 34, 38, 40
    on epistemology, 34–38

    on experience, 1–2, 4–5, 9–10, 12–13, 15, 69–70, 193, 227–228
    on explanation and justification, confusion of, 34–36, 38–39
    on incorrigibility, 15, 22–28, 40
    Kant and, 26, 35, 229
    on linguistic communication, 232–234
    linguistic turn and, 21–22, 26
    on Locke, 34–38, 225–226
    Myth of the Given and, 18, 30, 32–38, 166–167, 193, 225–229
    naturalism of, 232–233
    neo-pragmatism of, 1–2, 21
    objectivity, hostility of, 21–23, 26–27, 29, 34–41, 43
    on panpsychism, 230–231, 233
    on Peirce, 225–226, 231
    psychological nominalism of, 33–34, 38–39
    reason and, 229
    second Enlightenment of, 22, 27, 39–40
    Sellars and, 15, 23–24, 26, 30, 32–34, 38, 41, 231–233
    on sensation, 29–34, 38
    on triangulation, 37
    in two-pragmatist reading, 4–5, 9
Russell, Bertrand, 177, 187
Ryle, G., 196–197
Ryleans, 30, 98
    Descartes and, 35
    incorrigibility and, 23–25, 35
    psychological nominalism and, 33–34

Sachs, Carl, 82, 166
Santayana, George, 237
Särkelä, Arvi, 222
scorekeeping, 28–29, 46–47, 77, 94
    communication and, 87–92
    de re and *de dicto* ascriptions in, 89–90, 97, 99
    idealist error and, 96–99
    objectivity in, 92–93, 98–100
    perceptual-theoretic account and, 118–119
    phenomenalism and, 94–96
    rational constraint and, 73–74
    realist error of, 96
    reliabilism and, 71–74
    third-person attitude on, 97–98
    TOTE cycle and, 78
second Enlightenment, 22, 27, 39–40
second nature
    Bildung and, 219–220
    Dewey and, 192–193, 199, 218, 221–223, 239–240
    McDowell on, 218–221, 223–224

Sellars, Wilfrid, 2, 4–5, 223–224
   on Myth of the Given, 1, 9, 34, 50–51, 207
   on perceptual experience, 228
   on pre-linguistic awareness, 32
   psychological nominalism of, 32–33
   Rorty and, 15, 23–24, 26, 30, 32–34, 38, 41, 231–233
   Ryleans of, 23–25, 30, 33–35, 98
   on Special Creation, 231–232
sensation
   definitions of, James on, 144–145
   embodied, 59
   epistemic neutralization of, 33–34, 36–37
   Rorty on, 29–34, 38
situation
   conflicted, Dewey on, 176–178
   Dewey on, 184–189
   as environment, 189
   primary experience and, 188
   thought and, 185–186
   as unbounded, 187–189
space
   Cassam on, 111
   egocentric and objective, 114–115, 117–118
   Evans on, 111, 117
   in experiential-theoretic account, 125–126
   Kant on, 111
spatial concepts, egocentric and absolute, 113–118
spatial consciousness. *See also* consciousness; fringe or marginal consciousness
   answerability and, 119
   Berkeleyian view of, 146
   Evans on, 16, 110–111, 113–115
   James on, 144–156, 235–236
   presence and absence in, 152–156
   received view of, 145–147
   Strawson on, 16, 110–111
   temporal succession in, 150–151
   triangulation and, 108–109
Stern, R., 82
stimulus and response, 62–66
Stout, Jeffrey, 2, 21–22
Stout, Roland, 49
Strawson, P. F., 110, 125
   experiential-theoretic account and, 125
   James and, 126, 149
   perceptual-theoretic account of, 82–83, 110, 123
   on spatial consciousness, 16, 110–111
stream of thought. *See* thought
surprise
   Davidson on, 102–103
   Dewey on, 177

therapeutic practice, philosophy as, 220–221
thought
   characteristics of, James on, 128–139, 153
   constant change of, 128–130
   Dewey on, 163–169, 179, 185–186, 214
   experience as tribunal for, 158–159, 166–168
   introspection and, 141
   object of, 128–129, 133–134, 136–139
   presence and absence in, 153–154
   as sensibly continuous, 128–129, 132–134, 139
   situation and, 185–186
   stream of, 134–135, 138–139, 142, 151–152
   as unitary and singular pulse, 128–133, 139, 153
thought, topic of. *See* object-which-is-intended
thought's object. *See* object-as-it-is-intended
TOTE cycle, 43–44
   as algorithmic, 54–57, 62–63
   atomism of, 55, 61–63, 81
   commitments and, 53–57, 66–69, 75–78, 81, 86
   Dewey and, 55–56, 62–63, 65–66
   double-checking and, 77–78
   Erfahrung and, 66–67, 75–76, 78
   Erlebnis and, 77–78
   intellectualism of, 55–56
   Myth of the Given and, 56
   perception in, 79–81
   rational constraint and, 67–69
   reflex arc and, 62–63, 65
   scorekeeping and, 78
   world-involvingness of, 85–86
triangulation
   cognitive, 103
   of Davidson, 37, 101–108, 117–118, 203
   of Dewey, 203
   egocentric, objective space and, 117–118
   error awareness and, 102–108
   of James, 142–143
   linguistic communication required by, 107
   pre-cognitive, 103–104
   spatial-consciousness and, 108–109
tribunal, experience as, 174
   Dewey on, 17–18, 158–159, 166, 168, 175–176, 180–182, 192–193
   McDowell on, 10–11, 17–18, 158–159, 167–168, 176, 182
truth
   correspondence theory of, 8–9, 165
   Dewey on, 7, 179

truth (cont.)
  epistemic objectivity and, 8–9
  error and, Davidson on, 101–103
  Misak on, 6–7
  Peirce on, 7
two-pragmatist reading, 4–6, 9–10

unboundedness of the conceptual, 182–184
unboundedness of the situation, 187–189

Wanderer, J., 85–86
Willaschek, M., 182
Wittgenstein, Ludwig, 15–16
  Davidson and, 103–104, 108
  Dewey and, 201
  on interpretation, 88
  McDowell and, 220
  private language argument of, 201